PENGUIN BOOKS

# LEFT FOR DEAD

## Samantha and Laurence Barlow

Samantha grew up in Sydney's Eastern suburbs. She joined the NSW Police Force in 1994 and became a crash investigation and traffic expert. She rapidly gained promotion to sergeant and was primed to become a future commander. She was medically discharged from the police force in 2011. Laurence was born in Liverpool, England, and grew up in southwestern Sydney. He joined the NSW Police Force in 1984, going on to spend 23 years as a member of Police Tactical Units, attending sieges, riots and arresting some of Sydney's most violent criminals. He was also an expert Weapons and Defensive Tactics instructor, spending 6 years at the NSW Police Academy. He was discharged in 2013 at the rank of Inspector. Samantha and Laurence live with their three children in Sydney.

## Sue Williams

Sue Williams' first true crime book, *And Then The Darkness*, was shortlisted for the prestigious Golden Dagger Award in the UK for the international true crime book of the year. She is also the author of a number of other bestsellers, including *Outback Heroines*; *Father Bob: The Larrikin Priest*; *Welcome to the Outback*; *Women of the Outback*; *No Time For Fear* and *Mean Streets, Kind Heart: The Father Chris Riley Story*. Sue is an award-winning journalist, and lives in Sydney's Kings Cross.

www.suewilliams.com.au

# LEFT FOR DEAD

## A True Story of Resilience and Courage

SAMANTHA & LAURENCE BARLOW
with SUE WILLIAMS

PENGUIN BOOKS

PENGUIN BOOKS

Published by the Penguin Group
Penguin Group (Australia)
707 Collins Street, Melbourne, Victoria 3008, Australia
(a division of Penguin Australia Pty Ltd)
Penguin Group (USA) Inc.
375 Hudson Street, New York, New York 10014, USA
Penguin Group (Canada)
90 Eglinton Avenue East, Suite 700, Toronto, Canada ON M4P 2Y3
(a division of Penguin Canada Books Inc.)
Penguin Books Ltd
80 Strand, London WC2R 0RL England
Penguin Ireland
25 St Stephen's Green, Dublin 2, Ireland
(a division of Penguin Books Ltd)
Penguin Books India Pvt Ltd
11 Community Centre, Panchsheel Park, New Delhi 110 017, India
Penguin Group (NZ)
67 Apollo Drive, Rosedale, Auckland 0632, New Zealand
(a division of Penguin New Zealand Pty Ltd)
Penguin Books (South Africa) (Pty) Ltd
Rosebank Office Park, Block D, 181 Jan Smuts Avenue, Parktown North, Johannesburg 2196, South Africa
Penguin (Beijing) Ltd
7F, Tower B, Jiaming Center, 27 East Third Ring Road North, Chaoyang District, Beijing 100020, China

Penguin Books Ltd, Registered Offices: 80 Strand, London WC2R 0RL, England

First published by Penguin Group (Australia), 2013
This edition published by Penguin Group (Australia), 2014



Cover design by Adam Laszczuk © Penguin Group (Australia)
Text design by Samantha Jayaweera © Penguin Group (Australia)
Front cover photograph of Samantha Barlow by Simon Alekna/Fairfax
Other cover photographs by Jimmy Thomson
Typeset in Sabon by Samantha Jayaweera © Penguin Group (Australia)
Printed and bound in Australia by Griffin Press

National Library of Australia Cataloguing-in-Publication data:

Barlow, Laurence, author.
Left for Dead: a true story of resilience and courage /
Laurence Barlow, Samantha Barlow, Sue Williams.
ISBN: 9780143571421 (paperback)
1. Barlow, Samantha. 2. Barlow, Laurence.
3. Policewomen--Biography.
4. Police--Violence against--New South Wales.

Other Authors/Contributors:
Barlow, Samantha, author.
Williams, Sue, author.

364.1555092

penguin.com.au

MIX
Paper from responsible sources
FSC® C009448

This book is dedicated to the doctors, nurses and support staff of St Vincent's Hospital's Intensive Care Unit in Sydney, and their colleagues who work in critical care.

It is also dedicated to the men and women who have worn the 'mighty blue shirt' of the New South Wales Police Force and our brothers and sisters who work in emergency services throughout Australia and beyond.

*Samantha and Laurence Barlow*

# CONTENTS

# PART ONE:

# Left for Dead

# Chapter 1
# HUNTING FOR EASY PREY

It's a chill late-autumn night in Sydney's notorious Kings Cross.

Along the main red-light strip, doormen hustle passers-by for business. They stand outside the strip clubs, the pole dancing joints and the bars, imploring potential punters to 'Come and have a look,' to step in and view their wares which are, invariably, overpriced drinks and underpaid women.

In other doorways, skinny young girls sit on high stools, shivering in too few clothes, as loud music blares from shadowy corridors or down from forbidding flights of stairs behind them. There's often motley crews of kids hanging around too: the 'runners' for the drug-dealers, delivering little plastic packets of heroin, ice, coke or amphetamines – whatever's been ordered – and furtively pocketing the cash payments, ready to hand them over to their bosses later.

On a cold Tuesday like this, there's never much happening. There'll be a few stragglers wandering the street, the odd drunk, locals with heads bent against the wind rushing home after a night out, a couple of streetpeople with nowhere else to go. They're all used to the sight of emaciated hookers, faces marked with the tell-tale acne scars of a bad diet and an even worse drug habit, skulking in the shadows, hoping to spot a lone punter ready to pay for a little company.

Kings Cross, just 2 kilometres from the city centre and named after the intersection of three main roads, William Street, Darlinghurst Road and Victoria Street, has long been the one place in Australia where society's undercurrents both collide and combine.

A bohemian heartland of artists, writers and actors in the early twentieth century, it was also the centre for the sale of sly grog, sex, cocaine and the rights to illegal casinos. The rivalry between the two infamous brothel owners Tilly Devine and Kate Leigh helped fuel the razor gang wars of the 1920s, the organised crime turf battles over the spoils.

The influx of US servicemen visiting Sydney for a little R and R during the Vietnam War imported another major element into the already potent mix of crime, vice and corruption: heroin. Rapidly developing into a centre for its supply, followed by crack and ice, Kings Cross became a honeypot for the addicted, hopeless and helpless, and drug-related crime quickly came to dominate the streets. One of the world's first medically supervised injecting centres for drug users was opened in Kings Cross in 2001.

These days, Kings Cross is still that heady combination of rich and poor, a place where criminals rub shoulders with the cream of movie, TV and radio shock-jock stars, and bohemians break bread with bikies. But even more than this, it's where the rest of Sydney comes to party on a surfeit of bars, restaurants and strip clubs providing a never-ending flow of alcohol, sex and drugs. With one of the highest rates of assaults and robberies in the country, the feeling, quite wrongly, is that this is a place without rules.

For those who live and work in The Cross, the most densely populated area of Australia with nearly 20 000 people living in an area less than 1.4 square kilometres, the rules are very clear: you don't mess with the cops, you don't mix with the crims and you certainly don't shit on your own doorstep. But for the outsiders who drift in, up to no good, it always looks like a place of boundless opportunity.

And tonight, in a nearby street, one of those deadbeats paces, looking for easy prey.

The man is just under 6 foot tall, and looks wiry and strong. His dark hair is short on top, but with a long black ponytail, plaited at the back. He's unshaven and has a general unkempt air about him. He's also covered in tattoos, hidden away for the moment under a dark hoodie, black jacket and navy-blue jeans, while the insides of both of his arms are scarred from a decade or more of heroin use and abuse.

Just now he's broke, but itching for a heroin fix. It's gnawing away at his insides.

He's only a few weeks out of jail, freed on parole after two years served for breaking into houses and stealing whatever valuables he could sneak away. He had a big row with his girlfriend in Wollongong, 80 kilometres south of Sydney, and drifted into Kings Cross, hopeful of making a little cash on $5000 worth of camera equipment he recently thieved from a shop break-in. He's had some success too, selling it in a pawnshop no questions asked and, with the proceeds, buying some fresh heroin to feed his raging addiction.

Feeling flush, he then buddied up with two sex workers he met at The Cross, going back to the flat where one of them lived and sharing a fix in exchange for sex. He had a feed there too, tearing apart a hot chook they'd bought on the way back and heaping it between two slabs of bread. When one of the girls then split to look for more customers on the street, he stayed back and had sex with the other. This one was better. She hadn't asked him to wear a condom and so he didn't. He didn't bother to tell her about his hep C and being HIV-positive, either. Tough shit if she caught them, but she probably had them anyway, he reasoned to himself. Then he injected himself again with the last of his stash.

He would have liked to stay, but this woman was eager to get back out into the afternoon too, for the chance to earn more cash. Besides, there were two other men there, the woman's flatmates, somehow also sharing the tiny one-bedroom unit. They were sitting watching TV in the cramped lounge room and ducking into the bedroom's en suite to use the only toilet in the place. They'd glowered at him when he'd walked in and swore at the girls about bringing someone new back and making too much noise. Now the two girls were gone, they didn't look any friendlier.

He left one of his bags by the bed, slung his little daypack over his shoulder and slipped out after the woman, planning to stick close to her. She might get lucky and then hopefully she might share any smack she bought. As he came out of the rundown redbrick block of flats, he looked around him. He was slap-bang on the main road running from the eastern suburbs of Sydney, with their bays and beaches, directly into the city, 3 kilometres away to his left. To his right, he could see down the road to the illuminated side of a bus shelter on the edge of a park. Straight in front, he caught sight of the woman fast disappearing along the tangle of streets into Kings Cross.

He started hurrying, and strained to see her in the distance. He thought he glimpsed her again, but then she disappeared. He stopped and felt his irritation mount. The bitch had given him the slip.

Now, ten hours on, it's late at night and he's getting agitated, craving more of the drug, his body racked with the ache of withdrawal. He has no more money and with every passing hour, he feels his desperation grow. He needs to 'get well' and for a junkie that means only one thing: getting the money to score.

Before, he was bad. Now he's dangerous.

He's been lurking around this darkened neighbourhood for hours, on the hunt for a target to menace, to attack, to rob. Whatever it takes.

And then he sees her. A woman alone. Early twenties. Petite, slim, blonde and laden down with a bag in either hand. She seems comfortable, like she has money. The black leather bag she has over one shoulder looks expensive, and the black fabric one in the other hand is full of clothes and groceries. She doesn't look the type to be going anywhere with an empty purse. Even better, he can see headphones from an iPod over each ear.

He makes a snap decision: he's going to get her. If he's careful, she won't even notice him coming. She won't know what's hit her. He pulls his black hoodie down over as much of his face as he can and advances. Softly. Like a cat getting ready to pounce. Stealthily. His new Nike joggers, a present from his girlfriend back home in Wollongong, don't make a sound.

The woman is walking fast; she doesn't like being around these deserted streets on her own in the dark. Suddenly, she hears a soft footfall approaching from behind, pulls her left headphone off her ear and immediately quickens her pace. But she's too late.

Before she realises what's happening, two strong arms grab her from behind, a hand is clamped over her mouth and she smells the rancid breath of her attacker close to her face, hears his ragged breathing in her ear. 'Hey baby, don't you want to . . . ' she hears him whisper. She twists and tries to push his arms off her face to wrest herself free but is simply not strong enough to break his grip. Instead, she falls heavily to the ground in a desperate attempt to duck away. She cuts one knee badly but has no time to try to stem the flowing blood. 'Give me the money!' he barks at her. 'Give me the money!'

Instead, she lashes out at him, thrashing wildly with the bags she's carrying, tries to kick him, to punch him, to scratch him. She wants to hurt him before he can hurt her. And she knows, in this dark and lonely street, she may well be fighting for her life.

The ferocity of her reaction takes the man completely by surprise. He snatches his hand back from her mouth to defend himself and makes a grab for her arms. In that split second, she screams as loudly as she can, a shriek that rips, loud and hard, through the night-time hush.

It has an immediate effect. There's the sound of footsteps running up, and then she hears another woman shouting. 'Hang on!' she's yelling. 'I'm coming!' Almost simultaneously, she hears a window of an apartment somewhere above her being slammed open and a third woman yelling down asking if she's all right.

The man gives a sudden whimper of defeat, pulls himself away and runs off down the street. His prey slumps into the arms of the second woman, shaking with the fear of what she's just been through, and overcome with relief and gratitude. Even so, she has no idea just how lucky she's been.

The man vanishes into the darkness, licking his wounds, cursing his misfortune.

Next time, he tells himself, he'll do it right.

# Chapter 2
# THRILLED TO BE BACK

It's pitch black when Kings Cross police sergeant Samantha Barlow opens her eyes. She hasn't slept much; she's been feeling too restless. Her phone is just by the bed, and she leans over and cancels the alarm that was due to buzz in a few minutes' time.

After seven months off work on maternity leave with her two small children, she hasn't yet got used to getting up at 4.30 a.m. ready for the early-morning shift. But she loves her job so much, she was too excited to sleep. All morning she's been looking forward to the alarm going off so she could get up and spring into action. Today will be only her sixth day back.

Her husband of just two years, Laurence, stirs sleepily beside her. Normally, he'd wake at the same time and murmur, 'You're still here!' – his daily joke about being baffled that she's still married to him when she could have done so much better for herself. He'd then usually tell her that he loves her, and kiss her on the side of the head. But today he sleeps on.

A fellow police officer she got to know on the job during the Cronulla riots, Laurence is off sick this morning with an acute bout of tonsillitis, both upper and lower respiratory tract infections and back pain from three bulging discs, and she's anxious to let him keep sleeping. He won't have to wake properly for a good three hours yet, when he'll take their seven-month-old baby Ben to his first day at day care and drop off their toddler daughter Lily, who's due to celebrate her second birthday in eleven days. Samantha pauses for a second and hears the gentle breathing of the pair on the monitors she's put by the side of the bed. Good. Their two beautiful children are still sleeping soundly. No need to check in on them and risk waking either one.

Samantha slips quietly out of bed and runs lightly downstairs. She doesn't dare have a shower at home at that time in the morning for fear of disturbing the kids. She loves her sleep and if the kids can sleep through, she's more likely to enjoy an unbroken night. It's always hard getting up before dawn, still a good two hours away this morning, but the earlier she gets to work, the sooner she can be back home again with her family.

She laid her things out in the lounge room the night before, and now she pulls on a long-sleeved T-shirt and track pants, then squashes her PE kit and police boots into a pink Enviro shopping bag, folding her police uniform trousers and freshly laundered police shirt on top. She'll iron those when she gets to work; it'd be pointless ironing them now, knowing how creased they'll be by the time she reaches work and pulls them out of her bag. She doesn't bother with coffee or breakfast, either. She can pick up those at work too.

She quickly washes her face and brushes her teeth in the small downstairs bathroom, and does a quick check of all the kids' clothes, spare sets of outfits and sunhats laid out on the dining table. She spent the evening ironing name tags onto them, and making sure their bags, drink bottles and formula bottle for Ben were all clearly labelled too.

Then she swings her smart new grey and pink leather designer bag – a gift from her mum for her thirty-fourth birthday two and a half months ago – over her shoulder and picks up the Enviro bag. The front door always closes with a bang and, eager to get out of the house as silently as she can, she pushes open the back door, tiptoes out and pulls it closed softly behind her. By 4.50 a.m. she's at the wheel of the family's blue Holden Commodore sedan driving out of Sydney's southern suburbs, heading for Kings Cross.

There's little traffic on the road, and Samantha feels the old familiar hit of adrenalin of being on the way to a job she adores. Although she enjoyed her time off, it was no picnic being at home with two children under the age of two, and she's thrilled to be back at work in the police force – all she's ever wanted since the age of ten.

And while she loves her role as a police sergeant, working in the traffic division of Sydney's fast-paced Kings Cross, the job, in turn, loves her back. She reached the rank of sergeant quickly, remarkably after fewer than ten years' service, and although still in her early thirties, she's on the cusp of being promoted to inspector. Already she's passed three of the four components of the promotion system and is due to complete the final part in five months' time. That's by no means her limit, either. She's already being seen as a woman fast going places. One day, her bosses predict, the popular blonde with the ready smile, easygoing manner and iron resolve might well end up in the executive levels of the organisation.

This morning, however, she's totally focused on what the day ahead might hold. Her first five days back at the station have flown past in a whirlwind of trawling through the thousands of emails that came in during her time away, having a compulsory medical, catching up with her colleagues, attending lectures and picking up her management scores that, together with the exams she sat while on leave, will form part of her assessment for promotion to Inspector after sixteen years with the force.

'I loved my time off with my children, that was very precious to me,' Samantha says. 'But like anyone, it can be hard staying home all the time with two babies for company, especially when you're used to a challenging career. It was very hard leaving them, and I found I was missing them and wanted to know what they were doing all the time, but I was keen to get back to work too. I felt so excited to be back.'

Now, this Wednesday morning, 13 May 2009, she's on her way to take a fitness test to requalify for her part-time role in the Operations Support Group, which provides support for the riot squad. She knows she'll pass with ease. Almost as soon as her son Ben was born last October, she resumed the rigorous training regime she'd followed almost all her life, knowing that in a force still largely dominated by men, she's always determined to do at least as well – if not better – than the best of them.

This time it's been a tough call to find the time to regain her peak physical shape, but somehow she's managed. That spell of maternity leave proved incredibly busy. As well as looking after the kids, Samantha sat for and passed the second and third sets of exams for promotion to inspector, often getting up at 3 a.m. or 4 a.m. to study while the children were asleep. On the days Laurence, already an inspector, was off, she'd go into the spare bedroom to work, pretending to Lily that she was at the station and keeping up the charade by calling her at mid-morning to talk to her on the phone, and slamming the front door at around 1 p.m. and walking in as if she'd just arrived home. During her leave, the family also moved out of Laurence's house in one Wollongong suburb and into a rental home in another while that was sold. Then, when Ben was just six weeks old, they moved again into the dream home they'd just had built on the site of an old redbrick cottage Samantha had owned for years in southern Sydney.

While it's more than halved their travel time to work – from a drive of an hour and a half to the city to one of just thirty minutes on a good day – it's been hard going. The couple are mortgaged up to the eyeballs and the house feels terribly empty with little furniture and a big backyard that's not much more than a quagmire of mud. In order to raise a little extra money, both husband and wife are working overtime for a security company the police are aligned with to help make ends meet. Samantha has already worked one extra shift for them at Fox Studios that first weekend, and has signed up for several more. But hopefully, if she becomes an inspector in October, that will mean a not insignificant $25 000 increase on her annual salary, which will provide welcome relief, as well as a different location for work, and fresh and exciting challenges.

'We're no different to any other couple starting out with a young family,' says Laurence, forty-five at the time. 'Money's tight but you're happy to make sacrifices. We'd liked living in Wollongong, where we'd started our married life, but moving to southern Sydney cut our daily travel time to work by an hour each way. We knew the new house was a stretch but we've both always been hard workers, and we knew it was going to be difficult at first, but it'd get easier with time.'

So as Samantha drives towards Kings Cross, she is feeling excited by both work and her future. In between listening to music and chat on the radio, she thinks about her day ahead. After dropping in to Kings Cross station to pick up an official police car, she's due in Homebush at 8.30 a.m. for the fitness test. There'll be a number of shuttle runs – running between two markers at least nine times within an allotted number of minutes – push-ups and a few simple agility exercises to perform.

After that, she'll probably go for a run with a few of the guys at the centre before heading back to Kings Cross. She has a few errands to run, too. There's $200 in her purse ready to buy a birthday present for Lily and she smiles to herself thinking of the little girl's delight when she unwraps her gift at the party they're planning for her. Lily had a party for her first birthday, but she was still too young to really understand the fuss. This year, she's been looking forward to her second birthday party for weeks.

Eventually, Samantha hits the Kings Cross Tunnel and arrives in Rushcutters Bay at 5.20 a.m., driving along the dark streets, looking for an unmetered place to park that will allow her to stay all day till the end of her twelve-hour shift. She eventually finds a gap on McLachlan Avenue near the BMW garage, and pulls in there. She snaps off the radio, kills the ignition, grabs her handbag and pink shopping bag from the passenger seat, and climbs out of the car.

She then starts walking briskly down the road past the BMW garage. She can't help smiling to herself as she glances over to it. One of her happiest memories is when she was eight and a half months pregnant with Ben, and she and Laurence went there to buy a car, laughing as she struggled, with such a big belly, to get into the driving seat behind the steering wheel to check it out. That might not just be a distant memory, either. Last night, she and Laurence talked about her desire for a third child to complete their family, and decided to try for another baby so the three will be as close as possible in age.

Shaking her head in wonder at how good life can be, she then walks up to the traffic lights, turns left into Craigend Street by the eastern end of the Cross City Tunnel and begins the climb up the hill towards Kings Cross. It is the last time she is ever to take that route.

# Chapter 3
# OUT OF THE SHADOWS

It's a bad night for a hopeless junkie. There are so few people around and those who are . . . they're just too bloody determined to hang on to their money.

After failing to rob the woman in the back street, the man is growing more and more desperate. He creeps up behind one sex worker on a busier street but she sees him, turns to face him and immediately starts shouting and hurling abuse. Worried she'll attract attention from a few passers-by, he yells at her that he only wanted to know the time, and slinks back into the night.

Later, back close to where he lucked out earlier, he spots one of the prostitutes he had sex with, and who shared his fix. Back then, he told her his name was Rob, but she didn't look like she believed him. He doesn't really care whether or not she did anyway. He's used a number of aliases all his life, so many that sometimes he has trouble keeping track of them. One of his favourites is 'Spooner'. But he's keeping that one to himself.

Tonight, he greets her like an old friend. In truth, she feels a bit like his only friend. He doesn't know if his girlfriend will have him back after their fight and, because he jumped straight onto a train to

Sydney, he knows the police will now be looking for him to lock him up again for breaking the strict conditions of his parole. He didn't sleep at home the previous night, he hasn't attended any of the drug counselling sessions arranged for him, and he wasn't in when the probation officer called. He knows he's now in deep shit. He keeps a wary eye out for anyone in uniform.

Spooner walks up to the woman, wanting to talk. 'I just tried to rob a girl,' he tells her. 'I tried to put my hand over her mouth and she fought me off and I ran off.' The woman nods. She looks at him. He seems agitated, restless, twitchy. She can tell he's 'hanging out' – junkie talk for being in dire need of a shot.

He looks rough. Wearing dark-blue jeans, a checked flannelette shirt and a black jacket, he looks as though he's trying hard not to be noticed. She then peers more closely. She observes that he has a large rock in his right hand, about the size of a house brick. He sees she's noticed. 'I'm going to smash someone's jaw and head in,' he explains, 'and steal their bag.' He then walks briskly off.

He prowls around the streets for a few hours, looking for a suitable target. He can think of only one thing: getting enough money to buy drugs.

He doesn't doubt that he has the nerve to smash a woman, either. After all, he's hurt women – and badly – before. The first time he appeared in court was for violence, for maliciously injuring someone, back when he was just twelve years old. That was June 1982 and over the next twelve months he was busier still, committing no fewer than thirteen other offences, including injuring another person, ten break-ins and two thefts. He started drinking heavily at fourteen and began bashing his girlfriends from that point on. 'Women are easy victims,' he confided to a casual acquaintance. Gradually, the violence escalated.

Later that same year, he was committed to an institution for juvenile offenders and then continued relentlessly on his chosen path of drug-taking, robbery and violence. By twenty-two, he was serving a stretch in jail and, five years later, he was back behind bars after his first frenzied attack on a woman: punching an old girlfriend, the mother of his two little girls, then stabbing at her with a 30 centimetre carving knife, slicing one of her fingers as she tried to fend him off and lunging at her with such force that the knife became embedded in the wardrobe door next to her.

But he didn't have to know women to hurt them. Not at all. A much more recent four years inside had been for a random attack on a woman in the streets. This time, she was a young Irish tourist, in Australia for a holiday visiting friends for a month. He started up a conversation with her in the street, and then asked her for a kiss. She politely declined and walked away.

He followed her and approached her a second time a few minutes later. She brushed him off and walked away again. But this time he came up behind her, pushed her to her knees and slammed her on the back of the head six times with a blunt object.

The woman desperately tried to cover her head with her hands, but was bludgeoned three more times. That'd teach her to treat him like dirt.

She only managed to escape by crawling through bushes as she was bashed, and then falling over a retaining wall into a main street. There, she scrambled to her feet and ran until a taxi driver came to her aid. She was then rushed to hospital, where her injuries were found to be terrible – her fingers and knuckles were shattered by the blows and she was left with large gashes, grazes and hideous bruising to her head. She was forced to undergo surgery to both her head and her hand.

The police caught their man soon after. Spooner had left the beanie he'd been wearing at the scene of the crime and the DNA on it matched his. No one could ever accuse him of being a criminal mastermind.

After doing more time for that, he went back to jail for burglary. He's now been out for just twenty-five days since he applied for parole and the authorities granted it, and is already seeking out a fresh victim. This time, he's feeling even more dangerous.

As well as being a hopeless junkie hanging out for a fix, he's also a diagnosed schizophrenic who stopped taking his medication the day he was released. It's a potent mix.

He needs cold cash and he's determined to get it. He knows he's got it in him to jump a woman and do her some real damage. And this time he's not going to let her get away.

It's now just before 5 a.m. on Wednesday 13 May, and Spooner is on the hunt. He's loitering on Craigend Street, the lonely road that divides Kings Cross from Darlinghurst, just outside the door of the rundown unit block where he had sex and drugs fifteen hours earlier.

He sees a woman parking her car nearby and he takes a long, hard look at her. She has a small backpack over her left shoulder as she crosses the street towards Ward Avenue. As she reaches the other side of the road, she puts her bag down and starts going through her pockets, looking for something. Then she looks back at her car, and sees him standing at the entrance of an apartment building.

He looks at her, and she looks at him. He realises he's been clocked. She doesn't look too friendly, either.

In fact, there's something about the man that's making her feel uneasy. 'I didn't like the look of him, and I wondered if he was going to break into my car,' she says later. 'I thought I might have left my mobile in the car but there's no way I was going back there across the road. It was dark and the way he was standing there, just looking at me, didn't feel right.

'So I kept walking quite quickly. When I looked back, I noticed he'd moved closer to the front of my car and was still looking in my direction. I just kept walking and after a while, I lost sight of him. I wondered if I was overreacting. After all, he wasn't actually doing anything.'

Spooner has already decided not to go after her. He needs a victim who's not moving so fast, someone he sees before they notice him. He doesn't have long to wait. A few minutes later, another woman parks her car on Craigend Street and then starts walking over to Ward Avenue. She hasn't seen him, and he feels this might be his chance. He starts running towards her, trying to catch up to her.

At that point, she turns and looks directly at him. She then speeds up and takes out her mobile phone. She's still walking quickly but has now started talking loudly on the phone. It sounds as if she's on the phone to the police, saying where she is and that a man is following her. The man doesn't quite know what to do. She's now reached Bayswater Road where there are a lot more streetlights, and is walking along the edge of the roadway instead of on the darker footpath. The woman keeps using the word 'police' and it gradually dawns on him that she's actually a policewoman and is on the phone to Kings Cross police station, which is just a few hundred metres away.

Again, he can't believe his bad luck. She's obviously seen him and has probably memorised his description by now. He decides to give up on her, and drops back. The woman stays on the line until she notices he's now out of sight, and carries on her way to work at the station.

Spooner, meanwhile, is getting more and more antsy. What the hell is going on? He needs to be more careful, he tells himself. There are a few more people around here, and it's better lit, so he decides to go back to Craigend Street and continue his hunt there. Fifteen minutes later, on nearby Surrey Street, a quiet one-way street lined with parked cars, golden robinia trees along the footpath and elegant old terraces, he spots another potential target. This time, she's walking behind him, in the same direction. He halts and turns to face her. 'Do you have the time?' he asks her. 'What's the time?'

She moves over to the footpath to avoid him. As he comes closer, she summons all her courage. 'If you don't leave me alone, I'm going to call my boyfriend,' she threatens. 'And he works at Kings Cross police station.' Bloody hell! What is it with that station this morning? He considers that for a few moments, then turns on his heel and walks away from her. She's another one who looks like far too much trouble.

He then wanders down the hill a short distance, and discovers a small pocket park, little more than a grassy wedge with a few mature pepper trees around the edges and an old stone wall, topped with a graffiti-daubed wooden fence, separating it from the houses behind. A pedestrian bridge over the main roadway winds down to the park, and in the shadows by the pylons holding the bridge up is a green park bench. On the pavement in front of the grass and a little to its left is a bus shelter made of transparent perspex, with an illuminated ad for the Fred Hollows Foundation on its side and another bench inside it. To the back is a sharps bin for other drug users who regularly come to the park to shoot up.

Spooner sits for a moment on the bench in the park and ponders his position. Maybe he could pick off someone walking past? But he'd have to be careful: the pavement is right on the five-lane main road, with different filters going up to Darlinghurst, into the Cross City Tunnel and Kings Cross Tunnel towards town, and down in the other direction towards the eastern beaches.

Yet there's not much traffic and where he's sitting, he's also in the shadow of the overpass. But headlights from the odd car flicker over him as they pass by, and he can see some of the drivers looking. He feels too exposed here. A young man on his way home from a night-shift at work trudges past and, when the man on the bench glances up at him, he quickly looks away. The man knows, once again, he's been noticed.

It's now 5.15 a.m.; he's going to have to get a move on and find someone to rob before he attracts any more attention. It'll start getting light soon too, and there'll be a lot more cars on the road as the early risers start off for work. He simply doesn't have time to screw this one up.

He rises to his feet and stands for a few seconds, working out where to go. He feels anxious, and jigs forwards and backwards and sideways. A motorist driving towards the city notices him and makes a mental note to himself about how jittery the man looks, how suspiciously he's acting and how glad he is that he's not out there in the dark, having to deal with characters like him.

Finally, Spooner reaches a decision. He turns round and peers back into the park. It's dark there across the grass, around the edges, and he could hide away from the world. Those women have spooked him. He realises he's only going to be successful if he manages to catch a woman completely unawares, just like he did a few years ago with that Irishwoman.

He walks into the shadows at the back of the park and hunkers down against one of the walls, where he can't be seen from the footpath. Standing, he can see a little down the street, but crouching down, no one can see him. He stays there and waits. When he sees someone coming, he'll be able to dart towards the old robinia tree standing just by the pavement, hide behind its gnarled trunk and then sneak out of the shadows from there. Even better, he'll be standing on a slope downwards to the footpath, so he'll have the high-ground advantage. He'll be able to use the impetus of his movement to strike someone even harder.

His fingers tighten over the rough surface of the slab of rock he's holding in his right hand and he feels his body shaking all over. He badly needs a fix. And now he has the perfect time and the place, and the weapon, to get one.

Samantha Barlow doesn't stand a chance. As she walks briskly past the start of Arthur Park on her left, she can't see a dark figure slinking out of the shadows towards her. The first she knows of his presence is when she feels a blow, hard, to the back of her head, delivered with such force it actually dents her skull.

She crumples to her knees but the blows from the sharp edge of the rock keep coming. Her hands go instinctively to her head to try to protect it and her right hand is smashed and mangled as it now receives the full force of Spooner's rage. There's blood pouring from the back of her head, from her forehead and face, matting her hair, a dark stain seeping downwards through her clothes. She keeps fighting back, still gamely hanging on to her bags. Finally she falls forward, face-first, onto the ground, in agony from her injuries, still not understanding what's going on, confused and in shock. The man tries to wrench the bags from her grasp and then, infuriated, smashes her face into the stone wall. At last, she goes limp and sinks into unconsciousness.

At that, Spooner looks furtively around then, like a wild animal, grabs her and drags her into the park to his lair, where they can both be hidden in the shadows. An 8 metre trail of blood is left in their wake. He then rips open Samantha's leather bag and darts back to where items lay scattered on the ground from the struggle over the cotton bag. As he gathers them, he suddenly stops dead. One is a blue shirt, with the unmistakable epaulettes and crest of the NSW Police Force. Shit. This woman is police.

He stands motionless for a few moments. 'I'm dead,' he thinks to himself. 'I've just killed a policewoman. My life's fucked.' He glances over at Samantha, lying on her back where he's dumped her, and sees as if for the first time her broken, bloodied face, her smashed skull, her mangled hand. Her eyes are closed; she looks dead. He snatches up the shirt and throws it over her face so he'll no longer be able to see the damage he's caused. All that blood, all those injuries . . . he's starting to feel sick.

He begins to go through the leather bag, looking for cash, for any valuables he'll be able to sell. After a few moments, though, he suddenly realises he shouldn't be standing here next to the body. Anyone could see him. That wouldn't be smart. He feels panic rising. He's got to get out of here. He grabs all the woman's possessions and chucks them back into the bags, whipping the shirt off her face as an afterthought and stuffing that in too. He realises he's dropped the rock he used as such a lethal weapon and hunts around for that. He doesn't want to leave it on the scene – it could too easily lead police straight to him.

He finds it, covered in her blood and hair, and then he races away as fast as he can. Samantha lies crumpled at the back of the park, left for dead.

# Chapter 4
## LEFT FOR DEAD

The sight of Samantha Barlow's battered face has so unnerved Spooner that he can hardly think straight. He's sure she's dead, and that he's just killed a policewoman. He's not worried about her, though. He's more worried about himself.

He darts around the corner from the park and then forces himself to slow down. Don't attract attention. Try to act calm. He's sweating with the effort of smashing Samantha, of pulling her into the park and throwing everything back into her bags. And he knows he looks suspicious, with her blood on his hands and his jacket, and carrying a woman's shoulder bag and a pink shopping bag as well as his own little backpack. But he can't help that. It's too late now. What's done is done. He walks briskly along Oswald Lane away from Kings Cross, skirting the parked cars so he can walk close to the walls of apartment buildings and terrace houses, where the shadows are the deepest. It's on a downhill slope and soon leads into the hushed maze of streets behind Darlinghurst. He needs to find a quiet place where he can stop and go through the bags. He only hopes that he'll find plenty of cash and stuff worth selling.

He crosses one street. He's now about 100 metres from the park and the next little street, Womerah Lane, is deathly silent. He looks around. In the dim light of the odd streetlight, he can make out only garages with their roller doors down, back gates and overhanging trees. In one corner, there's a raised garden bed full of the large dark-green tropical leaves of fruit-salad plants under the shelter of a tall gum growing along one edge. This looks a good spot.

He perches on the side of the low wall around the garden and goes through the bags properly. He finds a purse with $200 in it – the money for Samantha's little girl's birthday present – and her mobile phone. It's not much, but it'll do. He stuffs the purse down the front of his pants and puts the phone in the left front pocket of his jeans.

He then pulls the blue police shirt from her bag and bundles it among the roots of a plant, stuffing it under a little tangle of geraniums sheltering beneath. He takes the pink cotton bag that still holds her police boots and hides that too, behind shrubbery. He then squashes up the leather bag and pushes it into his backpack. Finally, realising he's still holding the rock with which he bashed Samantha so brutally, he tosses that into the same garden and buries it under a pile of leaves he scuffs up with his foot. He doesn't notice a man walking to work nearby, who sees him and wonders idly what he's doing.

Confident he's covered his tracks, he then walks away. He doesn't fancy getting lost in these back streets, so he goes back the way he came towards Kings Cross, past the park. He resists even glancing at the corner in which he left the woman. Instead, he marches straight past, crosses Craigend Street and Kings Cross Road and peels off down another back street, Goderich Lane, between the back walls of apartment blocks and hotels. It's quiet and there's no one there to see him.

Satisfied he's again out of sight and a safe enough distance from the park, he takes out Samantha's purse and rifles through it, extracting the $200 in cash and her credit cards. He flips through them and stares at them. Weighing it up, he decides it's too risky to try using the cards. So he tosses them, together with the empty purse and her leather bag, into a skip standing on the corner and rakes around it to make sure other rubbish is sitting on top.

He then walks down the lane and back around to Bayswater Road to a small convenience store, sauntering in as if he hasn't a care in the world. He buys a bottle of water and hands over a note in payment. When he's pocketed the change, he leaves the shop and walks around to the nearby laneway. There, he unscrews the cap off the bottle, crouches down in the gutter and pours water onto each hand, then rubs them together. After everything that's happened, he feels soiled.

'I felt fuckin' dirty after what happened,' he says. 'I felt I needed to wash myself. I washed my face, my neck, everything. I just felt bad. I felt really bad.' Even the simple act of rinsing the blood and dirt off his hands makes him feel better, like he's washing his sins away.

Close by, he sees a taxi approaching and makes a split-second decision. He needs to get away from this area as quickly as possible. He puts his arm out to hail the cab and it rumbles to a halt right beside him. He opens the door, gets in and speaks to the driver at the same time. 'Central Station,' he says. 'And I'm in a hurry.'

Samantha is lying in the grass at the back of Arthur Park, drifting in and out of consciousness. She has no idea what she's doing there; she simply can't work out what's happening. All she knows is that she's in excruciating pain, which keeps coming and going as she blacks out and then wakes up again. She doesn't realise she's been left for dead.

Slowly, her survival instincts kick in. Somehow, she knows she just can't stay where she is. She's lying in a pool of dark blood and she can feel her life force gradually ebbing away from her and soaking into the soil. If she stays there much longer, out of sight of the world, something deep within her tells her she could just slip away. And she doesn't want to die. She has a husband and two gorgeous kids to live for. She needs to get help, and quickly.

She puts both hands on the ground to try to lever herself up into a sitting position, but the pain from her shattered right hand is almost unbearable. She leans harder on her left hand and, little by little, manoeuvres herself into a sitting position. She feels light-headed and dizzy and just sits there for a few minutes, hoping the sick feeling will soon subside.

The sky's beginning to grow lighter, and there are two men at the bus stop 15 metres away. They're chatting animatedly. One's sitting on the bench in the shelter and the other is standing, and they're both peering down the road waiting for their bus to come. Neither of them glances in her direction. Then there's the soft purr of the bus approaching, the blurred squeak of its brakes as it stops, the whoosh of its doors opening and closing, then finally the unmistakable roar of its departure. Samantha is still lapsing in and out of consciousness, with no idea what's going on. She looks like the loneliest person in the world.

She sits and tries to focus, to gather her strength. A car sweeps past and its driver notices her in the grass. He doesn't realise she's doused in her own blood. 'I saw someone dressed in red, with red hair and a red face, sitting on the grass,' he later tells police. 'I thought it was a man with long hair. I thought it was a man who'd been at a party and was now waiting for a bus to go home and he was so tired, his eyes were closed. It looked like the person was resting.' He drives on.

After a few more minutes, Samantha decides to try to get to the footpath, to the bus stop. It's the only way anyone's going to be able to see her, to call for help. She lies down on her front and slowly, inch by inch, drags herself through the grass towards the path, leaving a scarlet slick of blood on the ground behind her. Halfway there, she reaches one of the pylons supporting the pedestrian overpass above and clings to it, leaving smudged handprints of blood. It's about another 8 metres to the next one, so she focuses on that as her target. Her progress is slow and uneven as she drifts in and out of consciousness, but she's determined. She refuses to just lie down and die.

She finally reaches the second pylon and, by hugging it close to her body, manages to pull herself up. The bench is only a few steps away. Her legs are shaking with the effort as she lunges towards it but she makes it. She slumps onto it. It's only a metre from the footpath, so surely someone will spot her here and call for help.

A female jogger at that point turns into Craigend Street, running up the hill towards the city. She notices Samantha on the bench, but she's so covered in blood that the jogger also mistakenly thinks she must be a man. 'He was sitting with his hands up to his face and it looked like he had blood on his face,' she reports to the police when questioned that evening. 'He was sitting sideways on the bench facing the park, facing away from the street. He did look a bit distressed.' The runner doesn't stop; she carries on straight past.

'I kept running because I thought he was a junkie,' she later explains. 'I often see people around the area that are a bit dodgy. My first reaction was that it might have been red paint. I wasn't sure whether it was blood or not . . . I think he saw me, he seemed to look at me and then he looked back towards the park.'

At the same time, four tradies, one in a yellow safety vest, walk past. Not one of them notices the broken, battered figure on the park bench.

Eventually Samantha realises that she has to be somewhere more obvious. She looks over to the bus shelter, about 4 metres away. People will start going to work soon. If she can only make it there, maybe someone will finally see her. If she doesn't get help soon, she knows all may be lost.

She summons every last vestige of her courage and slips silently down off the bench. Then, on all fours, she crawls towards the bus stop, staining the footpath with scarlet. She's now feeling very weak and exhausted with the effort and the loss of so much blood, and she's chilled to the bone, but she knows she has to go further. She has to somehow find a way of making it to that bus shelter to get noticed. Otherwise people will continue walking past, while the last faint sparks of life leak out of her. She doesn't want to die this way.

With an almost superhuman effort, she crawls further into the shelter. Fluttering in the corner is an old blue insulation blanket that's obviously been used by a homeless person sleeping there at some time in the past. Samantha grabs onto the side of the shelter and tries to lever herself up onto her feet so she'll be able to wave down a passing car, or at least make it onto the bench. But just as she's almost there, she's overcome with dizziness and slides back down, leaving the glass smeared with her blood. When the light-headedness passes, she tries a second time, but again falls down. After a third time, she realises it's not going to be possible, and instead just hunches in the corner of the shelter, wrapping herself in the blanket, utterly spent.

It's now 6.40 a.m., just over an hour since she was attacked.

A car speeds past on its way to the city, and Samantha's so awash in blood, the driver thinks she's someone merely waiting at the bus stop trying to get home after a big night out. Why else would anyone be in a Santa suit at that time in the morning?

A few moments later, a woman walks along the street, with her dog. As she gets near the bus stop, she too notices Samantha. It's this passer-by who finally approaches her. 'Are you okay?' she asks. 'Do you need help?' Samantha doesn't have the energy left to respond. She doesn't say anything, but her eyes remain open.

'I could see a lot of blood on her back right side of her head,' the woman tells the police later. 'She had blood all over her pants and her jumper. It looked as though she had some injuries to her face.'

But, ironically, out of all the people who've seen Samantha this morning, this woman is the least equipped to help. She didn't pick up her mobile phone when she left home to take her dog out. So there is little she actually can do. Instead, she goes off, catches her dog and then races home to call the police from there, leaving Samantha all alone again, and perilously close to death.

Samantha's attacker has just bought coffee and a hot breakfast from McDonald's, and is now walking through the main gates of Sydney's Central Station with his brown paper bag, holding a baggy checked shirt in the same hand.

As the CCTV cameras catch him on his way, he looks comfortable, completely at ease. He ambles over to a rubbish bin and dumps his own blood-spattered jacket into it. He then studies the departures board for a few moments, buys a ticket to Port Kembla, a suburb of Wollongong 110 kilometres south of Sydney, and sits waiting for the 7.01 a.m. train. He's on his way home.

At Kings Cross police station, Constable Phil Scott, a relatively new recruit, is just starting work on the 6 a.m. shift. He's checking the equipment, the cars and the overnight log and, by all accounts, sees it's been a pretty quiet night and an even quieter morning. It's now 6.20 a.m. which, on a Wednesday morning, is one of the most uneventful times of the week.

Today, he's paired with Constable Teneille Keith, a very junior officer who's on her fifth day at Kings Cross on rotation from Rose Bay police station. Scott is always keen and has a reputation as an unfailingly conscientious officer, so he suggests to Keith that they go out on patrol to double-check everything's truly as peaceful as it seems. A colleague is finishing his shift and Scott offers to give him a lift to his car down on New Beach Road. It's a decision that is to have life-and-death consequences.

Scott takes a van and he and Keith drop off the other officer, then complete a wide sweep of the area. Driving up New South Head Road into Craigend Street, however, something catches his eye. As he passes the park, he slows, then stops and reverses back until he's level with the bus shelter. He's spotted a blue tarp and what looks like a woman covered in blood slumped on the ground by the bench inside the shelter.

He climbs out of the van, and immediately calls for an ambulance. Keith also gets out and approaches the woman. She's shocked by her appearance. She seems to be drenched in blood, and it's not immediately obvious whether she's dead or alive. 'It was the most horrible thing I've ever seen,' says Keith. 'To realise someone's alive but red from head to toe in blood . . . It's like someone had poured red hair dye all over her. I thought, Has she been hit by a truck? Is she the victim of a domestic?'

Scott takes a closer look at her. Despite the fact that Samantha's a sergeant who's been working at Kings Cross police station for more than three years, he doesn't recognise her. He hasn't a clue who she is.

'She had a large cut to the right side of her forehead, which was bleeding, the area around the cut was swollen, her hair was caked in blood, and I saw one of the fingers on her right hand had a nail partially torn off and there was a large swollen area across her right knuckles,' Scott writes in his log. 'I saw the wall of the bus shelter behind her head was covered in blood.'

Her injuries are so severe, he thinks she must have been hit by a car. 'She was barely conscious,' he says. 'I didn't know if she was going to live. I felt it must be a hit-and-run.'

Keith, meanwhile, is trying to talk to the woman. 'What's your name?' she asks her.

Samantha looks at her blearily. 'Samantha Barlow,' she whispers back.

Still, she looks so unlike their Samantha Barlow, they don't make the connection. 'Do you know where you are, Samantha?' Keith asks her gently.

'No,' she replies.

Keith continues. 'You have a large cut on your head,' she says. 'There's an ambulance on the way. Do you know how you got this cut?'

Samantha shakes her head. 'No,' she says. 'Can I have a tissue?'

Keith tries again. 'You've been bleeding a lot. Do you know why you're bleeding?' Samantha answers that she doesn't know.

The policewoman then tells her she's going to put gauze and a wad of bandages to the back of her head to stop the bleeding, as Samantha continues to ask for a tissue. Keith is puzzled as to why she's so focused on a tissue for her nose, when her head is bleeding so badly. She doesn't realise that Samantha's own brain liquid is actually leaking out from her nose. Finally, Keith asks her where she's from. Samantha is firm. This she does know. 'Kings Cross,' she responds.

At that, Scott looks at her more closely. 'Samantha Barlow,' he repeats to himself thoughtfully. 'That's a sergeant's name at work.' He stares at her.

'Shit!' Keith says, shocked. 'Is that her?' The gauze and bandages she's holding to the back of Samantha's head where the bleeding is worst are now also soaked a dark red.

'I don't know,' Scott replies. 'I can't tell.' Beneath all that blood and those injuries . . . He pauses then suddenly snaps to attention. 'Yes! I think that could be her!' he says. Shocked, he calls the senior duty officer back at the station to relay the news that the woman they've just found so seriously injured could well be one of their own. 'I've known her for a couple of years since I've been at Kings Cross, but I didn't recognise her at all,' he says. 'Then when she said she was Samantha Barlow, something clicked. We very rarely deal with anyone we know. It makes it all a lot more confronting.'

The officer he's called, Sergeant Simon Kirby, immediately jumps into a car and races to the scene. He's been working at Kings Cross for fifteen years and, out of all his officers, he has a special soft spot for Samantha. 'We're good friends at work,' he says. 'We're always joking around and she's always bubbly and happy-go-lucky but is a very hard worker at the same time. She's a lovely person, a top bird. As soon as I heard it could have been Sam they'd found, I had to get down there.'

But nothing could have prepared him for how she looks. 'It was extremely shocking seeing someone you're close to covered from head to toe in blood,' he says. 'It was like that movie *Carrie*, when they tip a bucket of blood all over Sissy Spacek. Sam was unrecognisable. I thought she must have been run over by a car.'

Keith, still tending to Samantha, sees the mix of shock and horror on Kirby's face. 'I remember looking at him, and seeing him standing there in absolute shock,' she says. 'He was, "Oh my God! Oh my God! It's her!" He just stood there for a moment. He didn't believe it could be her. I think the whole situation was so much easier for me as I didn't know her.'

Kirby then approaches Samantha, bends down and says, 'Sam, is that you?' She looks up. 'It was only when she said, "Yeah!" that I realised it must be her,' he says.

Meanwhile, Samantha's still asking for a tissue. Scott tries again to find out what's going on. 'Samantha, what's happened?' he asks her.

'Nothing,' she replies. 'I just need a tissue.' Two more police officers then arrive at the scene, and Scott gets back on the radio to the ambulance service, to tell them their patient's injuries are severe, and that she's a police officer.

The ambulance arrives from the Paddington station, 1.5 kilometres away, in just one minute and twenty seconds. Michael 'Taz' Rundle is driving and he well appreciates the urgency of the situation. He started his morning shift just a few minutes ago and although the job has technically come in for the night shift, he volunteers to take it to allow the night shift to go home. It'll be good karma for the next time a job comes in late on his shift, and maybe the next one will take it for him. Today he's paired for the first time with former New Zealand Navy medic and trainee New South Wales ambulance officer Seth Leon, but the pair have met before at the station and have formed a bit of a rapport. They're both experienced and highly skilled paramedics, and Rundle is confident they will work well together.

They've made it to the scene in record time to find Samantha propped up on the bench surrounded by police officers. 'At first sight, she looked like a bag woman,' says Rundle. 'She was so dishevelled physically and her hair was so matted with blood.

But then you looked more closely, and you realised she was actually a young woman. I talked to her and observed her, and I could see she could understand what I was saying. She went almost imperceptibly from that vacant stare of someone who's been severely traumatised to someone that I could see was still there, somewhere inside.'

The two men work quickly and efficiently to stabilise her. They place a brace around her neck to protect her spine, take her blood pressure and pulse, inject her with medication to stop her being sick, in case, with all her reflexes slowed down, she might choke on her own vomit, and help her to her feet so she can lie back down on a stretcher.

'All the time, I couldn't help noticing how mangled and deformed her hands were,' says Rundle. 'She was also bleeding from the head and the back of her skull was a depressed mess. We couldn't know what might be going on inside her head, how bad her cerebral injuries, or damage to the brain, might be. We could see the severity of her wounds – some of the worst I've ever seen on someone still alive – but she had a good spark of life there.

'We knew, though, that time was critical. We talk about "The Golden Hour" – the time you have between sustaining an injury when the body protects itself with certain chemical releases, and then the time when you start to bleed out and the body begins to shut down. We didn't know what time she'd been injured but we knew she must have been there for quite some time and we had to get her to hospital and into surgery straightaway if she was going to stand a chance.'

While the two men work on her, there's the constant encouragement of the police officers at the scene, who are now arriving in their droves to see if they can help in any way. 'She's one of us,' they're telling the paramedics. 'Take care of her; she's one of ours.'

Rundle knows how important it is that those in the emergency services – the 'blood and guts industry' as it's known – look after each other. They all face similar dangers in their jobs, and he often stops to help police or fire officers he sees having trouble. One of the paramedics from the night shift that he replaced has even been panicking back at the station since, going out with a female officer from Kings Cross himself, he fears the patient might be his girlfriend . . . despite having talked to her on her home phone shortly before.

As they carefully lift the stretcher into the ambulance, Keith and fellow Kings Cross officer and friend Sergeant Kate Merritt scramble into the vehicle beside Samantha. Merritt wants to make sure she doesn't feel alone. 'Where are you taking her?' asks one of the police officers as they close the ambulance doors on the pair.

'St Vincent's,' replies Rundle.

'And you will take good care of her?' the officer asks. 'After all, she's one of ours.'

Rundle races round to the driver's seat. 'Sure will!' he replies as he revs the engine and prepares to switch on the siren. 'She's one of mine, now.'

The first Samantha's husband Laurence knows anything is wrong is when the home phone, and then his mobile, keeps ringing. It's just after 7 a.m. and he's still in bed, drugged up on a double dose of antibiotics for his acute tonsillitis, and suffering a shocking head cold. Through the thick fog in his brain, he felt Samantha slip out of bed two and a half hours before but, since then, he's been dead to the world.

He sleepily turns over in bed, and idly wonders who could be ringing at this time in the morning. He left his mobile downstairs and doesn't think to go and get it. Whoever's calling can leave a message.

Then the doorbell starts ringing, there's banging on the front door and, simultaneously, there's someone hammering on the back door. Finally realising that something's going on, Laurence crawls out of bed and runs down the stairs to find out what's happening. He opens the front door to find his good mate and riot squad colleague Inspector Paul 'Condo' Condon, and goes to the back door to find their other great friend and workmate Sergeant Brendan Crowe. Laurence can see from the look on their faces that something's terribly wrong.

'Sam's been hurt,' Condon tells him bluntly. 'Get in the car. We're going to hospital.' They wake the two children, Lily and Ben, dress them hurriedly, and Crowe and Condon grab one each under their arms and put them in the car too. Crowe drives them all straight to day care to drop the kids off, explaining to the manager that there's an emergency, then puts on the blue light, fires the siren and races down the highway from Caringbah in Sydney's south towards St Vincent's Hospital in Darlinghurst.

Laurence is deathly quiet as he tries to take everything in. There isn't much to tell him: Samantha has apparently been involved in some kind of incident, maybe a hit-and-run, on the way to work and is now badly hurt in hospital. The doctors need her husband's consent to put her into an induced coma in the hope of saving her life, but things still look bleak. They want him there at the hospital as soon as possible.

As the police car roars through the suburbs, darting in and out of the way of huge trucks bearing down on them, driving the opposite direction along one-way lanes and speeding past lines of morning commuter traffic, Condon's phone keeps ringing. It's Kate Merritt, who travelled in the ambulance with Samantha and is now by her bedside, relaying the words of the doctors and nurses to the trio. The news is getting worse by the minute.

'Sam was drifting in and out of consciousness, but in the ambulance I kept talking to her about her children Lily and Ben to try to keep her awake and focused,' says Merritt. 'We'd chatted at work about our kids, so I knew about them. I just wanted to keep bringing Sam back by talking about something she really cared about.

'At the hospital, I'd left the doctors to it, but then they asked me to come inside the curtains to try and keep her calm. I think having a familiar voice there, someone she knew, helped her. I kept telling her that she'd have to get back to her kids, and talked about how much they loved her, and needed her. But I was also speaking on the phone to the guys driving Laurence to the hospital. The doctors and nurses kept asking me where they were, and when they were going to get there. So I kept ringing them, trying not to panic them, but letting them know things weren't good and they should hurry up.

'Nurses are usually cool and calm and collected but you could tell from their manner that they were really worried. They kept asking me, "How far away are they now?" I didn't want to speak to Laurence because I could be more upfront if I wasn't talking to him, and the situation was getting worse and worse.'

Laurence sits white-faced and tight-lipped in the car, hurtling towards the city. His world feels as if it's crashing down all around him. 'Up to that point, I'd forced myself to be controlled, focused on what we needed to do with the kids and to get to the hospital,' he says. 'But at this point, I let myself go a bit. It sounded like they weren't expecting her to live. Then I got it back together and along the way, spoke to the police officers who were waiting in emergency with her, and was told that the medical team in neurosurgery needed to see me straightaway. I also rang Sam's parents to tell them.'

The three know they're racing against time. The doctors need to put Samantha into an induced coma and to operate immediately and they want Laurence there, urgently.

For his sake, even more than hers, he needs to say goodbye to his wife, in case she never wakes up again.

# PART TWO:

# While You Were Sleeping . . .

# Chapter 5
# THE RACE TO SAY GOODBYE

At Sydney's St Vincent's Hospital, the emergency doctors tried to clean their latest emergency arrival up a little in order to complete their preliminary assessment. Without doing much, however, it was obvious that Samantha Barlow was severely injured, and in an exceptionally critical condition.

Doctors intubated her and attached her to a machine that breathed for her in order to take some of the pressure off her body. But her injuries were massive. She had multiple lacerations to the scalp and forehead, as well as a number of fractures to her skull and a badly broken nose. It looked as though she'd been hammered over the head and face with a blunt, heavy object anywhere between eight and twenty times. She'd lost a huge amount of blood from haemorrhages both inside and outside her skull, and was suffering from hypothermia from her time left lying in the park. Her right hand also had a number of fractures and was extremely swollen.

The neurosurgical registrar on duty, Dr Vanessa Perotti, ordered a CT scan of the brain to see exactly how much damage had been done. It didn't look good. On the plus side, the injury had just skimmed one of the two major arteries pumping blood to the brain, and missed severing it by millimetres. Had that vessel been ruptured, Samantha would have bled to death before anyone found her. It would have all been over in minutes. But the scan did confirm a comminuted fracture – where bones are broken, splintered or crushed into a number of pieces – with several fragments caved in and actually inside the head. 'The scan also showed a right frontal bone fracture extending into the right orbital roof and fractures of the nasal bones,' she wrote in her report. 'There was poor grey/white matter differentiation consistent with brain swelling.' In addition, an X-ray of Samantha's right hand showed serious fractures of at least two of her fingers.

Dr Perotti phoned her boss Dr Malcolm Pell, now the chairman of neurosurgery at St Vincent's Private Hospital, at home. A hugely experienced doctor who'd qualified as a neurosurgeon twenty-one years before, he'd been a consultant at the hospital since 1991. They discussed the case and he said he was on his way in. They both knew it was essential to slip Samantha into an induced medical coma as soon as possible and to perform the surgery that might possibly save her life. They wouldn't even have time for an MRI. The swelling on her brain was the most serious problem; that could cause permanent brain damage and possibly kill her on its own. As Dr Perotti prepared Samantha for surgery, a plainclothes detective clipped Samantha's nails and put the clippings into a bag to be checked for anyone else's DNA. Everyone hoped her husband Laurence would arrive in time to see her before she went into surgery. They knew he was on his way but they had no time to spare.

Almost as soon as the police car screeched to a halt in one of the ambulance bays outside the hospital, Laurence was out and running into emergency. As he was whisked to Samantha's bedside he vaguely noticed all the police officers – including some from the most senior ranks – gathered in the rooms along the way. But all his focus was on getting to see Samantha.

His friend Inspector Paul Condon, racing after him, was taken aback by the scene. 'Even though we were being told all the way there that Sam was getting worse, I don't think any of us realised exactly how bad it was until we went in,' he says. 'Then we saw all the police there and all the nurses standing with tears in their eyes. I'd never seen that happen before.'

Laurence continued forward, approached Samantha's bed and saw the doctors surrounding her, the machines and monitors pulsing and beeping all around, a stand at each of the four corners of the bed all holding some kind of drip. He took a deep breath and pushed through to find a way in.

Constable Teneille Keith saw him approach. 'I remember thinking he must be the husband, and thinking, Oh shit! His wife looks terrible. This is going to be so hard for him.'

And it was. In nearly thirty years of frontline policing, Laurence had seen many people with the most terrible injuries – people hit by trains, struck by cars, slashed with knives, even men with their heads blown off by shotguns – but that first sight of his wife shocked him to the core.

Samantha was almost unrecognisable. Her head was wrapped in a huge bandage, there were tubes in and out of all points of her body, including down her throat, she was hideously swollen and dark purple bruises were just beginning to appear all over her face. 'She'd been officially placed into an induced coma the second I'd arrived and looked more dead than alive,' says Laurence. 'I've seen dead bodies that looked better than her.

'But I could hear her heartbeat echoing through the monitor's speakers. Her face was wrapped up like a cocoon, her nose was broken with blood and clear brain fluid running from it, she had two swollen black eyes that were beginning to change colour, her lips were swollen, her gums were bleeding and her teeth showed signs of either having been chipped or ground down by the pain she'd been in. Her right hand had been placed in a splint, which was attached to the bed with Velcro straps to stop her using it, like we do to people out of control on drink or drugs. Her head looked like a smashed pumpkin; she'd been beaten to a pulp.

'I thought she'd never come back from that. I thought I was there to say goodbye to her. I thought she was gone.'

Laurence managed to get close enough to her to lay a hand softly, gingerly, on one shoulder. He didn't want to put any pressure on her as he couldn't be sure where else she was injured. He was also paranoid about getting too close to her as he was so sick himself with tonsillitis and full of cold, and was terrified of passing on his germs. He offered to wear a mask. The doctors shook their heads. 'That's the least of our worries,' one said in a tone that made his heart sink even further. He turned back to his wife as if he could will her to live. As far as fond farewells go, it was all hideously unsatisfactory.

Dr Perotti was pushing Samantha up to the lifts to get her into theatre quickly as her condition was so critical. But Laurence was given a seat, as they briefed him on her injuries and on what they proposed to do. 'They were very insistent about me sitting down,' he says. 'The last thing they wanted was another patient.'

Matter-of-factly, they related the log of the damage done to Samantha. They told Laurence her blood loss had been enormous, but they couldn't be sure of the extent of her injuries until they operated and carried out their exploratory surgery. They also didn't know how long she'd been lying there in the grass. In short, they really couldn't tell yet whether she was going to live or die.

Laurence's body sagged on the seat as he signed, in a daze, all the release forms presented to him. 'They said she was pretty bad but they couldn't yet tell the extent of her injuries,' says Laurence. 'But I've been to a lot of emergencies in my time, and I could tell from everyone's body language the urgency of the circumstances. They told me the surgery would last for three hours until 10 a.m., so I'd have to wait till then to find out how she was going to be,' he says.

'I knew this was going to be the longest three hours of my life. But I still thought, at that stage, she was gone. And I didn't feel like I'd really said goodbye.'

Back at Arthur Park where Samantha had been found, the area was quickly declared a crime scene. Constable Phil Scott, despite feeling sickened by the state in which he'd found his colleague, had opted to stay, and helped tape off the entire vicinity.

Sergeant Simon Kirby was in charge and he filled in the paperwork while directing his officers to find where Samantha might have been hit by a car. As everyone pored over every inch of the road, the kerb and the footpath for blood, tyre tracks, glass or any telltale shards of metal, somebody suddenly noticed the trail of blood across the park and everyone's attention was diverted there. The blood led to the edge of the grass, by the stone wall, into the shadows, where a sizeable patch of the park and a section of the wall was stained a dark red, with clumps of matted hair twisted over the surface. The ground had also been disturbed, as if there'd been a fierce struggle.

'So at that point, we realised it wasn't an accident; it must have been an assault,' says Kirby. 'We started calling in more resources and were on the phone to other officers to tell them. Everything kicked off from there.'

Other police officers from Kings Cross were first on the scene, closely followed by those from neighbouring commands and still more on their day off or on holiday who'd heard the news and wanted to help. Then the specialists started arriving: forensic services, the dog squad, Laurence's own Public Order and Riot Squad (PORS) to help with the search, the highway patrol to stop traffic and speak to motorists. The commander of Kings Cross, Superintendent Tony Crandell, was on annual leave, but he was phoned at his home on the Central Coast and immediately volunteered to come in. They tried to dissuade him, but wild horses couldn't have prevented him coming to work the next day. New South Wales Police Commissioner Andrew Scipione was visiting a remote part of the state but requested regular updates while he abandoned his schedule and drove straight to the hospital. The analytical lab at Lidcombe was advised to stand by ready for a truckload of forensic evidence.

Within an hour, police had saturated the area, speaking to every passer-by, knocking on nearby doors, calling on local informants, checking anyone known to have a record for violent crime. A Kings Cross intelligence officer came up with lists of names, addresses, photographs and other information on possible suspects, known offenders and previous places of interest in the neighbourhood vicinity. The operation was declared Strike Force Ferndell.

'We had people come from everywhere,' says Kirby. 'It was incredible. We had sergeants and high-ranking officers whose regular jobs were to delegate work to others who were offering to take on the most menial roles, guarding the crime scene, helping search, anything we needed. We had volunteers coming from all over asking, what could they do to help? One of our colleagues had almost been murdered and wasn't really expected to live, and everyone wanted to do whatever they could. Everyone was horrified about a girl being attacked from behind, and being so terribly injured. It was humbling to see how much people cared.'

Some police, particularly those who were friends of Samantha and Laurence, were in tears at hearing how critical her condition was, but after a few moments to recover, all got on with the job at hand. A line of ten officers knelt down on the ground, shoulder to shoulder, and crawled millimetre by millimetre through the grass of the park, looking for any clue they could possibly find. Every item discovered was carefully examined, logged and bagged. Experts studied the bloodstains on the pylons, the bus shelter, the bench and the stone wall at the back of the park. Then an angle grinder arrived, and was used to cut down the bus shelter and bench to be loaded onto a truck and driven off to the lab. Both the crime scene and the underpass were inspected for fingerprints and CCTV footage from the Cross City Tunnel cameras was seized. The footage showed Samantha walking up the hill in the dark until she eerily disappeared out of range, just seconds before the attack would have happened.

The PORS also regularly worked as a group of specialist searchers to complement forensic services and they were immediately deployed to comb the area, too. Its commander, Superintendent Steve Cullen, who'd known Laurence for years and was grooming him to take over his role one day, vowed that no stone should be left unturned in the hunt for evidence. 'If you want to find a needle in a haystack, we're the people you call in,' says Cullen, whose team has previously been pivotal in finding evidence in the cases of missing six-year-old Sydney girl Kiesha Abrahams and the murder of nurse Michelle Beets.

'We work closely with the Homicide Squad – and no one knew if Sam would live or whether this would be a murder case – and we're very thorough and determined. We wanted to make sure we got our man.'

When Samantha's parents Janice and Vernon Groves arrived at hospital, Laurence greeted them both with a bear hug. He then sat them down and explained what was going on. They looked baffled, uncomprehending. How could this have happened? Could they really have lost their only daughter?

'We sat there in a daze; we felt so helpless,' says Janice. 'We couldn't believe what was happening to our daughter. I've never seen so many police in that corridor of the hospital. But we couldn't see her as they were operating.'

They hunkered down with Laurence in a nearby coffee shop, just 100 metres down from the hospital on the opposite side of the road, to sit and wait. It was agonising. And they couldn't help thinking, talking and reminiscing about their beautiful girl, now fighting for her life among strangers.

Born in February 1975, three years after her brother Jason, Samantha Groves was a happy, sunny child who was high-spirited and boisterous. Mum Janice, who'd worked as a signwriter and florist until the children came along, plied her with dolls, but Samantha was never interested. Instead, she liked to play games and sport, particularly with Jason and his friends, and grew up a regular tomboy. Jason still bears the 4 centimetre scar between the thumb and index finger on his right hand from the day he found the adventurous tot playing with a Stanley knife, not knowing what it was, and tried to take it off her.

Later that same year, while the family were living in the Sydney coastal suburb of Malabar, her mum taught her to swim, which began a lifelong love affair with the water. She learnt at the age of two over one summer and didn't swim again through the winter but when spring came, she jumped straight into a pool at a friend's house. 'She was quite fearless,' says dad Vernon. 'But the trouble is, she hadn't realised she'd forgotten how to swim in the interim and she went straight to the bottom and nearly drowned. I had to jump in and save her.' Such an early brush with death didn't faze her, however. She was surfing by three on waves that most of the other kids wouldn't go near and, by four, she was regularly swimming over 25 metres and was taking part in races in the ocean at the Coogee baths.

Vernon was a real-estate agent working long hours with his own business in nearby Randwick, and her mum often lent a hand there to help him out. They had a strong work ethic, which filtered down to their kids. Samantha was taught that from an early age. 'Even from very young, she was always very determined and put a lot of energy into achieving what she wanted to achieve,' says Jason. 'Our parents also instilled in us the idea of being the best you can be. So whatever Sam wanted, she always put everything into it. She also knew her own mind about what she wanted and where she was going.'

It all simply seemed natural to Samantha. 'If I wanted something I knew you had to work to get it,' she says. 'There was no other option. And if you wanted to know how to do something, then you just practised and practised until you'd mastered it. There were no shortcuts, no easy ways. Giving up was just never an option. If you loved something, you worked at it, and if you didn't love it then you moved on to something else.'

That turned out to have both its pluses and minuses for her parents. Samantha was never terribly interested in school, so only ever did just enough to get by. But she loved sport, particularly swimming, and threw herself wholeheartedly into that, absolutely determined to do well. Her long-suffering father would end up getting up at 4.45 each morning to take her to swim training six days a week before school, and then pick her up from school to take her to training every evening, too. By the age of eight, she was in the elite Heffron Park high-performance squad run by legendary Olympic swimming coach Terry Buck.

'She loved swimming and worked hard at it, and we were happy to help her,' says Vernon. 'She was very determined and was prepared to make the sacrifices for that, so we were too.'

But it was a shame her enthusiasm didn't extend to her schoolwork, says Janice. 'She always did well, but she could have done much better. I remember one of her teachers saying she was a delight, but she didn't apply herself. She just wasn't interested in school.'

Her dad, as a kid, was sent to the private school Knox Grammar on Sydney's North Shore as a boarder along with his brother. Their parents, however, weren't prepared to pay for their four daughters to go to private schools. As a result, Vernon was keen to send his own daughter, like his son, to a good private school. Samantha first attended Claremont College in Randwick and then the girls' school Kambala in Rose Bay for years 6 to 12. 'Dad thought it was important to get a good education and learn discipline,' says Samantha. 'I did learn a lot of self-discipline, but not necessarily for lessons. It was more for what I enjoyed doing.' Samantha cruised through both schools, reserving most of her energy and enthusiasm for swimming.

Besides, she'd already made up her mind what she wanted to do for the rest of her life. At the age of ten, she'd decided she wanted to be a police officer, and wouldn't be swayed by anything her parents said. She was adamant. Nothing else would do.

* * *

Time at the hospital seemed to be passing agonisingly slowly as the surgeons laboured over Samantha's broken body.

Dr Perotti had started in theatre by shaving Samantha's head, and putting her hair, matted with blood, dirt, brick pieces and wooden splinters, into a bag for the detective. 'That was the first I saw of Sam's injuries,' she says. 'There'd been so much hacking to her scalp, it nearly came off in some places in my hands while I was shaving. It was a bit of a shock. When I'd first looked at her, I couldn't tell the extent of her injuries. She had this lovely long blonde hair full of blood and it looked like there were multiple skull fractures and the skull had all been crushed inwards. No one had told us what had happened, but the place was absolutely full of detectives and cops, and Laurence was as white as a ghost. When we took the hair off, we could see it was much, much worse than we'd thought.'

The surgery they then performed was both delicate and dangerous. First, they had to drill into her skull, creating a star-shaped incision to create space for the areas of her brain that were swelling, so they wouldn't put pressure on the unharmed parts and risk permanent brain damage. Through that hole, around 7 centimetres in diameter, about the size of a clenched fist, they also had the chance to remove the jagged fragments of the smashed part of her skull that had perforated the membrane protecting the brain, causing the brain fluid to leak through her nose.

'We had to make sure we got out all the shattered bits of bone that could pierce the lining elsewhere too, and cause underlying damage to the brain,' says Dr Pell. 'We also had to clean out all the other foreign objects in there – hair, gravel, dirt and bits of brick.'

Her time on the table gave the team the opportunity to assess her injuries more closely, too. There were multiple fractures to her forehead, with one all the way down her forehead to her right eye socket. Then there were the fractures to the vertebrae in her neck and upper spine to look at, her broken nose and the brain itself, to try to judge how badly it had been damaged.

'I thought at first she would be okay but it wasn't until we were in the operating theatre that we realised the extent of her injuries,' says Dr Perotti. 'I thought, Oh my God! What has this person done to her? It was like someone had attacked her with a small axe all over her head. He must have struck her fifteen, sixteen or more times. He'd almost scalped her.'

Dr Perotti had only once before seen injuries like that: four years earlier when she'd been helping in the operating theatre with lifesaving surgery on Lauren Huxley, the eighteen year old who'd been bashed in the head and body with a set of metal fibro-cutters and then doused in petrol by a neighbour, who'd then tried to set fire to the house.

'But with Sam, I didn't think she'd ever wake up out of her coma,' she says. 'And if she did wake up, I was worried she'd have brain damage. The damage that man did was manifold. The biggest problem in operating on her was all the soil and grass and leaves. We had to peel off half the back of her scalp to clean it out. It took us over three hours to put her scalp back together again. I was scared that if her scalp died, that would be it. It would be over. The other major problem was her loss of so much blood and the freezing cold of the morning. They kept putting the heat up in the operating theatre, so it felt like we were trying to operate almost in a sauna. Then we had to X-ray her mutilated hand.'

That right hand was severely injured, with her first and third fingers almost completely detached, and fractures to those as well as to her fourth finger. The paramedics who'd brought her to the hospital described the hand as looking like it had been removed and put on inside-out.

'Vanessa did most of the surgery, but I came in and double-checked everything,' says Dr Pell. 'It was a severe set of injuries, which were certainly life-threatening if she hadn't had urgent surgery. You've always got to be a bit cautious in these situations.'

Laurence was looking at his watch every few minutes, counting down to the magic time of 10 a.m., when he'd know the verdict on his wife and whether she'd live or die. But even if she were to live, he was aware that the news might not be all good. Her head had been so badly injured, the doctors feared she'd have permanent brain damage. She might never be the same again.

As Samantha's parents sat and waited, trying not to imagine the worst, Laurence paced. He was going through a maelstrom of emotions. There was fear and anxiety, of course, but they were coupled with such an overpowering sense of guilt, it threatened to suffocate him. 'I was overcome with incredible guilt that I'd not got up that morning, told her that I loved her and said goodbye as she went to work,' he says. 'Worse than that, I was safely tucked into bed, while she was forced to endure the most horrific and violent nightmare anyone can ever begin to imagine.'

When police investigators arrived to ask him a few questions, it was almost a relief to be doing something, to be helping in some way. They quizzed him about what Samantha was wearing that morning, what jewellery she might have had on, what bags she may have been carrying, what they might have contained, how much money she'd had on her, which credit cards. He thought carefully and answered as clearly as he could, although he knew, having not seen her that morning, that they were all merely educated guesses at best. They then asked him if he thought it might be possible that the attack on Samantha was an act of revenge from someone she may have arrested in the past. He didn't know the answer to that, either. But for a while, it was all a welcome distraction.

The police media office had provided information verbally earlier that day to journalists about someone being found critically injured in a park by Kings Cross, and had appealed for any witnesses or anyone who had any information to come forward. It was only later they discovered the victim was actually a woman, and then that she was a police officer. As soon as that news became public, the phones in the media operations room went into meltdown. 'It probably wasn't until 10 a.m. that we put out a press release that it was a female police officer,' says Joanne Elliott, the media unit supervisor. 'The media response was incredible. Everyone was very keen for any details, and they all wanted to help in any way they could. It would have been one of the most high-profile events that we'd ever had to manage, in that Sam was a police officer and had been assaulted so viciously that the information we had at the time indicated she wasn't going to survive.'

One of the New South Wales Police deputy commissioners, Catherine Burn, also arrived at that point. The media was clamouring for information and a press release had been prepared. She asked Laurence to go through it to check a few details, which he did, and it was handed out.

As the clock ticked on, Laurence, his in-laws and the officers left the cafe to walk back to the hospital. He was stopped on the way by a passer-by who saw he was with a gaggle of men in uniform, and said he had some information about that attack on a policewoman earlier that morning. He didn't realise who he was talking to, and Laurence didn't have the energy to tell him; he just pointed him in the direction of another officer and watched him go. By now, a crowd of media had gathered at the front of the hospital but a contingent of police kept them back away from the family. Laurence refused all requests for press interviews. He was totally focused on Samantha and her fight for life inside. There was simply no room for anything else.

Back in Kings Cross, the hunt for evidence was painstaking. Police were conducting searches of all the streets and laneways nearby, as well as the car parks underneath neighbouring apartment blocks and the yards of the houses in the vicinity. A police helicopter was buzzing overhead, looking out for any items that may have been discarded around the area, particularly Samantha's bags.

Meanwhile, the haul of objects found in the grass of Arthur Park grew by the minute. There were the expected things: innumerable cigarette butts, dried pieces of gum, discarded pieces of clothing, odd shoes, ID cards, make-up, syringe packets, keys, mobile phone covers, underpants, stockings . . . But among them were the treasures they'd been seeking to help with the investigation: dried blood, single strands of Samantha's blonde hair, a handcuff-shaped key ring, a button from her shirt, her car keys, tiny threads of cotton from her T-shirt, a pen from her bag, and a lone strand of black hair.

'Those guys did such a good job,' says Sergeant Simon Kirby. 'They went through that grass, blade by blade, to look for clues and evidence. They picked up hair, dried pieces of blood, everything. It was very stressful at the time, because it was a terrible thing to have happened, but you're also conscious of having to make sure everything's done properly. You're aware that a single mistake could be the difference between a successful conviction and someone going free.

But it's pleasing when you feel you're getting somewhere and are starting to piece together the jigsaw puzzle.'

There were other breakthroughs, too. Three City of Sydney parks labourers, whose jobs were to empty park bins and clean up and maintain garden beds in the area, were forced to change their usual routine because of the area taped off by the police. An officer approached one of them, telling them they were hunting for items stolen during an assault and if they were to find anything unusual, they should report it immediately.

At 11 a.m., the trio arrived at the garden bed on Womerah Lane. While ferretting through the shrubbery to clear it of any garbage, they came across a pair of black lace-up boots, a pair of navy-blue cargo pants, a single blue police epaulette, a hairdryer, a hairbrush and a pink cotton bag. They put the items in the bag and went straight to the police. Nearby, a riot squad officer found Samantha's soaked police shirt and a brick encrusted with her blood and hair.

Meanwhile, police were knocking on all the doors in the neighbourhood to ask if anyone had seen or heard anything, or knew anything about what had happened earlier that morning. One apartment in one of the blocks close to the park was well known to police as a place where a prostitute lived, and a number of various transients continually came and went. The doorway of that block was also where Sergeant Christy Jessep had seen a man loitering after she'd parked her car earlier that morning, and who'd then stood staring at her. After the attack on Samantha, she'd made a statement at the police station and described the man she'd seen. Her description was remarkably close to another given by her fellow police officer, Constable Cassie Shakespeare, the woman whom the man had followed and who'd phoned the front desk of the station to alert them.

While Kirby was overseeing the crime scene, he was approached by a man who pointed to the same unit and said there was someone who looked out of control there the previous day, in the company of the prostitute. Perhaps he might be the man everyone was searching for.

Detective Senior Constable Tanya Smith happened to be knocking on the door of that exact unit. Regarded by her boss Crandell as one of the brightest young detectives in the force, she knew the apartment by repute. 'It's seen as a bit of a doss house, where a number of prostitutes and recent releasees from prison stay, with people coming and going all the time,' she says. 'So I went there and had a chat with a woman who lives there. She's a sex worker and is pretty feral but she was good.'

That exchange happened in the early afternoon of the same day Samantha was attacked, and it was to become the major breakthrough of the investigation. The woman turned out to be the prostitute Spooner had been with, who'd shot up heroin with him and who'd seen him the next day boasting he was about to smash someone with a rock to get money for drugs. She thought his name was something like Rob, and he'd said he'd only been out of jail for a few weeks. She also remembered him talking about home being in the Illawarra.

'Her description of him fitted the other descriptions,' says Smith. 'The woman was very willing to give information without being pushed too much. I think once people had known what this guy had done to Samantha, it was so bad that they were willing to be helpful and give us information. At the hospital, they were saying she might not come out of this alive, and people like this woman, may not have liked the police much, but she was aware this guy was dangerous, that he wasn't a local, and she could easily have ended up the same way as Samantha.'

Crandell was delighted with the quality of Smith's police work. 'Tanya was the person who extracted the information from the local prostitute that gave us the identity of this person,' he says. 'She is one of the most brilliant detectives I have ever seen and that's a big statement; I've seen a lot of brilliant detectives in my day. I had total confidence in that girl. Then she went and took the next step and found out where this person was likely to be. So she set a chain of events into place that proved the turning point.'

After Smith reported her findings back to intelligence, she rang her fiancé, a fellow police detective who happened, coincidentally, to work in the Illawarra. She had a hunch he might be able to help. She asked him if he knew of any local called Rob who'd been out of prison a few weeks and who might have a history of violence. It didn't take him long to report back.

'He gave me a list of recent releasees and pointed out one called Roderick who fitted the description I'd given him,' says Smith. 'He said he was a pretty bad guy.'

The man's surname, however, wasn't Spooner. It was Holohan.

The file was sent over and the investigators started studying his details and his record. He had committed a lengthy list of serious offences over the years, starting from when he was just a boy. Smith also printed out the photo of him that was sent over with the file. 'He looked just like the description the prostitute had given me,' she says.

And there, on one of the pages of his voluminous dossier, was a list of the names he'd used over the years. There was Holohan, Holahan, Holohand, Hollohan, Cruickshank and Cruikshank. And in the middle of the list, one more pseudonym: Spooner.

* * *

At that moment, Roderick Holohan, thirty-nine, has just turned up at a drop-in centre in Port Kembla.

His girlfriend Sara is there, and the pair make up after their row of a few days earlier. They've been together for four years now, but it hasn't all been smooth sailing. They often row and split up for a while. When they are together, it's not terribly romantic either. They usually sleep at friends' places, in empty houses or sheds, and sometimes on the street or in parks.

This afternoon, Holohan tells her he's missed her and wants to spend some time with her. He takes a shower and has something to eat. He then watches TV all afternoon.

On the news is an item about a policewoman in Sydney who's been attacked and beaten half to death, who isn't expected to live. He doesn't say a word.

Laurence, Janice and Vernon were still waiting for Samantha's doctors to come out of surgery with news of her condition. The surgeons had said they'd be finished by 10 a.m. but when 10.30 a.m. passed, then 11 a.m., then 11.30 a.m., they grew more and more nervous.

There was also an ever-increasing number of police standing around the waiting rooms and in the corridors of the hospital, hanging out for news of their colleague. One of them mentioned to Laurence that they'd identified a suspect in the attack on her, but he wasn't really listening. 'I might still have been in shock but I made the decision early on to only get involved in information that mattered, and the only thing that mattered at that time was Sam,' he says. 'I knew the mighty blue army would kick into gear and would be looking for who had done this to my wife. Time was standing still. I was just waiting, waiting, waiting.'

Born in Liverpool in the UK, Laurence was brought over to Australia by his parents as a kid. He'd grown up listening to The Beatles, one of whom – Paul McCartney – had been in the same year as his uncle at the former Liverpool Institute High School for Boys. Now he thought back to them again. 'All around me was a big blur of activity, with the investigation, the media, the doctors, but for me, everything stood still,' he says. 'John Lennon had once described being in The Beatles as like being in the "eye of the hurricane", and for me that day was just like that. Around me, everything was completely out of control. There was nothing I could do but wait for it to finish and there to be some sort of outcome.'

Finally, shortly after midday, the doctors emerged from the operating theatre. Samantha was still alive but the surgery had taken longer than anticipated because of the extensive damage to her scalp, the expectation that her skin might not survive and need grafts, and the risk of infection from the dirt, blood, pieces of brick and other debris that had penetrated her wounds during the attack. No one could say with any confidence that Samantha would live and, even if she did, that she'd ever fully recover from her injuries.

'The surgeon then began to speak in percentages,' says Laurence. 'I tried to understand what she was saying, but what does it really mean when a doctor says there is a 40 per cent chance of this, or a 50 per cent chance of that? Does that mean Sam will be 45 per cent capable of doing everything she used to do, or does it mean she will be 100 per cent at some things and can't do others at all? What bits will be normal? Speech? Memory? Mobility? I felt numb. They said she could be in a coma for up to a month.

'But there was worse to come. The neuro team openly admitted that as much as they knew about the brain, there were still things they couldn't predict, good or bad. The thing that stood out from this initial conversation was that we were being told to prepare ourselves for the real chance that Sam would suffer some form of physical or mental disability for the rest of her life, and might not even know who I was or remember anything to do with her immediate family, even our two small children, whether long term or short term. And there was still that distinct possibility that I'd soon be making funeral arrangements for my wife.'

# Chapter 6
# WHILE YOU WERE SLEEPING . . .

Laurence Barlow led Samantha's parents into the Intensive Care Unit of St Vincent's Hospital for their first sight of their daughter since the attack. He tried to prepare them for the shock. It was hard, though. Privately, Laurence felt his wife looked like a skydiver whose chute had failed to open and who had landed on her head. How could he possibly describe how bad it was going to be?

Both parents paled visibly on approaching the hospital bed. As well as her injuries, Samantha's face was now a terrible dark rainbow of red to black, as the bruises began to bloom. 'It was a horrifying sight,' says Janice Groves. 'She had things in her mouth, and there were tubes coming out of everywhere. Her head was completely bound and her face was so swollen, it looked about three times bigger than she was. We just looked at her and thought, How could somebody do something like that? It's no wonder the police who found her didn't recognise her. I'm pretty tough but I found it so hard.'

Laurence moved towards the bed, touched her leg through the bedclothes and then gently took her left hand in his. 'Hello, Sam,' he said softly. 'It's Laurence. I love you.' He then kissed her hand.

'As useless as I felt, standing beside Sam's bed, it was reassuring to be able to hold her hand, look at the machines and know she was still alive,' he says. 'I'd been given her wedding rings that morning and was carrying them with me, waiting for the right opportunity to put them back on her finger. I was just hoping against hope that Sam would somehow come through this horror and we would again have the life we dreamed of. Miraculous things happen in hospitals every day, and I started to hope that we could see another one.

'I made a promise to myself that no matter how bad things got, I wasn't going to leave hospital until Sam was out of the coma and I was able to speak to her and apologise for not getting my lazy arse out of bed that fateful morning and tell her that I loved her, and see that she understood.'

No one really knows where Samantha got the idea of becoming a police officer. It might have been the influence of a cousin who was in the force, working in the dog squad, or it might have been the exciting stories she'd heard at the South Maroubra Surf Life Saving Club, where she'd become an accomplished and dedicated surf lifesaver, from a couple of fellow members who were serving police officers.

'I think it was the variety that appealed,' explains Samantha. 'There's so many different sections, so many things you can do. I liked the idea of learning different skills. And I also wanted to help people. Mum and Dad have always been nice to other people and very community-spirited. They open up their garden to raise funds for breast cancer, they run the local Meals on Wheels and if someone ever needed help, they'd always give it. So it felt very natural to me to want to help. Apart from that, the police force seemed like a lot of fun.'

After a pretty much iconic Australian childhood hanging out around the surf club and at the beach with her mates, Samantha had already established herself as good at sport and an even better team player. For thirteen years from the age of sixteen, she competed in state and national titles in surf lifesaving, and at the South Maroubra Surf Life Saving Club – the only one of the two in Maroubra at the time to allow women to become members – she achieved every qualification, including the coveted gold medallion. She devoted at least 100 days a year on her weekends and during school holidays, ending up being involved in over 100 rescues, some in as fierce as 4-metre-high surf. 'I've seen her get rolled in boats and come up as if nothing had happened,' says her friend Karen Maddock, who met and got to know her at the club. 'She'd get thrown out of the rubber duckie but nothing ever fazed her. She just dealt with it and moved on. I can remember massive surf one day rolling the duckie and sending her flying, but she then just grabbed her board and went out and saved someone. She was always so brave. I was scared of everything, but she was scared of nothing.'

She also competed in every event she could in the surf carnivals, including racing inflatable rescue boats and swimming the line in the rescue and resuscitation team, the toughest position in an event that uses a traditional belt, rope and reel for rescues. 'Sam's very easygoing but also very competitive,' says Maddock. 'She has a very nice balance between the two. She was very confident that whatever she wanted to do, she'd achieve.

'The surf club looked after us, it was like a family. It gave us a good foundation and discipline too. You'd have to turn up for patrols – otherwise, you weren't allowed to compete. So we learnt that actions have consequences from a very young age, which kept us honest!'

But joining the police force wasn't as straightforward as Samantha might have liked. At first, she decided she'd like to enter as a graduate and applied to go to Sydney University to study criminology. The year she enrolled, however, the course was dropped. Then she thought she'd go directly into the police, but she was still too young. Instead, her parents encouraged her to go to June Dally-Watkins Business Finishing College for a year to take an executive business diploma and learn secretarial skills like shorthand and typing, and to study Japanese, all back-up skills, they said, that might be useful one day.

Her brother Jason couldn't understand why the idea of a career in the police had become such a passion. 'It seemed an odd choice and I was fairly perplexed about it,' he says. 'I thought it must be a phase she was going through. This felt to me like it was out of left field. But our parents have a strong moral compass and contribute to the community and believe in giving back and helping others. Mum and Dad told her they'd do everything they could to support her.'

Indeed, her father then revealed to her that he too had wanted to join the police when he was young. He'd been on the waiting list when a friend had asked him if he'd like to do some work in real estate, and he'd ended up staying in that for the next forty years instead. 'He hadn't told me earlier as he hadn't wanted to influence me,' says Samantha. 'But he always thought that was something he'd love to have done.' Her mum confessed she'd also applied for the police but she was too short, as you had to be a certain height in those days. She had her doubts, though, that her daughter would enjoy the police. 'For one thing, Sam could never stand the sight of blood!' says Janice. 'Even if she had so much as a splinter in her finger, she'd faint. But then later on, she even applied to the crash unit, so people can certainly change.'

Vernon had also encouraged her to get her real-estate licence, just in case one day she might want to work in property or join his business. Jason had shown no interest, but Samantha was a natural and completed the studies for her licence at night.

'I was always very interested in real estate, but it wasn't what I wanted to do for a living,' Samantha says. 'At the end of the year, I was just as determined to join the police, but I was still too young. You had to be eighteen and three-quarters, and I was only just eighteen.'

It was November 1993 and she took a job to earn some money for Christmas. She got a position as an administrative assistant for a college, the Moriah War Memorial College at Bellevue Hill, and stayed there until she was old enough for the police. In the end, she finished her job on the Friday and drove to the New South Wales Police Academy the very next day, Saturday 19 November 1994. When she was finally sworn in as a twenty year old at a ceremony on 19 May 1995, her parents were thrilled to come along and watch.

'I think when I finally joined the police, my parents were actually very proud of me,' says Samantha. 'They are good people who like to help others, very structured people, with very definite ideas of right and wrong. I learnt that too from them.'

The news of the attack on a policewoman in the early hours of that morning disturbed and saddened many people. The level of violence on the streets of Kings Cross was already a matter of huge public and political concern at the time, with police complaining that the number of licensed premises in the area – more than 300 within just 500 square metres – had gone beyond saturation point, and something needed to be done urgently about the amount of alcohol-fuelled aggression. Talks were being held about introducing a liquor licence freeze the next month and debate continued to rage over the best way to curb the violence.

'So the climate was ready for a real outcry about the attack on Sam, and that enough was enough,' says Dave Owens, then also a New South Wales Police deputy commissioner. 'Although it later turned out that drugs were involved in Sam's incident, rather than alcohol, there was such a focus on violence on the streets that didn't matter. There was the feeling that this wasn't an isolated incident, and that violence was happening too often.'

Very soon, the Intensive Care Unit was swamped with flowers and cards, even from those who had no idea of Samantha's name. Everyone was horrified both by the fact that the victim was a young woman and the mother of two small children who'd dedicated her life to serving the public, and by the savagery of the violence inflicted on her. New South Wales Police Commissioner Andrew Scipione addressed the press. 'What sort of animal would do something like this?' he asked. 'It's beyond belief. That one of our own has been attacked in such a cowardly way only doubles the resolve to find the person responsible.' Owens agreed. 'It was a dog act,' he says. 'To assault a female from behind . . . Everyone hates that, and cops in particular. To think it was totally unprovoked, and that she hadn't stood a chance, and the extent of the violence. It was a terrible, terrible thing.'

Even people who might under normal circumstances not be fans of the police were appalled, and came forward to say so. At the Kings Cross police station, a steady flow of locals, including street workers, criminals, drug dealers, gang members and other 'colourful' identities, dropped by to express their sympathy. Officers were completely taken aback. Sergeant Perri Hayes, who'd joined the police at the same time as Samantha and has remained a close friend ever since, says there were dozens of bouquets coming in to the front office all afternoon and evening, as well as the next day, and the next.

'There were lots of flowers arriving at the station, and well-wishers coming in to say hello, and cards and people ringing up to express their sympathy,' says Hayes. 'They were just random people, and that went on for a long time. There were some who'd dealt with her, or saw her regularly on the street, and others coming in to offer information they thought might help, but mostly everyone just wanted to say how terrible that it had happened and to acknowledge how bad it was. It was a nice feeling that so many people were thinking of us.

'On the street, people who'd dealt with Sam, who'd spoken to her or said hello in the mornings, all wanted to know how she was, as well as those who didn't have any idea of who she was, but just wanted to let us know that they were thinking of her.'

The head of Kings Cross police, Superintendent Tony Crandell, was also stunned by the reaction of the local community. He'd been posted to Kings Cross just the year before after previously working in Deniliquin, a town serving an agricultural area of the Riverina region of New South Wales, close to the border with Victoria. So he was transferred from the second-largest police area in the state, 650 000 square kilometres, which would take him five and a half hours to drive across, to the smallest police area, 3 square kilometres, which took him five and a half minutes to walk through. But he'd fallen in love with the locale just the same: entranced by its diversity, and the way some of the most wealthy, powerful and privileged people in the state lived cheek-by-jowl with some of the poorest, most desperate and sometimes most dangerous.

The police station was the perfect example of that dichotomy, situated at the point where Darlinghurst Road, with its sleazy strip clubs, drug-injecting room, pubs, nightclubs and pavements lined with sex workers and drug-runners, ended, and Macleay Street, leading to the 'Paris' end of Potts Point with its upmarket apartment buildings, boutiques, cafes and smart restaurants, began.

'If you walk out of Kings Cross police station and turn left down Darlinghurst Road then you are in for the policing experience of a lifetime,' says Crandell. 'If you turn right, you are in for a very, very pleasant walk and stroll along Macleay Street and through lovely Potts Point. Where else in the world do you have that?'

But as much as he loved the area, the reaction of the residents of Kings Cross still took him completely by surprise. 'I've got to say on that day, as well as the days, weeks and even months following, I've never seen a community pull together like that. This was the remarkable side of it for me. The community of Kings Cross consists of prostitutes, drug dealers, drug users – both those using the injecting centre and those not – and really consists of the homeless, the most disadvantaged, poorest, most downtrodden people the world can produce, right next to people of affluence. You see that real division of poor versus rich every day.

'What I saw now was the poorest of the poor, the street prostitutes, the drug-addicted, the alcoholics, those people coming together to say to me, "We want you to know this was not one of our community that did this, you must understand that we would not do this to our police." I'm thinking, Hang on, under normal circumstances we are not really their friends. They see us and think they might be arrested, and often they are, yet they still have this underlying feeling of loyalty to their police. They saw the attack on Sam as something that really crossed the line, and they came to the police station in droves. We actually ended up putting out some big cards so people could write on the cards and express themselves, and we were inundated with flowers – I've never seen so many donated to a police station – and gifts, and some of those from the poorest of people to whom $50 would be like $1000 to most of the rest of us.'

Those gifts included replacements of everything Samantha was known to have lost, items like her wallet, make-up and handbag, as well as offers of money to help her family. One local gangster even offered to do the police a favour and personally 'look after' the person they might catch for the crime. Officers thanked him for his concern but, naturally, turned him down.

Laurence, also overwhelmed by the number of bouquets being delivered at the hospital, asked the police to relay the plea that perhaps people could make a donation to charity instead. But still the flowers, in quantities that reminded him unnervingly of a funeral home, continued to arrive.

'It was just remarkable,' says Crandell. 'It reinforced to me the uniqueness of that Kings Cross community because on an everyday basis those were the people we were arresting and pulling into line, yet in the face of adversity those people joined with us.'

Not everyone behaved quite as well, though. A few of the better-heeled members of the community complained about the inconvenience of having to walk around the taped-off areas of the crime scene, and being stopped and asked if they'd heard or seen anything.

'Some of those residents complained to us that we were in their way,' says Sergeant Simon Kirby of his time at the crime scene. 'Then a couple made snide remarks that we were only working so hard because it was a copper who was attacked. If it had been any old Joe Blow, we wouldn't have given a shit. Of course, they were wrong and most had no idea what was going on. But it was interesting to see that even the crooks had a code they lived by, whereas some of the other residents weren't quite so understanding . . .'

Owens felt much the same way. 'That's what pissed off a lot of cops at the scene,' he says. 'We go through all the same procedures with other people, but it's just there isn't usually as much press about those, so the public doesn't see what we do. A lot of cops work in their own time as a matter of course, preparing briefs of evidence on days off and writing up reports in the evenings. With the attack on Sam, they just felt very much as if she was family, because the police are a large family. But don't forget, at the start of this operation, we didn't even know who the victim was.'

It was still only the afternoon of the day of the attack but, with the police investigation progressing so well, it was now time to put a heavyweight in charge, someone from the State Crime Command's Robbery and Serious Crime Squad. The chosen man was Detective Sergeant Mathew 'Mat' Moss, someone who – coincidentally – knew better than most what Samantha was going through.

Fourteen years before, when he was just twenty-two, he was shot while conducting a raid with the former Tactical Response Group (TRG) at Bankstown in Sydney's south-west. He'd been only three years into the job when, as the fourth man of an entry team, he burst through a door and came face-to-face with a man holding a shotgun in one hand and his young daughter in the other. The man fired and Moss felt his own blood pouring down his arm as he backed off to warn everyone else of the presence of an armed gunman. Of the 190 pellets fired, 160 were embedded in his lungs and left arm, and he wasn't expected to live. The first time he awoke, it was to hear a chaplain reciting the last rites over him.

Moss ended up spending three months in hospital and had to take nine months off work, going through rehab. 'It's just the roll of the dice,' he says now. 'Maybe I was more scared after then every time we did raids on armed offenders, but I wanted to do that work. I looked at it as a small speed bump on the road.'

Now working as a plainclothes detective, Moss had heard about the attack on Samantha on the radio, and was asked to go along to a briefing at Kings Cross. There, he was told that Samantha's chances weren't good. But as he heard her surname for the first time, he sat up. 'I thought, Barlow . . . Barlow . . .' he says. 'I know a bloke called Barlow. But there's heaps of Barlows around, I told myself. But then as the briefing went on, and they mentioned that Samantha was the wife of another officer, Laurence Barlow, I thought, Shit! You poor bastard!

He and Laurence had first met when Moss was helping train new recruits to the TRG as part of his rehab, while Laurence was one of those new members. Later, they also worked for a short period together at the Witness Security Unit. Just months before Samantha's attack, both men had attended a meeting at Watsons Bay for a planned security operation connected with the death of model Caroline Byrne at the Gap, and the murder trial of the man accused of throwing her off.

'I hit it off with Laurence straightaway,' says Moss of his former colleague. 'He's a bit of a lunatic and has a great sense of humour; he's a really good fella. He's a very dedicated officer, highly motivated and very highly regarded. But it was only shortly after that I was told this would be my job. I was nervous. He was a mate and his wife had been viciously flogged to within an inch of her life and was not expected to live. And I had the responsibility for the whole thing.'

* * *

By that stage, all the information being gleaned from the crime scene, as well as interviews with the prostitute who'd been with Roderick Holohan, other sex workers, the woman who'd been attacked the night before Samantha, other women he'd approached and people who'd walked or driven past that morning, were beginning to paint a clearer picture of what had happened. Kings Cross was eerily hushed that evening, as if it were somehow indecent in the face of such a tragedy to be out partying, and others seemed to want to stay away with such an obvious lunatic on the loose. Moss was amazed, just as Crandell had been, at how quickly the community had come together to help. 'Everyone put away their differences for a common purpose,' he says. 'For the women working there, they knew it could have been any of them, there but for the grace of God. And it was valuable help, sincerely offered.'

Many were appalled at how many people had passed Samantha, either on foot or in cars, without trying to help, but Moss could somehow understand that too. 'Seeing someone in that area covered in blood isn't unusual – it can be a bit like gladiator school up there, and people have become desensitised over time,' he says. 'Also, they don't want to get involved. There's a lot of junkies around and some can be dangerous. But people were now actively volunteering to help us.

'They recognised the police were there to help them and, in our hour of need, they were ready to help us.'

As a kid, Laurence had loved nothing better than watching Australian cop shows on TV: drama series like *Homicide*, *Division 4*,

*Matlock Police*, *Cop Shop* and *Solo One*. The police officers on the screen were invariably handsome – for they were nearly all men – they were heroic, they were incredibly skilled drivers and they always got their villain, no matter what obstacles were put in their way. The baddies back then were easy to spot, too. They had shifty eyes and bad skin, they wore ill-fitting suits or track pants and they were never quite clever enough to get away with anything.

The US police shows could be a lot more exciting, like *Adam-12*, about two cops on their daily patrol of the streets of LA, and *CHiPs*, about two motorcycle officers of the California Highway Patrol, as well as *S.W.A.T.* and the classic *Hill Street Blues*. Then there were movies like *Dirty Harry* and anything starring Charles Bronson, but the Australian films and TV shows often felt a lot more real and attainable.

Laurence's mum had an uncle in the police she always spoke fondly of. 'So the police force was considered in our house a kind of honourable profession to strive for,' says Laurence. 'My interest in the police was always encouraged.'

For a boy who'd arrived in Australia as a twenty-month-old toddler from Liverpool, life felt pretty exciting in any case. Back then, in November 1965, his parents William, thirty-two, always known as George, and Elizabeth, twenty-nine, whom everyone knew as Betty, were eager ten-pound Poms looking for a new life with their older son Robert, seven, and his little brother Laurence. Liverpool had been bombed heavily in World War II, with nearly half its homes damaged, but much of the reconstruction work afterwards was deeply unpopular and seen as ruining the character and social cohesion of the city.

There was still plenty of pride in the place, particularly for its two top-class football teams Everton and Liverpool – with the former's ground set to be used for the 1966 World Cup held in England. It was also the centre of the 'Merseybeat' sound, with The Beatles and Laurence's dad's workmate Gerry Marsden, of Gerry and the Pacemakers, all becoming international stars. But the city's docks and many of its traditional manufacturing industries were in decline and unemployment was rising sharply. 'Our parents came from a poor background, and they wanted the best for us,' says Robert. George says it was a gamble, but it would work out better than if they stayed. 'We had no house, I didn't have a trade, we had nothing back there. I told my wife Australia was a land of opportunity and that it could work out much better for us. We moved mostly for the children.'

Australia indeed felt like a fresh new start and, despite the heat that hit them like the opening of a furnace door and their mum missing her family, they settled quickly into their first home in their new land: a Nissen hut at the East Hills Hostel, close, ironically, to Sydney's own south-west suburb of Liverpool. In between caring for her boys, Betty worked in the canteen, and George was given a job at the British Leyland car plant in Zetland.

After eighteen months, the family moved to Moorebank, near Bankstown Airport, into a rented home backing onto the Georges River. Laurence and his brother loved having a river behind their backyard for fishing, swimming and watching the speedboat races, but their mother was less keen. As well as their safety being an issue for their mum, the river broke its banks twice while they were there and flooded the house.

Laurence grew into a big, strong kid, tall for his age, and good at standing up for himself when he was taunted with being a Pom. Robert, skinnier, quieter and more studious, was occasionally bullied for his English accent and for wearing glasses and Laurence would rush to help his older brother defend himself. 'Because we had no relatives over here, we were a close family; we only had each other,' says Laurence. 'Ties of love were all we had. I think it was hard for our mother as she had no support and neither Mum nor Dad could drive as back in Liverpool you'd never needed to, with all the public transport.'

He was always into sport, and wanted to be in everything from an early age: running races, wheelbarrow races, sack races . . . On the soccer field, other parents complained that he was much bigger than anyone in his own age group, and said he should be playing with kids at least three years older. He soon found he could hold his own with pretty much anyone. 'No one ever picked on Laurence,' says George. 'He was too big, too strong, too popular. I was always very proud of him.' Laurence himself, however, found it occasionally tough going. 'I was regularly in scraps,' he says. 'I never felt accepted by the Anglo Aussies, and in the playground I'd be playing with the Italians, Croats, Serbs and newly arrived Brits, the other outsiders who also played soccer rather than rugby league.'

His first primary school was the Chipping Norton Public, then, in year 3, the family moved to a Housing Commission home in Villawood, a few kilometres to the north, and he switched to a primary school there. His parents hoped one day to buy their own home, but without the support of an extended family were never quite able to catch up. Instead, they had ambitions for their children, and both Laurence and Robert passed the exams to get into one of the state's top schools, the selective Hurlstone Agricultural High.

Laurence worked hard there, motivated by both the knowledge that his parents often went without to keep him there and the hope of going to university afterwards – his mother's dream for her boys. He enjoyed school too, and excelled in sport, playing representative cricket and soccer and representing the school in athletics at state level. 'He was bright and intelligent, and really good fun,' says old schoolmate David Searle, who met him in year 8 when they were both playing cricket. 'He was very good at cricket, captaining the first eleven cricket team and making the representative sides. In our last year, we played Steve and Mark Waugh's school team three times, and won twice.'

Laurence was always good at soccer too. He captained the Marconi Juniors under-14, -15 and -18 teams, and later played for them in the National Soccer League's reserve competition. He played against the likes of Robbie Slater, who went on to play for the Socceroos and won the English Premier League with Blackburn Rovers, and the Waugh brothers, again, who gave up promising football careers to play cricket.

Searle says he turned out, however, to have more talents than anyone suspected. 'I was always a rugby player and after we left school, a few of us played for the Liverpool Rugby Club,' he says. 'One Saturday morning, he'd come to watch and we were a couple of players short. The coach saw him and said, "What about your mate?" He'd never played rugby before, but he said he'd have a go. So he played on the wing and scored a try and kicked a couple of goals for us. He then went on to play 300-odd games for that club and ended up captain of the first grade. We won the comp that year, and he ended up the leading points scorer and set a new club record for the number of points scored!'

Laurence also continued to play guitar, which he'd started learning at the age of just five with musical theory lessons, taking part in local concerts and talent shows. 'I used to joke that if you were born in Liverpool, you came out of the womb with a guitar strapped to your back, and a football glued to your foot,' he says. 'You then had to play football and guitar. How could you not?'

As for his future ambitions, he was torn between a desire to join the police, with all the excitement and lack of a deadening routine that might entail, and a new ambition: to become a schoolteacher. 'I had visions of myself teaching social sciences or maths and coaching cricket or soccer after school while continuing to play myself,' he says. 'That was always my back-up plan.'

In 1982, Laurence went to Macquarie University to study for an Arts degree. His favourite subjects were philosophy, anthropology and cognitive psychology. After he passed all eight subjects of his first year, two with credits, he started thinking more closely about his future options. There weren't many jobs for schoolteachers at the time, and unemployment was rising, hitting 8.7 per cent in the November of that year with every sign of continuing to soar. The police force, on the other hand, had launched a series of recruitment drives in a bid to raise their numbers.

'It sounds corny but I do think that being a police officer is one of the most noble things anyone can ever do,' he says. 'You're standing up for the little guy against the big guy and enforcing laws, putting your life on the line. I like to think it's in the top group of two or three professions where you put the community first and that always appealed to me. Then, of course, there was the exciting stuff and the physical side of it.'

Onlookers weren't too surprised by his career choice. 'He was the type of bloke who really fitted the mould of a police officer, early on,' says his schoolfriend Searle. 'I knew he'd be good as a police officer. He was straight up and down.' His brother Robert felt he'd only really gone to university in the first place to keep their mum happy. 'Joining the police was a good choice for him,' he says.

'He was never going to be happy in an office. He needed to be doing something physical and sociable. He was pretty black and white too; my brother didn't see many shades of grey.'

But just like Samantha, he couldn't get in straightaway. He'd never applied for Australian citizenship and the rules back then precluded non-Australians from serving. His police career was put on hold for a year while he sorted that out.

So Laurence whiled away the next twelve months waiting on his nationality status, playing rugby and cricket, having post- and often pre-game drinks too, chasing girls and looking forward to joining the police. He played his guitar and sang at parties, with a repertoire of over 100 songs including those by – surprise, surprise – The Beatles, as well as the Eagles, Bob Dylan and Elvis, and he even performed a few gigs as part of a duo. 'He went busking at one stage on George Street,' says Robert. 'I don't think Mum was happy about that.' He also became one of the leaders of 'The Blind Nine', a bunch of friends who went along to Bachelor and Spinster Balls out in the country. When his time finally came, he completed the eleven weeks' training in one of the first classes of the New South Wales Police Academy that had relocated just that year from Redfern to Goulburn, 200 kilometres south-west of Sydney, and was sworn in on 14 September 1984.

'It was everything I always imagined it would be,' he says. 'I was twenty years old and I was fit, so physically it wasn't a challenge. I'd just been to university, so the lessons weren't a challenge either. Back then you had to pass a spelling test to get in and some of the older guys were having problems, so I'd run tests for them to give them a hand. I made a lot of good friends and cruised, really, still finishing in the top ten per cent. I was waiting for the excitement to start.' He didn't have to wait for long.

* * *

Roderick Holohan is feeling increasingly edgy. He doesn't want to visit friends, or stay over at a friend's house. He doesn't want to talk or risk being asked any questions about where he's been for the past couple of days, and what he did while he was away.

Instead, he tells his girlfriend he wants to go to the nearby suburb of Dapto, on the western edge of Lake Illawarra. They take a walk and then, with some blankets they've been given, set up camp at Reed Park, just 400 metres away from the mall. It's cold and there's a chill wind blowing, but tonight they'll sleep under the stars. After all, he has a sneaking suspicion that he might not be free for much longer.

With the main suspect for the attack now known to be from the Illawarra, late that first afternoon a new line of inquiry opened up.

Laurence had recently worked in that region for six years as a member of both the State Protection Support Unit and the Operations Support Group and, in the course of his duties, had probably arrested dozens of its worst and most violent offenders. In addition, before moving back to Sydney, he and Samantha had been living in Wollongong, not far from the stamping ground of the suspect. Could the attack on her have been more than simply a random, opportunistic piece of thuggery?

A security expert was immediately sent to the Barlows' home in the Sutherland Shire to change the locks, and conduct a check that all was secure. The local police were told to include the house on their routine patrols.

For Laurence, it was all beginning to feel overwhelming. He was still not well himself, on a steady diet of antibiotics for the tonsillitis and painkillers for his back to keep himself going. As the attack on Samantha hit all the evening TV news bulletins, his mobile started to ring constantly with shocked family and friends inquiring after her. Many of those drove straight to the hospital and, not allowed into intensive care to see her, they spent hours in the waiting room outside instead, joining the battalion of police officers who were also sitting waiting for any updates. Everyone fussed around Laurence, and a number of visitors burst into tears as soon as they arrived, meaning he had to break away to try to comfort them – an exhausting task, especially when he was in such excruciating emotional turmoil himself. He managed to keep a tight lid on his own feelings, wanting to stay strong for Samantha, but he felt he was being sorely tested.

Happily, one of Samantha's friends offered to pick up their children Lily and Ben from day care and take them home, and her parents agreed to stay over in their house to look after them. They also volunteered to give Samantha's beloved but ageing dog Maddie, a Shar Pei, the medication she'd been prescribed the week before by their vet, which had to be crushed then sprinkled over her food. As a result, Laurence decided not to go home to see them all himself. 'I knew the kids were being well cared for, and they didn't really need me,' he says. 'Lily would miss her mum but Ben was at the age where he just needed to be fed and have a cuddle, and there were plenty of people around to do that. Out of them all, I knew Sam needed me far more, so I wanted to stay close for her.'

A well-meaning official at the police union, the Police Association of New South Wales, arranged for Laurence to be able to stay in a private room at the hospital, but he wouldn't hear of spending any time away from his wife. 'There's no way I was going to leave Sam's side to go to bed when she was so critically injured,' he says. 'They couldn't have dynamited me out of there. With everything that had happened that day, I was living on adrenalin supported by an hourly fix of coffee, just as I would be at a large emergency police operation. I'd already accepted that I wouldn't sleep for several days and had braced myself for the long haul. I needed to be with my wife. I needed to know everything. I hadn't said goodbye to Sam and I promised myself that I wasn't going home until she either woke up or died. I wasn't going anywhere. And if this was to be the end of her life, and of our life together, I wasn't going to waste those valuable last few hours in bed.'

He wouldn't have got too much rest in any case. In the middle of the night, Ben started coughing and couldn't stop and ended up being rushed from home to the paediatric ward of Sutherland Hospital with an acute respiratory infection.

Laurence, beside himself with worry, was given the choice of hospital beds to sit by all night. 'I chose to stay with Sam,' he says. 'She was in a critical condition. I knew if anything got worse with our son, I could be there in a police car with the siren and lights flashing within fifteen minutes.'

That night, the only time he left his wife's side was to visit the hospital chapel to say a prayer.

# Chapter 7
# HOPING FOR A MIRACLE

The next day – Thursday – was going to be critical for Samantha Barlow. While she was still on life support and in a deep coma, hospital staff knew that the swelling of the injured part of her brain could end up damaging the good tissue that was left. No one knew how it would turn out, or if she'd even wake from her sleep.

The nursing unit manager for the general neurological trauma section of the Intensive Care Unit, Nicky Glenister, kept a wary eye on the patient. 'She'd been in surgery for a long time on the Wednesday because there'd been so much damage to her scalp as well as the internal injuries, but the main problem with head injuries is always the swelling afterwards,' she says. 'The head is like a closed box, and the swelling increases the pressure on the brain and so you expect a patient to get worse before they can, hopefully, get better.'

Samantha was hovering in a no-man's-land, somewhere between life and death, and Laurence felt absolutely powerless to help her. But at least in this state of suspended animation she seemed to be finally out of pain. He sat by her bedside as the ventilator breathed for her, watching her chest rise then holding his own breath until her chest fell again on the exhale.

New South Wales Police Commissioner Andrew Scipione had been working away in the bush when the news had reached him about Samantha, and he'd immediately turned his car round and driven straight back to Sydney to see her. He'd known Laurence from when they both worked in Bankstown but got to know him better through the 2005 Cronulla riots, during which Laurence had played a central role in containing the trouble and restoring order. He'd then worked with him at setting up the new Public Order and Riot Squad to ensure the police could never again be caught out unprepared for that level of turmoil on the streets. 'I knew Laurence as a no-nonsense, get-on-with-the-business kind of guy,' says Scipione. 'He's got focus, he knew what had to be done and knew he had to deliver.' He didn't know Samantha but had received glowing reports. 'She was very well spoken of,' he says. 'When I talked to people, she was often referred to as the perfect officer.

'When I came in to see her that first day, she looked terrible. She looked, for all intents and purposes, as if she was already deceased. Her hand was a mess and her face was terrible. Someone doesn't get much worse than that without having a funeral.'

Scipione sat at Samantha's bedside for a while, then went and sat with his officers outside. 'They were all terribly traumatised,' he says. 'When someone like Sam or anyone in the organisation gets that badly injured, you're all hurting. It's the least you can do to be there with them.'

A police chaplain stayed nearby for most of those first few days, as well as a nun from Mary MacKillop's order, the Sisters of St Joseph. While their presence at times seemed to Laurence a grim recognition that his wife might not make it, at other times he took some comfort from them. When his mother, a Catholic, had died, the family had made sure her coffin contained a much-loved picture of Mary MacKillop, long before she was canonised as the first Australian saint. So for her son, it was a reminder that miracles can happen. 'And that's exactly what we were hoping for,' he says.

One day, the chaplain said a prayer over Samantha, with Laurence, his dad George and her parents all holding hands by her side. 'We were standing there with our eyes closed, but when we opened them, he was gone,' says her mum Janice Groves. 'Apparently he was so overcome by emotion at the thought this had happened to such a beautiful girl, he broke down in tears and left crying while we couldn't see him.'

Now Laurence was constantly checking each of the monitors, even though he had no idea what they were, and asking questions of the doctors and nurses, despite knowing he was probably just getting in their way. 'But it was what I had to do,' he says. 'If this was goodbye, then I intended to cherish every last second, learn as much as I could, hang on to every memory. It was only what Sam would have done for me too, if the situation had have been reversed. In fact, I think she'd have been even worse.'

Samantha took to the police force from the day she joined in 1994 as if it were a second skin. 'Policing is one of the most honourable professions in the world,' she says today. 'You go to work every day and you risk your life to help people. As dumb as it sounds, I wanted to serve, and I was really proud of my job.'

She enjoyed her training at the New South Wales Police Academy at Goulburn and did well at assessment time, despite being, at nineteen, the youngest of her class of 250 new recruits, with an average age of twenty-five. She found all aspects of policing fascinating and so, unlike at school, she was hugely motivated to study and learn.

'She's not naturally academic but she studied incredibly hard for her exams and she finished in the top rank of graduate police officers,' says her brother Jason. 'She was still so determined to be the best she could at everything!'

She also loved being able to see how much of the theory could be immediately put into practice and she liked the physical challenges, like the obstacle courses. The only part of the training she didn't excel in was in firearms. It would be many more years before she discovered her basic mistake was choosing the wrong eye – her weakest one – to be the eye she used in lining up her targets, and no one had corrected her. She hadn't realised she was in a minority of people who are 'cross-eye dominant', a right-handed shooter whose left eye was the dominant one.

At the academy, Samantha became a member of her 'gang of four', making firm friends with three other female probationers, Perri Hayes, Belinda Jacob and Sam Harrison. 'We became really close friends and had probably the best time of our lives, drinking and socialising,' says Jacob. 'Sam was popular and high-spirited and great fun.'

Yet she could also be a little more restrained than the others, says Hayes. 'She could be quite a private person too, and she was very ladylike – she never swore. I think she got that from her mum. But she was very friendly and approachable and she was also very career-minded.'

Samantha's first posting in 1995 was to Maroubra, close to home. She had the advantage in knowing the area but it felt odd at first giving orders to members of the public often twice her age. 'It felt weird telling people much older than me what to do,' she says. 'But I found that as long as I spoke to people appropriately and didn't come over all high and mighty, they'd respond well.' The first uniform she was supplied was at least two sizes too big but, she was reassured, 'You'll grow into it!' She had no intention of doing that. She also liked walking around in uniform, smiling and chatting to people, and found it hard to adjust to not doing the same when she was back in civvies. But she was rarely thrown by anything. Her first dead body was of an elderly lady who'd died of natural causes but who'd collapsed on her heater and, when discovered, was stuck to it, a sizzling mess. Samantha took that in her stride. For someone who'd grown up fainting at the sight of her own blood, she found she could tolerate all manner of gruesome sights and scenes involving other people.

Her second posting was to Mascot in late 1995. One of her very first jobs there on night shift was to go to the scene of what was reported to be a minor road traffic accident at Port Botany. When she arrived, there was a crowd of people standing around, out of their cars, staring at a man who'd just rammed his partner's car into a concrete barricade. As she walked closer, she also saw a woman covered in blood slumped on the ground. It turned out that the couple had rowed after she'd announced she was leaving him, he'd driven into her car, she'd climbed out and then he'd stabbed her a number of times. Inside the car, their ten-year-old daughter was crying. The man was still brandishing a massive knife but, concerned for the woman and her child, Samantha walked up to him and started yelling, 'Drop the knife! Drop the knife! Drop the knife!'

At that, the man looked straight at her, calmly raised the knife and then slit his own throat in front of everyone. He slid down the back of the car and Samantha ran over, kicked the knife away, and attempted to take his pulse at his neck. As she knelt on the ground, cradling him, she was horrified to realise his head had nearly come away in her hands. She then called for an ambulance and went to look after the woman and her daughter, later having to take their statements at the hospital. 'It was all pretty horrible,' says Samantha, who was then just twenty years old. 'But I never panic. You're thinking about everyone else and what you're doing, and I'm weird but I have a very strong stomach. While he was obviously dead, luckily the woman recovered so it turned out okay but it was hard. That was the very start of my shift and I still had another eleven hours to go . . .'

Rarely did Samantha get upset by the things she saw in the course of her work. Even when she had to help at the crime scene of a woman so severely bashed by her partner that they'd left a trail of blood from one end of the apartment to the other, she found she was able to avoid becoming emotionally involved.

'I'd often go home and tell my parents what I'd been doing, and then I'd sleep so well!' she says. 'They were always interested and asked questions and never really cringed at anything. They were as weird as me!'

Her parents remember those days well. 'She loved to come home and wake us up and tell us about her day,' says her mum Janice. 'We were always very close. She told us about a horse which had got injured in its float in an accident and how she'd had to sort it out, or about how she'd had to chase someone. I suppose she got a bit more blasé as she got older, but in the early days she was always very excited. Then she'd go off to bed and sleep, and we'd be left wide awake!'

On Christmas Day 1995, Samantha attended another altercation, this time nearby at Eastlakes. When she arrived, neighbours reported a gunman holding a child hostage on the top floor of a twelve-storey unit block. She called in the Tactical Operations State Protection Group and they kitted her out, asked her to come to the top floor with them and armed her with a sledgehammer so heavy she couldn't even lift it. After five hours waiting there, officers managed to capture the man and rescue the child without her, thankfully, having to attempt to swing the hammer.

Samantha was then immediately called off to help at Bondi where thousands of backpackers had left their traditional beach party to mill around the streets and were set upon by gangs of men in cars. Violence erupted with up to 1000 people fighting and throwing missiles and, when the police intervened, mobs started attacking police cars and throwing bottles. 'The riots were full-on by the time I arrived,' she says. 'There were probably only fifty police and a good few hundred protesters just throwing things at us. It was all alcohol-fuelled, but it was more a surprise than anything. You didn't know what was going to happen, but I wasn't scared. We had shields and batons, but no helmets, just our soft cloth hats – but I always felt my head was pretty hard, so that was all right.'

Doctors hovered around the bed, discussing the state of Samantha's scalp. The neurosurgeons had done what they could for her brain, but they were still worried about the possibility of infection. The level of trauma to her skin and blood vessels had been so great that they fretted there might be insufficient skin left to knit together to form scars. This would mean she'd need skin grafts. One of Sydney's leading plastic surgeons, Dr Damian Marucci, was called in to take a look.

He carefully peeled off the dressings covering her head, examined what was left and decided to operate. 'It wasn't like there were just simple cuts to her scalp and face,' he says. 'All the cuts were really jagged with underlying fractures of her skull and facial bones, too. I could see how battered and bruised and swollen she was, with incredible black eyes. It was a terrible situation but I thought I'd be able to help. Of course, she was still in a coma, unconscious, and it was unclear whether she'd wake up again. I'd be operating on her not knowing how she was going to be, and if her brain was still working. If it wasn't, what I'd be doing would be purely academic.'

On the plus side, Dr Marucci could see there was good blood flow to the skin that was left, so he carefully worked to reconstruct her face, reopening and restitching the deep lacerations of her forehead, and piecing back together the patchwork of her scalp. He examined her fractured nose, which was pushed to one side, and discovered that the fractures extended back from her nose to the base of her skull. He gently tried to straighten the nose as best he could at that stage and decided, if she were to live, he would perform rhinoplasty further down the track.

Finally, he turned his attention to her shattered hand, the broken middle finger and the crushed index finger. He lined up the broken fragments of bone of the middle finger using a portable X-ray machine, and held the bones in position using stainless-steel pins, or K-wires. He repaired the crushed nail bed of the index finger but left the underlying smashed bone to heal by itself. He knew more surgery would be needed on those later, too.

Laurence was heartened by how up-beat Dr Marucci was about this second round of surgery but even as he began to relax – just a little – he was approached by two sexual assault counsellors from another hospital. They said they'd like to conduct a vaginal swab to make sure Samantha hadn't also been the victim of a sexual assault. Laurence was appalled. He knew it was routine, but he didn't want his wife to be subjected to any procedure that he couldn't be sure was absolutely necessary. He told them he'd only permit the test to be done if they had a request form signed by the senior police investigating the crime. After a heated argument, they left and he immediately contacted one of the officers in charge. No, he was told, sexual assault as a motive had been ruled out; the test didn't need to be done.

For Laurence, it felt like one small victory. He hadn't been there to protect Samantha in her time of need but he sure as hell was going to do everything in his power to safeguard her now. While he looked as if he were staying strong on the surface, underneath he was absolutely devastated by what had happened and fearful of how it might end. In his working life, Laurence was the tough one, taking control of the most volatile and dangerous of situations on the very frontline of operational policing, helping other people in their hour of need. But now he was in a position totally beyond his control, helpless and utterly powerless to influence the outcome.

He stepped up the number of questions he was asking the doctors and nurses. Every time they came to check on her, he asked what they were looking for, how they were doing that, what they proposed to do next. Every answer, every explanation, he committed to memory, and then, in the occasional breaks he was forced to have from Samantha's bedside, he looked up what they were saying on his laptop, studied the medical texts, trawled the internet for alternatives and then returned to intensive care with a whole new set of questions. It was exhausting not only for him, but also for the doctors. But it was his own way of trying to compensate, and of making absolutely sure Samantha was receiving the best possible care he could guarantee.

But as well as the guilt, he was also beginning to feel very angry. He was enraged that someone had done something so terrible to his wife, and would quite possibly rob her of her life, his children of their mother and him of the love of his life. He was incensed too that so many people had apparently seen her lying battered and bloodied in that park, yet did nothing to help.

'Even if they didn't want to stop and ask her if she was all right, even if they didn't want to get involved, they could have used their mobile phones to report it to the police,' he says. 'Why couldn't anyone even have done that? If someone had phoned the police earlier, that could have made such a difference to how quickly she was found, and whether her life was going to be saved.'

Luckily, his best mate Inspector Paul Condon, a tactical commander at the riot squad and one of the two colleagues who'd brought him to the hospital the previous morning, opted to stay with him and do everything he could to help. He sensed Laurence's shifting moods and tried to intervene whenever he saw him getting close to breaking point. He had chosen not to go into intensive care to see Samantha. He was too worried he might be so affected by the sight of her that he'd fall to pieces and then be of no use to his friend.

'Laurence was stunned,' he says. 'He becomes very stoic when things go bad, and tries to take himself away from the emotional side and deal with the facts. But I think he was convinced we were going to lose Sam. He was behaving like she could go at any minute or that she'd actually died, which put a lot of strain on him, and on our friendship.

'He's an excellent police officer, a natural leader, but that somehow made it so much harder when the trouble was personal.'

Laurence's police career began at 19 Division, Bankstown, in south-west Sydney, on the weekend following the 1984 Milperra Massacre. If he'd hoped for his police life to be exciting, it couldn't have got off to a more action-packed start than dealing with the fallout from the gun battle between rival bikie gangs the Comancheros and the Bandidos, which left seven dead and twenty-eight injured. He didn't know it then, of course, but his career would continue very much as it began.

He encountered his own first dead body a few weeks later when a pedestrian was knocked down by a car and killed on a zebra crossing. His second came not much later when he answered a call at the station from a man threatening to kill himself. Shortly afterwards, there was a report over the police radio of shots fired. He raced to the address to discover the body of a young man who'd placed the muzzle of a gun in his mouth and pulled the trigger. The walls and floor were covered in his blood.

Sometimes, however much he tried to help, he couldn't avert tragedies. He often used to try to help an alcoholic and obviously mentally ill man who would wander the streets of Villawood and Chester Hill, trying to have him admitted to a psychiatric ward of the local hospital. One day, after yet another unsuccessful attempt – the examining doctor turned him away, declaring he was as sane as any of the medical staff there – the man went home and hanged himself from the branch of a tree in the front yard of his house.

'I suppose I grew up very quickly as a result of many of the things I saw in those early days,' says Laurence. 'One of the most horrific things was being the first to find a man, an illegal immigrant, who seemed to have jumped or fallen – or been thrown – from a moving train. His face had come into contact with the brick wall of the rail bridge overpass and he was still alive, although a large part of his face was either missing or significantly disfigured. As I leant over him, I could hear a loud slurping sound as part of his face would be sucked in every time he inhaled, and then the same sound when he exhaled. He later died, but I've never been able to get that sound out of my mind . . . or my nightmares.'

A very drunk man another evening brandishing a long, serrated bread knife posed a completely different kind of threat. He'd been fighting with his equally intoxicated brother, but when Laurence arrived, he lunged at him instead. Laurence backed off behind a kitchen chair, drew his long police baton and then hit the man's arm as hard as he could to try to make him drop his weapon. He held on to the knife for a while, but was later disarmed, arrested and taken to hospital to be treated for a broken arm.

Laurence again found himself a target when a riot erupted at New South Wales's maximum-security juvenile jail, the Minda Detention Centre at Lidcombe. Buildings were destroyed and fires lit, and the main instigators barricaded themselves in the main recreation building. The Tactical Response Group (TRG), the riot and siege squad set up in the early 1980s to tackle serious incidents, was going to take too long to arrive so Laurence, even though he'd served in the force for less than four years, was chosen to lead a team of highway patrol and general duties officers into the fray. Armed only with a baton, and using a steel garbage bin lid as a shield, he raced in and was immediately set upon by the group, who were hurling snooker balls. 'I remember a pool cue being smashed over my head as a second one crashed into my makeshift shield,' he says. 'But I still managed to arrest the main culprit, who turned out to be an eighteen year old convicted of murder.'

Yet that was by no means the scariest incident the young officer was to encounter in his early years. The TRG had originally been created in response to the Australian Motorcycle Grand Prix at Bathurst degenerating into a series of bloody riots between 1980 and 1985. Laurence's first visit to the races was in 1987, tipped to be another bad year. And it was. 'That stands out as one of the scariest times of my life,' he says.

'I remember sitting in the police bus whilst rocks, bottles, lit tree branches and Molotov cocktails rained over us, whilst holding a perspex police riot shield against the inside of the windows to reinforce them as glass began to crack and shatter. I still have vivid memories of looking out and seeing shirtless and bearded men, standing on the side of the road, chanting, yelling, throwing rocks and other objects at us, with campfires and broken glass everywhere. Once you experience something like that, it stays with you for life. You remember people being injured, set on fire, the smell of diesel and chlorine that filled the air from the homemade form of napalm which had been reported to have been mixed with large elastic bands to enable it to stick to your skin whilst on fire. It was terrible.' Things weren't much better the following year at the street-car championships, the Summernats, in Wagga Wagga over Easter. About 3000 people rioted after a car drag-racing event.

Laurence made some good friends within the force, and also married in 1986. But he found his career was almost all-consuming and in 1988 made the decision to join the TRG. He'd seen the squad, and often worked side-by-side with them at various incidents, and felt he'd very much like to be a part of one of the 25-strong units whose primary role was to respond to riots, protests, disasters, sieges and hostage situations. 'It felt like the kind of frontline policing I'd always wanted to do,' says Laurence. 'You were really putting your life on the line to protect the public, and I felt I'd be good at it.'

Laurence spent the next three years with the TRG, dealing with a huge variety of incidents. Many of these involved sieges. His first was in Seven Hills in Sydney's west where, after the failure of negotiations, the decision was made to force entry into a house to try and disarm the gunman inside. He was part of the team that ran up the driveway, smashed their way in with a 6 kilogram sledgehammer and confronted the man. After a tense few minutes, Laurence stepped forward and took the loaded rifle from him. Another siege, this time in Summer Hill in the inner west, ended less happily when the instigator killed himself with his own shotgun. A third in Drummoyne nearby became a tense stand-off after Laurence entered the lounge room of the house to discover a woman sitting on the floor with a handgun. He talked to her for more than an hour to persuade her to give up her weapon, using his own experiences to advise her on her family and relationship issues.

The squad also carried out a number of searches. By now, Laurence, a tall, strong man with broad shoulders and a seemingly endless store of stamina, had been designated 'the hammer man', the one yielding the sledgehammer. In the first raid, on a first-floor flat from which drugs were being dealt and where one of the dealers was known to have a rifle, the order was given to gain access in three – or fewer – strikes of the sledgehammer. If that failed, or anyone heard the sound of a rifle being racked or actioned, the exit plan was to smash a window then dive out into the bushes, 5 metres below. Luckily, it took Laurence only two strikes, and the loaded rifle was seized from its position slung across the inside of the front door.

Another drug dealer's unit, this time on the top floor of a block also in the inner west, was much better protected with a metal door inside a metal frame. This one took fourteen strikes of the hammer, with two shotguns and five handguns covering Laurence as he laboured, before it finally gave way and the man inside was arrested without a shot being fired. A similar raid, this time on a bikie gang's clubhouse, also happened without incident, and machine guns were confiscated from the premises.

Laurence received a bravery award, a Deputy Commissioner's Citation, for his next arrest. A man was wanted for a sex-related incident and had been hiding out in a caravan at the back of a house. Laurence tore off a screen door from its hinges with his bare hands and was first into the caravan, yelling, with his gun drawn, to find the man lying in his bed, reaching beneath his pillow for his .357 Magnum handgun. Laurence kept shouting for him to leave it alone, when he suddenly noticed a young woman lying in bed beside him. At that, Laurence stepped over, grabbed the man with his left hand, dragged him from the bed, forced him up against the wall and arrested him. The Magnum was later recovered, fully loaded.

It was yet another close call in a career that was rapidly becoming a constant flirtation with danger and death.

The police involved in the investigation into the attack on Samantha were working long hours, and were desperate for any news about their colleague. Towards the end of the second day, Laurence agreed to attend the daily 6 p.m. muster at the Kings Cross police station to find out how things were going, and to update everyone on his wife's condition.

Kings Cross Superintendent Tony Crandell picked him up from the hospital and, on the way to the station, was taken aback when Laurence asked him to drive past Arthur Park. 'Are you sure you want to do that?' Crandell asked him.

Laurence nodded, a grim look on his face. 'Yes,' he said. 'Yes I am.'

Crandell pulled over when they reached the park and let Laurence gaze out through the window. 'That's where the attack would have happened,' Laurence said, gesturing towards the footpath by the tree, 'and that's where the offender would have run.'

He stared at the scene for a few more minutes, then looked back at Crandell. 'Okay,' he said, 'I can't stay here any longer. Let's go.'

The pair drove on in silence. 'I think Laurence thought it would be therapeutic, to look at where it had happened,' says Crandell. 'But it wasn't. I don't think he found any solace in that at all. He's a big, rough, tough man, but I could see that it hurt him to go there, that he was struggling.'

When they reached the station, they parked, entered through the front doors and walked downstairs into the training room. The place was so packed there was barely space to move, but the crowd divided to make way for him. Then, as he reached the front and started speaking, there was an absolute hush; they hung on his every word. He struggled to keep his composure as he recited the list of Samantha's injuries and relayed what the doctors were doing to try to save her life.

'I said that Sam was so far miraculously defying the odds and was still alive,' he says. 'I told them if she lived, there was still a good chance that she might suffer some form of long-term mental and physical disability but at least there were signs she was weathering the worst of the storm. There was still hope.'

Everyone in the room was moved by both what he said about Samantha and his own demeanour, Crandell among them. 'He captivated his audience,' he says. 'Here was a fellow who was clearly distraught but who was giving them this information and they were hanging on every single word he said because they so desperately wanted her to survive. Police being police, they wanted to know whether we were likely to detect the offender, but I've never seen greater concern from a group of people in my life. And the courage shown by Laurence was just remarkable.'

In turn, the team briefed Laurence about their inquiries. Police had worked many extra hours of unpaid, voluntary overtime and the investigation was in very good shape. Detectives had by now upgraded Roderick Holohan's status from 'suspect' to 'wanted', and the investigation was feeding information to police in the Illawarra. They'd begun contacting registered sources, visiting and watching the places Holohan was known to hang out, supported by security officers reviewing CCTV footage from railway stations on the Illawarra line, as well as from security cameras around Wollongong. They'd also received an anonymous tip-off in a phone call about where he might be.

As they finished, Laurence went over to Detective Sergeant Mat Moss, running the investigation, and shook his hand. 'Thanks, mate,' he said softly.

Moss's face softened and Laurence could see him trying to hold back tears. 'We won't rest till we get him,' Moss replied, his hand on his heart. 'We will get him.'

Laurence smiled, also doing his best to keep his emotions in check. 'I know, mate,' he said. 'I know.'

In truth, Moss desperately hoped it would work out that way, but had no real guarantees. 'I'd said it with a degree of confidence, armed with a lot of information,' he says. 'I'd wanted to give him some reassurance. I only hoped it would be true, that we would get our man.'

Roderick Holohan wakes up on Thursday at about 8 a.m. in Dapto park. In the bright sunlight of morning, however, his girlfriend notices something strange – his shirt is speckled with blood.

After a few minutes, she dismisses it. She's having her period and it may be her blood on his clothes. She doesn't think any more about it.

Gathering up their blankets, they walk into Wollongong, buy some breakfast and hang around in town. With nothing much else to do, they then decide to visit Rod's sister who lives nearby. They spend an hour or so at her house, then decide to go back to Wollongong. The sister drives them to the railway station at Dapto.

The couple are sitting on the bench on the platform when a friend of theirs approaches. She sits down too, and the three sit, happily chatting.

At 9.15 p.m. that evening, a posse of police pounce on Roderick Holohan as he's sitting on that bench at Dapto railway station. He's startled but doesn't seem surprised. This is the moment he's been dreading, but he had little doubt it would arrive.

The police tracked him down to the park where he'd slept, and then followed the trail to the station. They then rang the Strike Force Ferndell detectives in Sydney and asked them to come up to Port Kembla police station for a briefing. They all raced there, hopeful of finally getting their man. He fitted all the descriptions, matched every line of inquiry they'd been following.

Then, as he's arrested, he immediately admits to the attack on Samantha. 'I thought I'd killed her,' he says.

'Not yet,' is the tight reply.

And the reason for such a savage beating? He needed money for drugs, he explains. It was as simple as that. Nothing more, nothing less.

# Chapter 8
# FACING THE DEMONS

As the night sky began to lighten early on Friday morning, Samantha Barlow's third day in a coma, her husband Laurence went into the staff bathroom at the hospital to wash his face and have a quick shave. He lathered up with soap and took out the razor someone had brought him, holding it in his right hand, ready to start. In the mirror, he could see himself looking ghostly pale after a second night without sleep.

But as he raised the razor to his face, he noticed his hand trembling violently. He tried to hold it still with his other hand, but that seemed to be shaking almost as much. He willed himself to stop, but couldn't. Finally, he flung the razor into the sink and collapsed onto the floor, curled up into a foetal position, and sobbed and sobbed and sobbed, as if he'd never stop.

'I'd spent the night imagining what Sam had gone through,' he says. 'From her injuries, the attack would have been so ferocious. I just couldn't come to terms with how that had happened, and no one had tried to intervene. This was a beautiful woman dressed in casual clothing with a bag on each shoulder, walking along the streets of Sydney, an off-duty police officer, simply trying to get to work.

But no one had stopped the attack, and no one had helped her when she needed it most. I was angry but at that point, I'd just fallen to bits. I'd been trying to keep it together, but inside, I couldn't cope.'

Eventually, Laurence did manage to pull himself back together and went back into the tiny interview room, just by the Intensive Care Unit, which he and his mate Inspector Paul Condon had commandeered for themselves with the hospital's permission. They'd taken a couple of tiny mattresses off gurneys and thrown them onto the floor so they could lie down for a couple of hours at night when the nurses insisted he leave. He couldn't bear being away from Samantha for any longer than that. Neither man had slept, though. Condon listened as Laurence talked, reassured him when his fears about Samantha threatened to overwhelm him, and tried to calm him when he became too agitated.

Now completely exhausted, Laurence asked Condon to organise for them to go and look properly over the crime scene. He felt finally ready to face his darkest demons. Condon phoned the head of the investigation, Detective Sergeant Mat Moss, and then walked with Laurence over to Arthur Park. The sun hadn't yet risen and, in the thin pre-dawn light, Laurence stopped and stared at the small patch of green where his wife had faced the fight of her life. 'There was a chill in the air, and the cold was coming up from the concrete path through my shoes,' he says.

'Everything seemed so cold and still. I thought of Sam and imagined how cold she must have been, left to die for over an hour, and the terror and confusion she must have gone through, lapsing in and out of consciousness. My wife is the most strong-willed and determined person I know. I knew she would have fought like a Wallaby forward pack. A less determined person would have no doubt been lying in a morgue fridge, not still fighting on at hospital.'

As soon as the police guarding the crime scene saw Laurence, they all came over to shake his hand and touch him on the shoulder, many openly in tears. He acknowledged them, and then ducked under the crime scene tape, where orange cones marked every spot where forensic evidence had been found or photographs taken. Moss arrived and the pair hugged. Having been close to death himself, he knew much better than most what Laurence must be going through. Moss then showed him around the scene, walked him through what he believed had happened and took him to where Samantha's bloodied police shirt had been found.

On his way back out, Laurence noticed where the bus shelter had been, where Samantha had lain, wrapped in a blanket until she'd eventually been found. He'd been told she'd been slumped against an advertising panel for the Fred Hollows Foundation, with a kindly image of the late lifesaving ophthalmologist smiling down. Later, Laurence was to receive a card from a member of the Hollows family saying they'd been comforted by the thought that Fred had been watching over her. Strangely enough, he felt that too.

Laurence missed Roderick Holohan at that park by just three hours. Shortly after 10 a.m., detectives drove Holohan to Arthur Park. He'd agreed, when arrested the night before, to show Moss exactly where he'd been, what he'd been doing, and where he'd launched his attack on Samantha. He'd said he wanted to help, but no one was in any doubt about who he thought his cooperation would benefit most.

In his first interview with Moss that night, in the charge room at Port Kembla police station, he made no attempt to hide his crime. 'Man, I can't believe what I've done,' he said. 'I'm a fuckin' idiot.

I just started hitting her and I took her bags and ran away.' He didn't ask, however, how Samantha was faring; he was too busy feeling sorry for himself. 'My life's fucked,' he said. 'What's going to happen to me now?'

Moss quietly asked him if he'd be prepared to assist the investigation. He nodded. 'Man, I'm sorry about what I did,' he replied. 'I just want to help you. I'll show you where I threw the mobile phone and the handbag. I'll do whatever I can to help.'

Holohan was sleepy, however, and Moss guessed he was still coming down from heroin he might have taken earlier that evening. He instructed the officers to give him something to eat and drink and left him alone. When he returned, he asked him what he'd done with Samantha's mobile. Holohan told him it was locked so it was no good to him, and he'd tossed it into the lake at the park at Dapto. They drove him out there and, in the light of the watery moon and their torches, he showed them where he thought he'd thrown it from. Police divers later recovered it, intact. 'Look, I want to help you guys any way I can,' Holohan insisted. 'I've done a bad thing and I want to make good what I've done.'

Moss pressed home his advantage, telling him that if he genuinely wanted to help, he would come back up to Sydney and agree to be filmed showing them exactly what had happened early the previous morning. Holohan agreed. 'For a short time, I believe he was sincerely sorry for what he'd done,' says Moss. 'I've seen a lot of crooks in my time who've never meant what they've said. But he certainly didn't have to do a video run-through. He could have exercised his right to silence. But I'd managed to get a bit of a rapport with him. I told him he was doing the right thing in being open and honest and frank.'

Holohan's failure to comply with the conditions of his parole gave investigators the right to keep him in custody without any additional charges – strategically buying them more time to eliminate other suspects from their lists, while still making sure Holohan was no longer on the streets, posing a danger to anyone else.

His parole was successfully revoked and, a few hours later, early on the Friday morning, he was driven back to Sydney. As he was escorted into Kings Cross police station, the place fell silent. Everyone knew exactly who he was and what he'd done to their colleague but, by the same token, they all knew they had a job to do. To show their anger towards him, to give him any clue of how they were feeling, might give him grounds for complaint and potentially damage the case against him. And that was the last thing anyone wanted.

After an hour, he was driven to Arthur Park. There, with the police videoing every move and every word, he went through exactly what he had been doing that morning, where he'd first seen Samantha, how he'd approached her. 'He said he didn't know she was a policewoman,' says Moss. 'She wasn't in uniform, so he said he couldn't have known.'

He then demonstrated how he'd lunged at Samantha and crushed her skull with the brick. Everyone who saw him that day will never forget it. Local resident Laura Good, out for her daily morning walk from a nearby apartment block, saw the figure crouched down over his imaginary victim, smashing his hand down, again and again, as if bludgeoning someone to death. She shuddered to see it.

'It was quite a weird and shocking sight, like watching a scene being filmed, or a play that was real but not real,' says Good. 'I asked a police officer standing nearby what was going on, and he told me it was a re-enactment. I can't imagine how the police would have felt watching him go over it with a brick or whatever he had in his hand, especially seeing as he'd attacked one of them. It made me feel quite defenceless.' After that morning, she always avoided walking anywhere near that stretch of path.

As news got around that the man who'd beaten a policewoman almost to death was back in the park, a small crowd gathered beyond the crime scene tape. A few onlookers started shouting out to him. 'Scumbag!' yelled one. 'Mongrel!' shouted another. And a particularly burly man called to the police, 'Bring him over here, and we'll do him for you now!'

The officers looked on stonily, studiously avoiding reacting to anything. Moss didn't even seem to hear them; he was carefully watching, and noting, everything Holohan did. 'It was hard as, knowing Laurence, it was impossible not to be touched by everything,' he says. 'He's a mate, and you always help your mates. But I couldn't afford to be hostile towards the suspect at all. You have to be professional. To show my feelings would have contaminated our relationship and would be counterproductive. He would have picked up on that, and I wanted him to cooperate.'

Holohan said he'd hit Samantha around four times. Moss, like everyone else watching, knew full well from the hospital records that it was in reality many more, at least twelve, maybe as many as twenty.

But there was little doubt that Holohan thought he'd killed her. 'I thought she was dead, mate, fair dinkum,' he told Moss. After putting her police shirt over her face, he took it off again as he was about to go, 'to get rid of it because it had the police badge on there. I don't really know why I done it . . . I really wasn't thinking rational or anything, mate, at the time . . . I'm fuckin' insane at this fuckin' time. My body's screaming for heroin, I've done this to this lady, then realised what I've fuckin' done, freaked out . . .'

On the outside, no one could see much change in Samantha. She was still breathing with the aid of a machine, her heart was still beating and while the swelling to her face had started to go down just a little, her face, neck and shoulders were still a mass of bruises, cuts, stitches and bandages.

Laurence continued to spend long hours at her bedside, holding her one good hand, stroking her shoulder and talking to her constantly, telling her how much he loved her, how much he and their children needed her, how all her family, friends and colleagues were also keeping vigil in the waiting room outside.

From time to time, he broke away to escort her parents or close friends into intensive care to see her. One was Samantha's close friend Robin Williams, who got to know her through the Coogee dive shop she runs with her husband Scot. 'I don't do very well at things like this, but he told me he thought I should go in, and that he'd help me, he'd be there the whole time,' she says. 'He guided me through it. It was very difficult because we thought she wasn't going to make it, but he held my hand the entire time and talked to Sam and to me. He made a very difficult thing bearable. The next day, I took my daughter Casey who was eleven at the time to the hospital. She said she wanted to go in, so he helped her too. He knows how to deal with people and help them through their fears.'

He also escorted Scot to Samantha's side. 'It was very confronting,' says Scot. 'It was horrific to see her like that. I would never have known her. But he walked me in and said, "Hi Sam, it's Laurence. I love you. Scot's here to see you." He then told me just to talk to her, talk about anything.'

Samantha's good mate from the police college, Sergeant Perri Hayes, was another of the first in. She'd been working from home the day of the attack but had received a call telling her Samantha had been attacked and was badly injured. Hayes immediately dropped her small daughter off at kindy and headed over to the hospital. Halfway there, she had a call from someone else who hadn't realised Samantha was such a close friend.

'They told me a policewoman had been assaulted and that they thought she was going to die,' says Hayes. 'I pulled off the road. I was completely hysterical. I had to sit there and re-gather myself. Then when I thought I was safe to drive again, I continued. But my sister works on the police radio and she was hysterical too. She used to run past that park on the way to work every day . . . But we were all really worried about Sam. We didn't know, even if she lived, what the long-term outcome would be. We were just all waiting around for updates from the doctors.'

That Friday morning saw the first piece of good news, the first glint of hope. Neurosurgeon Dr Vanessa Perotti had just taken a third CT scan of Samantha's head and sat Laurence down to show him how it looked. Even to an untrained eye, the change in her condition was obvious. The first scan on the Wednesday had shown the areas of her skull that had been smashed like an egg shell, and the two holes in the dura through which the brain fluid was leaking out, while the next one the following day illustrated where the fragments had been surgically removed. Now the new scan confirmed no blood clots, no sign of a stroke, no infection and no evidence of bleeding inside the brain. What's more, the pressure inside Samantha's skull seemed to have peaked, and to be on its way down. Perotti had, for the first time, abandoned talking in statistics and now sounded cautiously optimistic.

'Monitoring brain pressure is very specific,' explains her boss, the chairman of neurosurgery Dr Malcolm Pell. 'If the pressure is high and it doesn't respond to drugs and ventilation, then the outcome can be bad. But Sam's pressure had responded and was quite reasonable. There were no wound or infection problems, and she was young, which means the brain has more elasticity than with older patients, and very fit.' He felt the time had come to be a lot more positive about Samantha's chances and went to see her husband in the intensive care ward.

Laurence regarded him nervously as he approached, but Dr Pell smiled and stretched out his hand. 'He came in, shook my hand and before letting go, told me his prognosis, that Sam was recovering well and he thought she was going to be okay,' says Laurence. 'I heard the words but couldn't accept them. I weakened my grip, teared up and looked at the floor. He responded by grasping my hand more firmly and repeating himself, staring at me eyeball to eyeball. He refused to let go of my hand until I acknowledged what he was telling me.'

That was a deliberate move on Dr Pell's part. He was well aware that anxious family members often have trouble understanding what's said, particularly when they've prepared themselves for the worst. 'You've got to calm the person down, otherwise it just goes over their heads,' says Dr Pell. 'You've told them a significant amount of information and they hear the first few words and the rest becomes a blur. So you have to go through it slowly and carefully to make sure they understand.'

Yet Laurence still had trouble digesting his words. 'I felt numb and in shock again, disbelieving Sam's recovery in such a short period of time,' he says. 'Three days before, she was on the verge of death. Now I was being told that she would probably live. It's all we ever wished for, but now I was too scared to embrace it.'

* * *

Samantha was always eager for new challenges in her career, and early on she'd set her heart on joining the highway patrol. 'I loved the thought of being out and about instead of stuck in an office,' she says. 'Then if you see something happening, you can respond straightaway. And if you are stopping people, it's for doing something wrong.'

As part of the training, every officer was supposed to serve a week in each specialist unit, but Samantha had begged to be allowed to spend a month at highway patrol, expecting to love it. She did, and the day she returned to general duties at Mascot, she applied for a transfer to highway patrol, back at Maroubra. Her boss told her she was far too junior for a place – maybe in a year she'd be experienced enough – but that he'd let her send off her application in any case. In the meantime, she volunteered for every highway patrol operation that came up. Then, to everyone's surprise, within two months her tenacity won through, and her transfer was approved.

'I was very keen and went above and beyond what they asked to show that I was really capable and that I really wanted it,' she says. 'I was just very pushy. But no one would believe I'd got it, even when I told them. On my last day, I said goodbye and they were still saying, "Yeah, yeah, we'll see you on Monday!"'

It was only on her first day in the job, in May 1997, that they discovered Samantha had never actually driven a highway car before. Fortunately, however, she'd always been a good driver, loved driving and passed all the tests on her first attempt. As she'd imagined, she adored her job, patrolling the highways for trouble, conducting random breath tests, checking the roads and traffic around events, and providing medical escorts, particularly for heart transplant teams.

Her bosses noticed her early on. 'For a start, she was one of the few females in highway patrol!' says Dave Owens, the former commander of Maroubra who went on to become a deputy commissioner. 'But she was good. She was very professional, she was always well presented and nothing was a problem for her. She always responded, and never backed away from any job. She'd jump in whenever she could to give anyone a hand.

'You always get a lot of complaints from the public about highway patrol because they're the ones giving out tickets, but we never received many about her. She was always so bright and bubbly and people warmed to her immediately. It was a male-dominated area but the guys were always happy to be with her.'

Samantha occasionally had a bit of fun on the job too. Her brother Jason remembers being pulled over twice on one night for breath tests by members of her unit. 'She thought that was amusing,' he says. 'And once, she actually pulled me over. I was coming back from a party and saw the siren behind me and pulled over. A young policeman got out of the car and tapped on my window. He asked me if I knew why I'd been pulled over. I asked if it was because I'd gone round a roundabout too fast, or had gone through the last traffic lights on amber. He looked at me, and then said, "No, it's your sister in the car behind." I looked back through the rear window, and Sam was there, killing herself laughing.'

She also trained to be part of the Operations Support Group (OSG), the part-time support act to the riot squad, made up of officers who could be called in at the last minute to assist the full-timers in riot response, hand-to-hand fighting, bomb searches, chemical and biological defence and important security operations. It was a three-week course, and a tough one to pass, but she was determined to grab any new opportunity. 'She was always very motivated,' says her colleague Senior Sergeant Belinda Jacob, who later married Laurence's mate, Brendan Crowe, and took his surname.

'She could be stubborn too if she wanted something. She'd try anything once. I did surf boats for a while. To her, it was very natural; to me, it was terrifying. But that's what I liked most about her: she'd give anything a go, she was always trying new things, and she'd usually be very good at them too. I always thought she'd climb the career ladder.'

As part of the OSG, Samantha was drafted three months before the Sydney 2000 Olympics, as well as during the event and after it, to help search all the sites and maintain security. 'They like to call on the highway patrol as you're in a car and can get anywhere quickly,' she says. 'But the atmosphere was wonderful and it was hard at times not to get carried away when Australia was winning and remember you weren't meant to be watching!'

Always keen to do more than her fair share of the work at hand, Samantha was popular with her male and female teammates alike. The force might have been dominated numerically by men, with a culture still determinedly macho, but she seemed able to straddle the line between being one of the boys and remaining one of the girls. 'She seemed to manage that effortlessly,' says Judy Cohen, who'd gone to school with Samantha and also been a competitive swimmer. 'If anyone said something wasn't for her, she'd ask, "Why the hell not?" She had a lot of confidence and didn't get bothered by anything.' She was always popular with the men too. 'The guys knew she could do anything they could do, and often probably better,' says Crowe. 'She never tolerated fools, either, which everyone respected. She worked in a lot of male-dominated areas, and the guys loved her.'

It didn't hurt Samantha's popularity at work that she was always keen to take on the night shifts, as they gave her more free time over the weekends to continue to compete in swim races and surf carnivals. 'Then I could compete all day and work all night,' she says. 'It suited us all.'

In 2000, at the age of twenty-five, she married a fellow police officer from highway patrol, a man six years older. He was a keen scuba diver and she also qualified as a Divemaster so they could enjoy the sport together, and she ended up diving all around Australia, both with and without sharks, and leading dives at night. It was through him she met Robin and Scot Williams. 'We thought she was incredible,' says Robin. 'She was driven and a perfectionist but she was also so much fun, and lively and interesting. She was also the best-looking policewoman we'd ever seen – especially in that one-piece blue jumpsuit. We knew her boyfriend first but when we met her, we liked her more!'

For a while, the couple were happy, but it wasn't to last. 'I think we were just very different, and enjoyed different things,' says Samantha. In 2002, the pair divorced. Her parents were secretly relieved. 'He was young and immature,' says Janice. 'He rang her later to say he was sorry, he'd just been young and silly.'

In 2001, she took a month's secondment to the crash unit, which investigates 'significant' car crashes over a wide area of the state: any vehicle accident, including cars, buses and boats, where someone is grievously injured or killed. Samantha found she loved that even more than highway patrol, and applied to transfer there. She was accepted immediately. It was a tough gig: there were often long distances to drive to reach the scenes of the accidents and Samantha usually found herself travelling throughout the State by herself in the middle of the night, which often proved challenging. 'I got to know the duty operations inspectors pretty well after phoning them for help to find out where I was going,' she says.

After the drive, there'd then be six to eight hours of painstaking investigations of the sites, with measurements, photographs and witness statements, then the long drive back again afterwards. Following that, there might be charges, court appearances, and even appeals to work through. 'But I loved being responsible for the whole of a crash investigation from start to finish,' she says. 'It can be very gory, particularly when you're literally standing in someone's blood where they've been thrown from a car, but I found it very worthwhile.'

The first investigation Samantha did by herself was one where a drug-affected driver had a head-on crash with a car being driven by a woman who was thirty-eight weeks pregnant. As soon as the man realised what had happened, he leapt out of his vehicle and ran off, leaving the woman trapped in her car. Bystanders gave chase and despite him tearing through gardens, jumping fences and ripping clothes off washing lines to try to disguise himself, they caught him and marched him back to the police. The woman's child was born prematurely as a result of the crash and died, and the woman herself had to undergo a complete hysterectomy because of her injuries. The man was successfully charged, convicted and jailed for manslaughter. Sadly, the woman was diagnosed with cancer during the subsequent appeal, and died soon afterwards.

'I'd never really had any trouble with junkies up to that point,' says Samantha. 'Working in the eastern suburbs of Sydney, most of the people I'd met were recreational users. I'm not condoning their use of drugs, of course, but that incident and that poor woman was my first experience of a real scumbag kind of junkie. I hoped I'd never come across his type again.'

* * *

From the moment Laurence knew that Samantha would now probably live, he went into overdrive. No one could tell him, because nobody knew, whether she'd still be the same woman when she eventually woke from her coma, or whether she'd be left with permanent physical and mental disabilities. But either way, Laurence redoubled his efforts to protect his wife. Every time a doctor approached her, he wanted to know why, and what they were looking for. Every time a nurse gave her medication, he asked them what it was, and what effect it might have. Every time a monitor blipped, he questioned why it was doing that, what it indicated and how it might compare to what was considered normal. The flood of questions, as well as his constant presence at Samantha's bedside, soon began to wear everyone down.

'I knew I was being a pain in the arse but I had an insatiable need to know more,' says Laurence. 'I would regularly refer to my notebook and ask several questions at a time, commencing with, "I don't expect you to answer this right now, but . . ." I needed to share every second of Sam's life.'

It was now three days since he'd seen their children, Lily and Ben, but he'd been told Ben was now much better after his trip to hospital, and he knew they were being safely cared for by Samantha's parents, helped by a voluntary roster of their mates in the police force. Laurence worried about the kids, and how they were faring, but felt that Samantha's need for him was far greater. He continued sitting by her bed all day and most of the night.

The doctors found his behaviour understandable, but still hard going. Dr Pell tried to explain they needed room to work on Samantha. 'Laurence was difficult in the sense that he was very caring and over-protective, and wanted to be by her side the whole time,' he says. 'He was distraught but we had to explain to him we needed the space to do our job.'

Dr Perotti also urged him to take a break from his wife's bedside. One day when she came in, he looked particularly glassy-eyed. 'He was very sleep-deprived and was becoming a bit manic,' she says. 'I felt he was coming close to losing it, big time. I kept telling him to go home, but he refused. He said I couldn't force him to. It was then that I called one of his bosses at the police and asked them to help.'

By that Friday afternoon, things were coming to a head. Laurence still wanted to spend every moment he could with Samantha, and refused to leave. So Deputy Commissioner Dave Owens came over to the hospital, fully prepared. 'Laurence had been pushing the boundaries and questioning everything the doctors did,' he says. 'He was asking them what they were doing, and whether that was the best course of treatment, or whether there might be something else they hadn't thought of. And they were looking at him and thinking, Shit, mate, you wouldn't understand even if we told you. Laurence is such a big guy, and so tough, people assume that's all there is to him, but he's actually very intelligent, very smart, with university qualifications and a fine brain. Still waters run deep, as they say. So they'd tell him something and he'd immediately go off and research it, and then come back and ask more questions.

'The hospital were fantastic to him, they couldn't have done more, but he was wearing the welcome out. He was driving the doctors mad. We had to limit his access. Someone had to stand in front of him and tell him it was intensive care and he couldn't come and go as he wanted. But the problem was, no one was prepared to tell him that because they thought he might belt them, and that would hurt. In the end, I said I'd tell him, believing he wouldn't hit me, and I wore my uniform especially – just in case. So I told him and we had a fairly heated discussion, then he marched off. He came back a couple of hours later and said he wouldn't interfere again.

'But by the end, the doctors had started talking to him in medical language, because they accepted he wasn't a dope. Laurence had made it his purpose to fully understand what was occurring with Sam, and became very knowledgeable. They talked to him as if he were a medical professional too. I'd listen to them and then ask Laurence if he understood what they were saying. I had no idea.'

But slowly, gradually, Laurence began to relax just a little. The nurses started getting used to his presence and even joked with him about getting him to make the beds or asking him when he'd be taking his nursing exams. 'I was on the ride through hell, but I couldn't have been in better company, with such highly qualified, committed and caring people,' says Laurence. 'Then one senior nurse who could draw from many years of experience smiled and confidently predicted that, in her opinion, Sam would be okay. That was the point I felt like I was beginning to climb out from under the rock I had been carrying since the day of the attack.

'I knew there was still a long way to go, but that became a turning point for me. For the first time, I began to allow myself to accept that Sam wasn't going to die, I wouldn't be arranging her funeral, and that I would definitely be taking her home with me.'

Samantha's funeral wouldn't have been the first Laurence had ever organised. In 1989, while he was still serving with the Tactical Response Group (TRG), his first wife gave birth to their son, Kyle. But what should have been the happiest event of their lives ended tragically when complications during delivery resulted in the baby suffering brain and other terrible damage. While Laurence's wife underwent emergency surgery for the massive internal injuries she'd incurred during the birth, Kyle was transferred to the Camperdown

Children's Hospital and Laurence stayed with him for the thirty-three hours of his short life.

'I was just twenty-four but there I was choosing a burial plot and preparing to bury my son,' says Laurence. 'It was a terrible time. I wrote a song, which I dedicated to Kyle, and while I could play it on the guitar, I could never sing it as I kept choking on the words. I still do today. Two years later, Eric Clapton released 'Tears in Heaven', a song for his own son who died young. In the twenty-four years that have passed since Kyle died, whenever I hear his song, I stop what I'm doing and for a couple of minutes reflect on what might have been. Sometimes I cry, sometimes sing along, but for me, this song is Kyle's, too.'

Laurence had a few weeks off, grieving his son's death. His friends came to his aid, but the experience certainly changed him. 'He used to be the life of the party, always doing silly things,' says schoolfriend David Searle. 'But from the point he lost his first child, he became more serious about life.' Then he threw himself back into work with a vengeance. While he'd always enjoyed his police service, now it also served as a valuable distraction from his heartache.

He never failed to be surprised by some of the situations in which he found himself. One of the tasks of the TRG was to escort dangerous prisoners between jail and court. Laurence decided on the additional precaution of conducting a strip search of one prisoner, well known for a long criminal history that included an escape from court after injecting heroin supplied by his mother during the lunch interval. To his amazement, he discovered that this man had inserted a number of objects into his anus, including pins, nuts, bolts, a piece of metal shaped like a spanner and a handmade key, all wrapped in paper and plastic. The individual items were discovered, when bolted together, to form a crude dagger, while the key, when tested, opened the cell door.

Another notorious villain to cross Laurence's path was Danny Karam, a violent, drug-using nightclub bouncer. Karam had viciously assaulted his girlfriend in her flat and the TRG was called in to arrest him. Laurence was the second officer into the unit, wearing full protective gear and carrying a shield. As he turned left into a bedroom, Karam was standing there, yelling and swearing. As soon as he saw Laurence, he hurled a glass vase at him. Deflecting the shards of glass with his shield, Laurence instinctively ran towards Karam and pushed the shield at him, and the pair crashed through a glass dressing-table mirror. After a violent struggle, the team arrested him and took him in. Karam went on to become one of notorious underworld boss Bill Bayeh's brutal standover men, and formed his own gang selling cocaine in Kings Cross. He was murdered, allegedly by members of his own gang, in 1998. His character was featured in the 2010 TV series *Underbelly: The Golden Mile*.

There was just no shortage of dangerous incidents. One Friday night out on patrol in Liverpool, a car started revving its engine loudly and, as Laurence walked towards it to speak to its occupants, it drove straight at him. He leapt to one side, drew his gun and, when the vehicle still failed to slow down, discharged one round. The driver swerved at the last second, brushing Laurence's left thigh. The car was found abandoned in the early hours of the morning with a gouge in the bonnet directly in front of the driver, showing how it had been heading directly for Laurence. 'I genuinely believed I was going to die that night,' he says.

But the late 1980s and early 1990s were also a time of increasing tensions in the relationship between police and the Aboriginal community, with criticism levelled particularly at the deployment of the TRG in both country areas of New South Wales and in Redfern on the city fringe. There were a number of incidents that inflamed the situation. In April 1989, an Aboriginal man had opened fire on two police officers in the street, fatally wounding one, Constable Alan McQueen. A few days later, the Special Weapons and Operations Squad (SWOS) – a unit similar to the TRG but with its members drawn from the ranks of detectives – was searching for the gunman, and launched an early-morning raid on the Marrickville home of another Aboriginal man, David Gundy. During that raid, David Gundy was accidentally shot and killed, with a later Royal Commission being told that he'd tried to pull a gun off an officer and, in the struggle, it had gone off.

Despite a number of inquiries, as well as a huge amount of media examining police procedures and their activities in Aboriginal communities, a series of major TRG raids on homes in Redfern took place in February 1990 as part of Operation Sue. Laurence, who'd been on a six-month secondment to the witness protection program, had returned to the TRG and participated as the hammer man again in three forced entries into homes. The operation, however, was later widely criticised as being too heavy-handed, with not enough justification. In June 1990, there was outrage again when another unarmed man, Darren Brennan, was shot and injured in Glebe in similar circumstances to those of David Gundy's death.

The resulting uproar led to the New South Wales Government closing down both the TRG and SWOS in June 1991, cutting the number of officers and divvying up their tasks. Laurence went on to join the Fairfield local area command, where he became part of the OSG.

Laurence was disappointed at the loss of the TRG, but felt this might be a good time to take a breath in his whirlwind career. After the heartbreak of losing Kyle, his wife had given birth to their daughter, Olivia, in 1990, and another son, Ryan, the next year.

But the couple were still struggling. 'In truth, the wheels fell off our relationship with Kyle's death,' says Laurence. 'It was very hard to come back from that. I still remember the doctor and Stillbirth and Neonatal Death Support counsellor at the children's hospital telling us that very few relationships survive the death of a child.'

The waiting room was still crowded with police and friends waiting for updates on Samantha's condition, and Laurence decided that Friday evening to go back to the Kings Cross police station and share the good news with everyone all at once.

Addressing the same downstairs room packed with many of the same faces, he looked around, smiled and announced, 'She's back! The doctors tell me they think she's going to live!' At that, there were gasps of disbelief, tears and a spontaneous round of applause. No one could have been more delighted. Laurence finished by thanking everyone for their support and asked them to do him a huge favour: to spread the news, tell others and ask them to tell more. He was buckling under the weight of requests for information, and that's how they could all help him best.

'I also told them to try and block out what they knew and had seen in the previous few days,' he says. 'When they thought about Sam, they should recall the good things instead. They should remember a funny story, her beautiful, infectious smile, or some other positive memory. They should try to finish any conversation they had about her with a smile and a hug.'

While the couple had received tremendous support from many friends, family members and the wider police 'family', there were a number of other friends who didn't make any attempt to contact Laurence or who didn't call by at the hospital to say hello. They said they were giving him room. 'But room for what?' he asks. 'That was always disappointing.'

Equally, though, there were always the surprises. Late one evening, the security phone in intensive care rang, and a nurse brought the phone over to Laurence. On the other end was a man who, in a faltering, nervous voice, kept apologising for troubling him, but said he just wanted to know how Samantha was doing. Laurence didn't recognise his name and, curious, left the unit to see who it was. It turned out to be a man with an intellectual disability who had walked to the hospital from his home a couple of kilometres away as he'd been so upset to see what had happened to Samantha on a news bulletin.

He presented Laurence with a message to Samantha carefully written by hand on a faded yellow Post-it note, expressing his sympathy and saying how sorry he was. He then delivered a little speech about how much he admired the police, who'd always been good to him, and how he hoped Samantha would get better soon and go home to her family. He'd obviously spent a lot of time rehearsing his speech, and avoided Laurence's eyes as he choked back his emotion at a couple of points.

When he finished, he shook Laurence's hand as firmly as he could, and walked off with his head held high, proud at what he'd achieved. Laurence watched him go, feeling enormously grateful for his kindness.

# Chapter 9
# CURSING LAURENCE

There's a strange combination of hope and dread when someone's in a coma. You long for them to wake up but you're terrified that they may not be all right when they do. It's a question that hangs over the sleeping patient that can't be answered until they open their eyes and recognise the faces of their loved ones . . . or don't.

On Saturday, at the start of Samantha's fourth day in her coma, Laurence Barlow's darkest fear was that his wife might not know him when she finally emerged. 'After it was clear Sam wasn't going to die, my biggest worry was that she'd wake up and not know who I was,' he says. 'I needed her to wake up and know me so I could tell her I loved her. That was my mission: to see her understand that. Everything else could look after itself.'

The early hours of the morning were the worst. During the days, at least things were happening, with doctors and nurses coming round and visitors dropping by, but in the stillness before the start of the day, it was hard to keep the fear from taking over.

Laurence and Inspector Paul Condon would sit in the little room they were using, and just talk. 'He had to vent and the only way for him to vent was to me, after everyone else had gone,' says Condon.

'His days were full of sitting with Sam and speaking to the specialists, as well as dealing with a constant flow of people trying to do the right thing. They meant well, but often they'd ask him the same questions, over and over, like, "Are you angry?", "Are you upset?" What was he supposed to say to that?

'The hardest thing for him was having no control over the situation. All his career, he'd been involved in the biggest police challenges going, and he'd step in, take control and manage the situation. But this was all quite foreign to him. Sometimes he'd take his anger and frustration out on me and that was fine; that's partly what I was there for. We had some arguments sometimes, we got physical and I got hit a few times. But that's how we dealt with it.'

It seemed to Laurence that people were trying to wrestle what little control he did have away from him. They generally meant well, he knew that, but they'd usually express it by trying to tell him what to do: Sit down . . . Relax . . . Go home . . . Sleep . . . Visit your kids . . . Don't worry. It only served to make him even more tense and frustrated. 'Helping someone through a life-changing incident is about building relationships based on respect, empowerment and trust,' he says. 'Too many people were guilty of well intentioned but unformed and unsolicited advice. They fell into the trap of thinking I needed them to fix my life when all I needed was a hug. The more people tried to tell me what to do, the more isolated I felt and I began to spend more time with the families sitting in the waiting room of the Intensive Care Unit who were less judgemental and we became our own peer support group.'

But Laurence did find other ways of biding his time. He shared the flowers being delivered for Samantha with the other patients in intensive care and offered around all the food he was being given, too. One night, he saw a woman similar to the age his mother would have been had she lived, sitting alone in the waiting room outside intensive care. He heard her trying to phone her family in Canada and the US but not being able to make contact. Her husband had suffered a heart attack while they were on holiday in Sydney, and now it was touch and go whether he'd make it through.

Laurence went over and started talking to her, learning her name was Margaret. Over the days and nights that followed, he always kept a careful eye on her, making sure she was coping. He'd often bring her a bouquet from Samantha's massive bank of flowers, a cup of tea, a blanket or a cushion, or just sit with her for a chat. One night, he arranged for a 'blue-and-white taxi' – a police car – to drop her at her hotel when he realised how nervous she was going out after dark by herself in a strange city, particularly knowing Samantha's story.

'It made me feel like a son looking after his mother,' says Laurence. 'We shared a laugh, some sadness, told each other stories about our lives and families and, for a moment while I was helping her, I could forget about my own problems. I was helping Margaret but, in truth, she helped me far more. For nearly thirty years in the police force, I'd been helping people in crisis. It's extremely difficult when you have that "helper" mindset to become the helped person. Now being able to help her made me feel useful again; it restored some of my pride and dignity.'

Condon looked on, pleased that Laurence was taking the initiative again. 'The way he spent all that time talking to Margaret and others in intensive care, it just showed how caring he really is,' he says. 'Most people never saw that side of him: how much he cares about others and he tries to help them, especially when they're going through a similar situation. He's a born teacher and he's always trying to help people to understand things, and to make things better for them.'

For Laurence, his time with Margaret felt like a great gift. When her husband finally recovered enough to be transferred to the main hospital, and then to fly back home, he was thrilled for them both. And he's never forgotten her husband's attempt to show his gratitude.

'It was an honour to meet Margaret's husband during his recovery and I will always remember the look in his eyes, when he was still hooked to his life support system, with tubes hanging out of his nose and mouth, when he saw me taking care of his wife. On the last day, he thanked me so warmly for showing his wife so much humanity.'

Working in crash investigations in 2002, Samantha was in her element. Many of the crashes were quite grisly, with a number of decapitations of motorcycle riders, but she relished the challenge of getting to the bottom of each accident that came her way.

At one point, she even took a TAFE course in mechanical engineering in her own time so she'd be able to set up her own reconstructions of crashes, taking into account speed, distance and the friction of roadways, instead of outsourcing the task to expensive outside experts. 'I was always not so good at physics,' she says. 'But I got a distinction on the TAFE course, so I must have been doing something right!'

Ever eager to get ahead, Samantha also took her sergeant's exams in mid-2003, and applied for promotion to a position that had become available in highway patrol in Griffith in south-western New South Wales, 580 kilometres from Sydney. In truth, she knew it was far too early to expect to succeed. By now, she had nine years' service under her belt, and had completed several courses to acquire additional skills, but most people still had more like fifteen years' experience before they made the grade. 'Not being overly patient, I thought I'd start the ball rolling and then maybe after twelve years, I might get it,' she says. 'I didn't tell a soul at my office what I was doing. But then, to my shock, I was told I'd got an interview. I didn't know which way to turn. So I went to my boss, who'd just won a sergeant's position after twenty years' service, and told him. His reaction was, "Oh my God! You've got an interview! And for highway! But you know you won't get it . . . " He did tell me, though, that the interviewers would ask me nine questions about highway patrol, so I'd better be ready. So I downloaded everything I could find to do with highway patrol and learnt as much as I could off by heart.'

At the interview in July 2003, the panel of five asked her their questions, then told her the position had received 105 applications. Samantha assumed they were turning her down gently. She'd forgotten all about it by the next month when, competing in a surf carnival on Sydney's northern beaches in an inflatable rescue boat in dangerously wild surf, the boat rose high on a giant wave, then crashed down again. Her left foot was fastened in the strap, so she couldn't stop the movement severely twisting her left knee. She went to the medical centre but it had swelled so much, they couldn't see what was wrong. They gave her the week off for the swelling to subside and then she consulted an orthopaedic surgeon who told her she needed a full knee reconstruction. With half her work performed on her hands and knees at crash sites, she knew that would cause problems. And just as she was about to go in for the operation, she received the call: congratulations on her promotion, and new position. After just ten years in the job, she was, remarkably, to become a sergeant.

Samantha went to Griffith in January 2004 shortly after the operation with her knee in a brace for some time, hidden beneath her uniform, but tried not to let it affect her work. 'It was killing me, but I didn't want anything to get in my way,' she says. 'I was determined to do everything as well as I could. I was in a lot of pain, but it was always my philosophy to suck it up and get on with things.'

It's not as if her new job started quietly, either. In her new position, she had responsibility for traffic and highway patrol for the whole of the Griffith local area command, as well as a huge chunk of New South Wales that included fifteen separate police stations with twenty highway officers located in four main stations: Griffith, Leeton, Narrandera and West Wyalong, 154 kilometres away. On her second night, she was called to the site where two cars had just crashed head-on in a 110 kilometres-per-hour zone, killing two adults and a child. 'It was pitch-black and I had no idea where I was,' she says. 'It was so hard writing down a description of the roads when I had no idea what they looked like in daylight, either.'

But the hardest thing about being away from Sydney was the pace of life. She'd be saying, 'Okay! Let's go!' and it would take everyone else a while to stir. 'I was so used to going a million miles an hour. It took me a long time to slow down . . .'

Even though she was a sergeant at such a young age, she immediately started relieving as an inspector too. Samantha was also the only member of the Operations Support Group (OSG) in Griffith, so she had to stay on top of her game for that too. She knew her annual re-accreditation course back at the academy in Goulburn would be tricky, however, with her knee still strapped up and very sore. So she trained extra hard beforehand to be able to run faster during the shuttle runs but take the turns more slowly to avoid pivoting too heavily on the knee. She passed, despite choosing to be paired with the biggest man on the course, an amateur boxer, for the hand-to-hand defence tactics part of the course, to test herself against the best.

The knockout blow came later, though, when the course instructor, a giant of a man called Senior Sergeant Laurence Barlow, refused to take her with a troupe of twenty to quell trouble that had broken out in Balranald, about 250 kilometres west of her own patch at Griffith, leaving ten people, including her, behind. 'He said I had to stay and finish the course,' says Samantha. 'I thought he was the biggest scumbag not to take me. I argued but that was the first time I hadn't been able to talk someone around to change their mind. He'd told me no, and I don't like people saying no to me. I cursed him in his absence for the rest of the course.'

She had absolutely no idea how impressed he'd been by her. Friends in the police had mentioned her before, saying what a great job she'd been doing in Griffith, what a good team leader she was and how he should make a trip there to look her up. 'But I'd thought that no one could be *that* perfect,' he says. 'But when I finally met her on that course, I thought she was awesome. But there was an eleven-year age difference between us, and I thought she was out of my league. I tried to impress her in the way I went about my job, but it turns out all I'd managed to do was persuade her I was a pig!'

Once she'd re-qualified for the OSG, life was full-on back in Griffith. As well as her normal highway patrol and crash duties, the OSG was busier than ever. There were protests and then trouble at a local mining site to deal with, and then she was called on to help in 2005 in the search for a man believed to be hiding out in Dubbo's Western Plains Zoo, an open animal park set in 300 hectares of bushland. His name was Malcolm Naden, and he'd disappeared from his home after the body of a young mother was found in his bedroom. The police sealed off the zoo and for three days Samantha joined the battalion of police trudging nervously on foot around the zoo searching for him, but without success.

'I thought if any of the animals were to go for us, they would have chosen me,' she says. 'I was the smallest thing there . . .' Naden was later to become one of Australia's most wanted fugitives and evaded capture until March 2012.

But back in 2005, unrest seemed to be spreading and riots broke out in Cronulla in December after a fracas between two racial groups exploded into a series of violent assaults. On Sunday 11 December, 5000 people gathered at the beach and attacked a man of Middle Eastern appearance whom the crowd suspected might be a Muslim. Police and ambulance officers were also attacked, there was a stabbing and many people were arrested over the next week of riots.

Samantha had been called in to help towards the end of the troubles and, with Laurence in charge, was instructed to patrol the beach and the area around it over the next few days. The police contingent all stayed in Wollongong and, on the last evening, Samantha and Laurence had a few drinks at the bar together. 'We got chatting, and I thought he was actually quite nice,' says Samantha. 'We were literally the last ones to leave. Then we met up quite a few times after that, travelling between Griffith and Wollongong where he was based.' It was a quiet start to a romance that would irrevocably change both their lives.

On the last day of 2005, Samantha also helped at riots in Dubbo centred on a housing estate where two officers were set upon and their police car set alight after they stopped a suspected stolen car. The police shut down the area and the trouble was finally quelled.

But always looking ahead to the future, she started planning her next move. She knew she wanted to return to Sydney, but had to find a vacant sergeant's position to apply for. There were only two she was interested in: one in highway patrol in Mosman, a quiet, upmarket suburb on the city's North Shore, and the other as an educational officer in Sydney's red-light district of Kings Cross. She knew nothing about that job, but thought if she couldn't get the post in Mosman, then she'd do her damnedest to work out the Kings Cross job as she went. 'I thought I could give anything a go,' she says. 'I wasn't qualified for that at all, but I knew I would give it my best shot.'

Both interviews went well but, as fate would have it, she was offered the Kings Cross job first. She asked if she could wait a few days to find out if she was going to be offered the Mosman position, but was told no, she had to either accept Kings Cross or reject it immediately. She accepted it.

The very next day, Mosman phoned to offer her their job, twenty-four hours too late.

Detective Sergeant Mat Moss, in charge of the investigation into the attack on Samantha, was studying the video of Roderick Holohan's re-enactment of what he'd done, and felt an enormous sense of relief that they'd got their man. Everyone had worked together to solve this crime quickly.

Of course, they still had a way to go, other lines of inquiry to discount and people who'd seen Holohan to interview, not to mention a possible murder charge if Samantha died, but it was comforting to know, at least, that he was off the streets.

'Everyone had done an amazing job,' says Moss, who himself had worked thirty-six hours straight since Holohan was arrested. 'I think we were all absolutely buggered.

'Of course, it had helped that he'd made such a full and frank admission, but that didn't change my feelings towards him at all. I still thought he was an absolute maggot. He had more form than Black Caviar and Makybe Diva combined, and it was my job to lock him up.'

* * *

Everyone was rallying round to look after Samantha and Laurence's children Lily and Ben, with rosters drawn up for Samantha's parents, her friends and Laurence's workmates to pitch in. Some of them felt Laurence should make an effort to see his kids, but in truth he was far too caught up looking after Samantha to even try. He received regular reports on how they were doing and while both youngsters were missing their parents, particularly Lily who'd always been so close to her mum, they both seemed to be thriving with so many different carers keen to look after them and keep them amused.

'Often it was amazing to see all these terribly rough, tough guys who'd worked with Laurence in the Tactical Response Group or the riot squad dropping off those kids at day care and pre-school and then picking them up again,' says Dave Owens, the former deputy commissioner. 'These are guys that could really hurt you, you don't mess with them, but here they were looking after those children with such a degree of care. Underneath, they were real softies, but they'd say, "Don't ever tell anyone!"'

With Samantha's parents Janice and Vernon Groves staying at their house most of the time, the police also did everything they could to make life easier for them. They delivered nappies, baby food, dog food and then, as well as other food, a new deep freezer to store it all in.

'It was chaotic but we all muddled through,' says Janice. 'We had a hell of a lot of assistance, even from neighbours. One day, they brought round a baked dinner of meat and vegies and sweets. People really rallied round; they were wonderful. The police picked us up and took us to hospital as we would have been lost in all that traffic.

'The children were a bit bereft and Lily sensed that something was amiss even though we desperately tried to shield her from it.

She would ask, "Who are these people?" and "Where's Mummy?" We'd just say, "She's coming home soon . . ."'

On the Saturday, three days after the attack, Samantha's close friend from her police college days and Kings Cross workmate Sergeant Perri Hayes took a break from sitting at hospital to look after the children and brought them to the hospital car park so Laurence could see them. Ben still wasn't back to 100 per cent after his respiratory infection, and Lily threw up in the car. But Laurence still couldn't bear to face them, even after half the week away. 'I just couldn't,' he says. 'It was very kind of her to do that, but I didn't have the space in my head for them.'

His brother Robert, looking on, couldn't understand that, and urged him to go down and to say hello to the children. But he wouldn't budge. Apart from anything else, he didn't know if he'd be able to hold his emotions in check when he saw them, which he was sure would distress them even more. Besides, he had no words to reassure them about when Mummy might be coming back home, which would be just too heartbreaking for them all.

Friend Robin Williams felt she understood. 'He was in such pain, he was a broken man,' she says. 'He said he just couldn't look at them right then. He was needed by Sam. He had to stay by her side. I got that. He's a strong man, and incredibly protective, but you could also see such vulnerability there, too.'

After his spell in the TRG, Laurence had returned to mainstream policing in 1991, based in Fairfield, covering the area of south-west Sydney that bordered Cabramatta. It was much less action-packed than his old job, but life in the police force was still never dull.

Even guarding a prisoner in a detective interview room could prove a challenge. Laurence was looking after someone once who started chanting, yelling and slamming his fist on the table. Then the man made a sudden rush for the door, trying to headbutt Laurence out of the way. 'His forehead came into contact with the top of mine near the hairline,' he says. 'But I held on to him, wrestled him to the floor, handcuffed him, then dragged him out of the room, blood streaming down my face, across the driveway and into the dock of the police station, which was located in another building. The contact split my skin and I have a permanent vertical scar around 3 to 4 centimetres long in the centre of my forehead as a permanent reminder of that day!'

Members of the public who called at the station didn't always want to talk about routine matters. One night a man burst through the door yelling he'd been shot. Laurence jumped over the front counter and put his arms around him to hold him up, as the man pointed to several gunshot wounds in his chest.

In the early 1990s, drugs were a huge problem in the area with nearby Cabramatta fast becoming Sydney's heroin supply centre. A lot of people were injecting drugs on the street and there was community concern about the dangers of HIV/AIDS, which was starting to become more widely known, too. 'We also had a lot of people on methadone, a thick, gluggy substance intended to be taken orally, who would break into a local pet store and steal animal syringes so they could mix their methadone with heroin or speed to increase their "high",' says Laurence. 'You would often find them in the toilets at the car park, the shopping mall and the railway station toilets, with animal syringes still hanging out of them, blood on the floor or on the walls. It was always a tough situation, particularly with people panicking that they could catch something from them.'

Overdoses, fights over drugs, violent crimes, including armed hold-ups to get money for drugs and robberies were all commonplace. Laurence gradually developed an ingrained hatred of drug pushers and everyone who traded in the misery they caused. He also deplored the 'victim culture' that grew up around some of the drug users. 'They aren't victims; they *cause* victims,' he says. 'Life is about choices and how you deal with the challenges that come your way. You can't tell me it's a result of poverty or of being brought up in a Housing Commission home. I know. I was one of those kids.'

In 1993, Laurence changed direction again and went into education services at the Sydney Police Centre in Surry Hills. Torn in his early days between policing and teaching, this seemed a perfect way to combine both loves. He took pleasure in drawing on his varied experiences in the field to teach the new recruits, and giving back to the police service in a completely different way. He also enrolled in a Bachelor of Policing degree through Charles Sturt University via distance education, taking three elective subjects within the faculty of education to help with his teaching.

Yet there was also personal anguish when his mum's cancer returned, just as she was coming up to the magic five-year clear period. She'd previously had breast cancer and a mastectomy, and the family hoped she'd made a complete recovery. But shortly before she was due to be declared safe, the doctors told them her cancer had returned and spread. She was just fifty-seven. Laurence's brother Robert returned from the UK where he'd been working in accountancy, and Laurence visited his parents as often as he could before her death, a month before her fifty-eighth birthday in 1995. 'My mother had extensive amounts of medication, including the morphine I would administer to her,' he says. 'Towards the end of her life, I would carry her as she was too weak to walk. It was a tragedy, the way my mother was forced to spend the last years of her life.'

Five months after her death, Laurence returned to the New South Wales Police Academy at Goulburn, this time as the team leader in charge of operational safety training. He enjoyed the change and felt it would be a healthier environment for Olivia and Ryan to grow up in. Two years before, a good mate had been killed in a firearms training exercise when he'd run towards a student to demonstrate the length of time it takes to draw a gun and fire at an assailant – and the student's gun turned out not to have been unloaded. Laurence wanted to do his best to make sure nothing like that ever happened again. He even named a firearms shield presented to the best in class in his honour, the Juan Carlos Hernandez Shield, as a permanent reminder of the need to be ever vigilant.

But of course, it was impossible to control everything. During one live fire session, a student accidentally shot himself in the thigh while re-holstering. Laurence went straight to the range to help staff look for an exit wound from the bullet, typically the area where most blood is lost. It could not be found; the bullet had lodged in his quadricep, and doctors at the nearest hospital said it would cause more damage to take it out than to leave it in. 'He remains the only student to leave the academy range with a round of ammunition without getting into trouble!' says Laurence.

Another incident came completely out of left field. In January 2000, a police officer was shot at the Eagle Vale police station in south-west Sydney near Campbelltown, and died of his injuries. The man who shot him turned out to be another officer at the station – and one of the star pupils of Goulburn's firearms training course. An investigation found that the victim, Constable Matthew Potter, had played a deadly practical joke on his mate, Constable

Brian Duffey, taking his pistol from its holster and pretending to unload the magazine. When Duffey reached for a safety plug to show the gun was safe, it discharged and fatally wounded Potter as he re-entered the room. 'As the Operational Safety Training Unit team leader who had taught the police officer responsible for the shooting, I spent significant time assisting in the preparation of this court matter,' says Laurence, who was promoted to sergeant while at the academy, and started studying for a graduate certificate in teaching. 'I later also spent an entire day in the witness box giving evidence before the district court where he'd been charged with manslaughter.' In June 2002, the court acquitted Duffey of all charges.

Laurence tried to help his students in other ways, too. Discovering that one of his students had just lost a baby, he sat him down and talked to him about his own experience with Kyle. Then, together with another instructor at the academy, he took him down to the shooting range in his own time to help him complete the necessary training to ensure he'd graduate, despite his distress.

But his own losses continued to mount. In 2001, after a separation, he and his first wife finally divorced after fifteen years of marriage. 'We just wore each other out,' he says. 'By the end, we had nothing left. There are always winners and losers in divorce, and it broke my heart that I didn't get to tuck the kids into bed every night. So instead, I decided to throw myself into work. There was a hole in my heart, and I needed to plug it with something.'

It was time now, he felt, to return to the frontline, and get back into tactical policing.

The strain of Samantha's condition was by now really beginning to tell on Laurence. The steady flow of visitors to intensive care wanted regular updates, and often people would see Laurence, say how sorry they were, and then break down and start sobbing. He found that the hardest thing. Trying to keep himself positive and energised for Samantha was becoming tougher and tougher. It had been inspiring in the beginning, seeing how much she was loved, but by the Saturday it felt like an incredible drain.

Everyone was asking what could they do to help, but he just didn't know. He and Condon, working together at 3 a.m. every morning, divided up the tasks that had to be done that day between the group of mates they nicknamed 'Team Samantha'. That took care of things like giving her parents a lift to the hospital and having spare clothes brought in to him. But it was fabulous when people just did things off their own bat, like Samantha's friend Senior Constable Suzie Schwass, who went and picked up the children from kindy, and another mate Brett Lloyd who turned up, unbidden, in the back garden of their house to mow the lawn.

The Police Association of New South Wales, the officers' union, was also offering assistance. Its president Scott Weber had known Laurence from his days as a member of the OSG and later the Public Order and Riot Squad (PORS), and says he was now seeing a completely different side of the man. 'Laurence is a very hard and forthright police officer, he's staunch, no one wants to mess with him,' he says. 'He's as hard as nails. But now you could see his heart was breaking. He wanted to protect his family and his wife, and he did that very well. Laurence was an example to all of us the way he kept fighting. He showed such great character. But when you looked at him, you can see that even the toughest of police officers are human and that they hurt just like anyone else.'

Laurence was certainly hurting. He was growing more and more tired from the lack of sleep and the anxiety and, as well as still battling his tonsillitis and back pain, he had a festering purple lump on the rear of his right hip that his GP feared was cancerous. He'd been waiting to see a specialist for that when Samantha was attacked. But far worse was the psychological pain of worrying about Samantha. 'I felt as though I was trying to run while sinking up to my knees in quicksand,' says Laurence.

Condon recognised the danger signs and suggested he take an hour out to go and have a meal with his two eldest children, Olivia and Ryan, who'd arrived at the hospital to see Samantha, and a small group of friends. Olivia was by now in the middle of her first-year exams at Sydney University but was having difficulty studying with the enormity of what was taking place. Ryan was preparing for the HSC and also struggling. Laurence agreed, and they decided to go eat at the nearby Una's, a German–Austrian–Swiss restaurant famous for the generosity of its helpings and friendly service. It was one of the first places Samantha had taken Laurence to dinner in the inner city, and they'd been there many times since.

The little group wandered down to the restaurant and stood outside chatting while arrangements were made for a table inside. When the waitress came out and beckoned them in, they all followed. Laurence, however, suddenly became overwhelmed with his memories of the place and, as he realised the table they'd been allocated was the same one he'd sat at with Samantha that first time, let out a moan and began shaking and crying uncontrollably. He was having his first-ever panic attack. Hastily, another group of tables was set up, the group was moved and Laurence managed to stop and pull himself together.

But he knew that he really couldn't take too much more.

# Chapter 10
## A SECOND CHANCE

Samantha Barlow started her new job in Kings Cross in January 2006.

She liked the area immediately. There was always something happening, the locals were a mixed mob and there was a real community feel within the station. It was an exciting area, a great place to learn. She came to know some of the residents well, and was soon on nodding terms with many of the more colourful characters around The Cross. 'It's an amazing place and it was often a real eye-opener walking around there,' she says. 'You never let people get away with anything, but it's always easy to have a chat with someone. It isn't hard to be nice to people, to be polite, never talk down to them and to treat them with consideration, and in return, they were usually nice back to you.

'There were a lot of drugs around, so you'd just have to pick your mark. But I never felt vulnerable. If there was trouble, you had your baton, capsicum spray, your gun and your handcuffs, and if you needed help, you could just call on your radio for assistance and someone would be there in twenty seconds. But I got on with everyone. I was happy to be back in the eastern suburbs and I'd see the same people every morning, say good morning, and have a coffee and a chat.'

In addition, she was back with her old gang-of-four mate from the academy, Sergeant Perri Hayes, who'd been at Kings Cross for ten and a half years. 'I was really excited when Sam came down,' says Hayes. 'The four of us still saw each other regularly, staying in touch through marriages, kids and separations, and when Sam came back to Sydney we started a tradition of going away for a long weekend together every year. I knew she'd love Kings Cross. The police are always highly motivated and there's a great variety of people in the area, the alternative gay and trendy community, the families, the working-class people . . . all sorts.'

But as much as Samantha enjoyed Kings Cross, she didn't particularly warm to her role as education officer. She didn't really know what was expected of her and, with fifteen probationary officers reporting to her in her first week alone and having to oversee everything they did, she felt a huge weight of responsibility on her shoulders. It was a world away from zipping around the state with highway patrol, investigating crashes or attending public order incidents with the Operations Support Group.

'I felt I knew nothing, but I couldn't tell a soul that!' she says. 'I winged it. I pretended I enjoyed it, but I actually hated it.'

Then, three and a half months into the job, the station's traffic sergeant hurt his shoulder and was put on permanent restricted duties. The then station boss, Superintendent Mark Murdoch, later to become an assistant commissioner, called Samantha into his office. 'How are you enjoying the education officer role?' he asked her.

Samantha smiled back at him. 'Good, thanks, sir.'

He frowned. 'Do you *really* like it?' he asked again.

She looked as enthusiastic as she possibly could. 'Yes, I *love* it!' she said.

'Oh!' he said. 'So you wouldn't like the traffic sergeant's role then?'

Samantha did a double-take. 'Yes please!' she said quickly. So the very next day, she moved into the traffic spot.

'She clearly enjoyed the operational side of policing and she was a good operator, with a good head on her shoulders, and she knew her craft,' says Murdoch. 'She was also in the Operations Support Group, and the tactical training for that stood her in good stead in an environment like Kings Cross. She was a very solid, very effective sergeant.'

Murdoch moved on in 2008 to head the City Central area, and Superintendent Tony Crandell came from Deniliquin to run Kings Cross, meeting Samantha as his traffic sergeant. He didn't really expect much. After all, despite the volume of traffic at The Cross, particularly on Friday and Saturday nights, it was all crawling at a snail's pace so there tended to be very few accidents, and hardly any of them serious. He imagined Samantha would spend all her time sitting at a desk going through the motions, but she surprised him time and time again.

'She was a very competent officer and someone who had a real desire to make a difference, and so she did,' he says. 'She organised some really, really good initiatives. Vehicle noise is always a big issue for Kings Cross residents from motorbikes and cars that are unlawfully modified, and she developed a system for police to actively go out and seek defective vehicles because of noise, and refer them to the EPA [Environment Protection Authority] for inspection. How she came up with that, I don't know, but it was her initiative and she drove it and it was extremely successful.'

An additional initiative started around the same time was Operation Elvis, with police targeting modified and defective vehicles, and drink-driving, to cut down on hoon behaviour, checks of people driving towards The Cross from Garden Island, as well as the Friday- and Saturday-night closure of Cowper Wharf Road to further deter road racers. 'These all made a dramatic difference, and really satisfied a lot of our community members,' says Crandell. 'Sam continually took that extra step and that's why I was always impressed with her. She had such a good work ethic, always pristinely presented, always professional, a high achiever. I knew if I gave her a task or needed something done, I never had to follow that up. From a command position that's gold.'

It was a pretty busy time for Samantha in other ways, too. Previously, she'd been seeing Laurence Barlow regularly, and their friendship had quickly developed into something far more serious. On a driving holiday along the Great Ocean Road in Victoria, they'd stopped off at a viewing point and, overlooking the Twelve Apostles, Laurence had gone down on one knee and proposed. They'd only been together a few months, but they felt they'd known each other for years.

'We'd both made bad decisions before, and we both felt we'd know now when it felt wrong and when it felt right,' says Samantha. 'And this felt very, very right. We were very easy together and we think very similarly. It's pathetic really, how well we get on! He's a much deeper thinker than me, but we both love sport and being healthy. We had so much in common.' With Laurence's children by now aged sixteen and fourteen, they were fully accepting of Samantha too.

Most of their friends were surprised at first, thinking them an unlikely match, but thrilled at how blissfully happy they both seemed. 'I sort of smiled when I heard they were together, and thought, That's an interesting combination!' says the deputy commissioner of the time, Dave Owens. 'But it did show a softer side of such a strong, tough guy that he didn't show to many of his fellow cops. At first, I thought it was an odd match, but they really do complement each other very nicely.'

At Kings Cross, Crandell was surprised too, but then pleased. He'd quickly developed a soft spot for Samantha as such a conscientious officer and happy personality to have around the station, and had first encountered Laurence seventeen years before, when he'd gone through the Tactical Response Group (TRG) training course. Laurence had been the instructor and they'd remained friends ever since.

'I think I was one of the smallest, if not *the* smallest, applicant to do that course, and it was the hardest five weeks of my life,' says Crandell. 'Laurence was back then even bigger than he is now, with a full beard and big blob of black hair. I can still remember, when I graduated, he said to me, "You now qualify to buy – *buy*, not get given! – a TRG shirt." I said, "That's fantastic." He said, "What size would you be?" I was actually smaller than I am now. I had no fat on me at all because I'd been running around for five weeks like a lunatic and it took me about three months to prepare to get into the course in the first place. So I said, "I think I'm a medium." He said, "No, sorry, we've sold out of those." So I asked, "Have you got a small one?" He said, "No, we don't stock small." So I said, "Well, I suppose I'll have to have a large!" And then he said, "That's a shame because there are no more larges left. In fact, if you want to be in the TRG you will wear an XL to an XXL. You don't have the option to have anything less than that." I said, "You're kidding me!" He said, "Well, the fact that you are small is not my problem; they are the options you have." But I really wanted a TRG shirt so I ended up having to buy an XL. I've still got that shirt and it's like a dress! After that, we had a *special* relationship!'

The pair crossed paths again when Crandell was in Deniliquin and Laurence was in the Southern Region. If there were any protests, problems or big events, Crandell would call on him for extra police and resources. 'So I've had contact with him on and off throughout both our careers,' Crandell says. 'He's a good man, and I felt they'd go well together.'

Samantha's friends, Robin and Scot Williams, who hadn't liked her first love much, were much more enthusiastic about this boyfriend. 'We met Laurence, and knew he was a winner,' says Scot. Adds Robin, 'He's a big, gentle giant and is very, very wise. He loved Sam unconditionally, he worshipped her, he cherished her, which is exactly what she deserved. He was madly in love with her and always spoke so beautifully about her. He's always treated her with the utmost respect and decency.'

Her family was all totally onside too. When Samantha asked her brother Jason if she could bring him to dinner, he shook his head in despair. 'Not another bloody policeman!' he exclaimed. But when she brought him, and the pair started talking, Jason was instantly won over. 'I told her he was the best thing she'd ever dragged through the front door,' he says. 'He was a sensitive, caring, thoughtful person. Both me and my partner got along with him well from day one. When my parents met him too, we were all in agreement that this was definitely the best pick Sam had ever had.' Her mum nods. 'Yes, we've grown to love Laurence,' she says. 'He's a lovely person.'

Laurence's brother Robert Barlow liked Samantha as soon as he met her. 'From day one, we were all in favour,' he says. 'She was very independent, very outgoing, very confident. Laurence probably needed someone like her, someone who'd stand up to him.' Their dad, George, was in love with her too. 'She was a great girl,' he says. 'I immediately thought the world of her.'

The couple married in November 2006, in a ceremony at the quaint old Meroo Union Church at Meroo Meadow, a small town between Nowra and Berry in the New South Wales Southern Highlands where her parents had retired to in 2000. Laurence's brother Robert was best man, his son Ryan was his groomsman, daughter Olivia was bridesmaid and Senior Sergeant Belinda Crowe was matron of honour, while Robert's daughters Lauren, Josie and Victoria were flower girls. The reception was held in a marquee erected in their garden.

Samantha made a glowing bride, particularly as she was four months pregnant. Unable to conceive naturally, the pair had decided to try IVF and their first attempt had worked, with their daughter, Lily, born in May 2007. Samantha took nine months off to spend with Lily, combining both her maternity and annual leave, and returned to work in February 2008. She then worked up until the month the couple's second child, Ben, was born in October 2008.

This time, Samantha took seven months off to be with her son and daughter, and relished the time spent with them. But by the end of her leave, she was ready to get back to the police. She'd missed both the job and the camaraderie that went with it. But it was only on her sixth day back that everything went terribly, unimaginably wrong.

Roderick Holohan was led into a cell at the Sydney Police Centre in Surry Hills. There was already another prisoner there when he entered. The TV was on, and he immediately asked if there'd been anything on the news about Kings Cross.

'What about?' the man asked.

'The copper that's on her death bed,' replied Holohan.

'Why?' asked the man. 'Was that you?'

'Yeah,' Holohan replied. 'I'm fucked.'

The man asked what had happened. Holohan wanted to talk. It seemed half boasting, half confessional. There was little doubt he felt very sorry for himself. But the cold way in which he recited what he'd done struck a chill in the heart of the other man.

'I just had to get on to some gear,' Holohan began. 'I went up to her from behind. I seen her and I started attacking her. I hit her once and she didn't go down and she started fighting back. I thought I hit her five times and broke her hand when she was trying to defend herself. I was told I hit her twenty times. I seen a police shirt. Once I knew that she was a police officer, I knew I couldn't let her live.

'I had to go on with it. I don't know how many times I hit her. There is a witness who is a working girl that saw me stalking people carrying either a rock or a brick earlier. I'm not worried about her though, 'cos she's scattered. Then I remember being back with my girl down the coast. My girl knew that something was wrong but I couldn't tell her what had happened.'

The other prisoner started to feel nervous. He'd heard snippets about a police officer having been brutally attacked in Kings Cross, and it had just dawned on him that he was locked in a very small cell with an extremely violent man.

'So how did they get you?' he asked.

'I think they followed me on the surveillance cameras,' Holohan answered. 'I think it's pretty much like England now, they can follow you everywhere.'

Holohan asked the man his name. The man gave him a false one. He didn't like the look, or the sound, of this bloke at all. He wanted nothing to do with him. Holohan had been talking in a voice completely without emotion, as if he were chatting about nothing more significant than going to the shops and buying a newspaper. The only time he demonstrated any emotion was when he mentioned that the police had taken his new Nike trainers. He was angry about that.

'So what are you going to do?' the man asked him.

Holohan looked thoughtful. 'I'm going to go under the forensics act and mental health, and blame it on the ice,' he replied. 'That's all the rage at the moment.'

The doctors had been gradually reducing the amount of medication Samantha was on and, during their 10 a.m. review that Sunday morning, decided the time was right to finally attempt to bring her out of her coma. Originally, they'd predicted she'd be sleeping for ten to fourteen days, but the speed of her recovery had surprised everyone, and they saw no reason to prolong the process. The less time spent in a coma, they reasoned, the better the chances of a complete recovery.

Laurence felt the hairs on the back of his neck stand up. This was the moment he'd been waiting for, hoping for, dreaming of, for the past four and a half days, but suddenly he felt gripped with nerves. What if Samantha woke up and didn't know him, didn't know anyone? Would she still be the same woman he'd fallen in love with?

The staff asked him to move away from her bedside while they brought her around. Laurence didn't want to, but they insisted. In the end, he agreed to a compromise – he'd stand at the other end of the Intensive Care Unit while they worked on Samantha. He stood nervously waiting. One of the wardsmen was standing nearby, and the two men had a conversation about Gymea lilies, the flame-red Australian native flowers the wardsman was growing back home. Laurence was happy to talk about anything to try to distract him from what was happening at the other end of the ward.

When Laurence's first marriage broke up and he left the academy, he'd gone over to the Wollongong local area command, starting his new job in 2001. There, he had two main roles. The first was as part of the local Target Action Group (TAG), a new series of crack 'flying squads' that the New South Wales Government had announced would be blitzing crime not only where it was worst, but also where it was emerging. The second was as the Southern Region operations coordinator of the Operations Support Group (OSG) and the State Protection Support Unit (SPSU), formed to contain emergency situations in regional locations, such as sieges, hostage situations, outlaw bikie gang activities and drug plantations, as well as conduct armed escorts and suicide intervention. The SPSU was intended to be a part-time unit that supplements or complements the Tactical Operations Unit – the group that replaced the old TRG. To Laurence, it was a move back to the kind of policing on the frontline he'd become so used to a few years before.

'I knew this was a job where I'd not be home often, and that suited me at the time,' he says. 'I took time off to complete my teaching qualification as a post-grad student at Charles Sturt University but the rest of the time, I could throw myself into the job, and become totally absorbed. It was exactly the kind of challenge I'd been looking for.'

For the next five years, he was permanently on call for high-risk duty, twenty-four hours a day. There was a siege in which the offender committed horrific assaults on his female prisoner until the unit stormed the house to free her. A while later, a child was abducted and Laurence ended up arresting the perpetrator at gunpoint, talking him out of his car and ordering him to lie on his stomach, where members of his team handcuffed him. Another operation – as part of the same team as Samantha – involved the massive manhunt launched for Malcolm Naden in the grounds of the Western Plains Zoo.

Laurence also had to deal with a number of suicides, like the father under investigation for the sexual abuse of a family member who hanged himself in his garage, a woman suffering a terminal disease and a young man who overdosed in a toilet block at a well-known beach.

He barely took any time off, only one big block of three months to take his dad George back to the UK in 2004, to mark his own fortieth birthday. It was good meeting up with his relatives, and he had plenty of fun. At a cousin's wedding, he volunteered to sing a karaoke song and told the crowd, 'This is a song I sing at home in Australia; maybe a few of you might know it.' There was a hushed silence until the musical introduction and the opening line of The Beatles' cover 'Twist and Shout', at which the place erupted. There were more sober moments, too. He and his father had travelled to the village of Abergwyngregyn in North Wales, where George had spent the war. One evening, he and his father got talking to a local called Tom Jones in a pub, who remembered driving trucks into Liverpool through the Mersey Tunnel and seeing barefoot kids in rags jump on the back to spoon sugar or flour or whatever else he was carrying into tin cans because they were so hungry. At that, George started softly crying. He'd been one of those kids, he revealed.

Returning to Australia, Laurence went straight back to work. As part of the TAG, he helped out with a murder investigation where a terminally ill woman was killed by her son, wrapped in a carpet, placed in the boot of his car and then disposed of in a remote area of the Illawarra hinterland. He also took part in many drug operations.

Yet he still found time for other interests. A long-time blood donor, in 2005 he decided to become a bone marrow donor too, and almost immediately was contacted by doctors who'd found he was the perfect match with a seriously ill young person interstate, in urgent need of a bone marrow transfer. Laurence agreed without hesitation and was given a series of daily injections to increase his blood's platelet count. 'Having lost a child myself, this was something I really wanted to do in the hope that this person's parents wouldn't lose him,' he says. 'No one should ever have to go through that.' While he sat in hospital receiving the jabs, he also came up with the idea of making the Leukaemia Foundation the beneficiary of the Illawarra Police Charity Ball, to raise more funds for their lifesaving work.

In his professional life, he still tended to relish the higher-level challenges of his OSG role the most. There was certainly no shortage of those. In February 2005, there were a series of riots in Macquarie Fields in south-west Sydney, sparked by a high-speed police pursuit that ended in a crash killing two young people. The violence that followed lasted four nights, with rioters hurling petrol bombs, rocks, bottles and bricks at police and setting cars alight, injuring several officers. Laurence was sent in and performed a command role, working shifts of over fifteen hours each, every night for a week.

His immediate boss, Chief Superintendent Steve Cullen, was impressed. 'You need experts in the field and when you're talking about riots, you need to know when to go, when to hold, and when to disengage,' he says. 'He was one of the best in the business, if not *the* best. He was very focused, very committed to the task, and both gives directions and takes direction very well. If he said, "All good here, boss," you'd know that it was all under control.'

He very soon came to the attention of those even higher up. 'He was at the Southern Region at the time he came up to Macquarie Fields and my staff officer said, "You have to look at this bloke!"' says then Deputy Commissioner Dave Owens. 'He had what looked like a wheelie bin as a helmet, and grunted hello. I found out he was an extremely smart person, and dedicated to the cops. Where strongarm tactics were required, you could trust him to do what he was legally allowed to do. He was a real tough guy, but he certainly wasn't dumb. When I look at any of the major protests and demonstrations, he just kept popping up. He was always up there at the front. He was one of those blokes you take notice of. I asked for his résumé; I wanted to know what we were dealing with.' Laurence was named favourably in the parliamentary reports that followed Macquarie Fields.

A new unit was set up in September that year: the full-time Public Order and Riot Squad (PORS), under Cullen's command. Both police and politicians accepted that there hadn't been enough officers, equipment, training and coordination at hand to nip those riots in the bud. It was hoped the new squad would be able to handle any other such large-scale public order problems much more efficiently.

It wasn't long before it had its first major test. That December the Cronulla riots broke out, and Laurence was again drafted in, often assuming the role of senior tactical commander at night when Cullen stood down. 'I call it Australia's fortnight of shame,' he says. 'Anglo-Australians targeted Islamic Australians in an incident that was fuelled by racist debate in public domains and the media. I remember there was a catchcry that a lot of the white supremacists were using: "I grew here, you flew here!" One night, in the middle of it all, one of them looked at me, obviously saw I was white, and said, "You're on our side surely?" I looked back at him coldly and said, "No. I flew here too."'

Laurence spent a week in Sydney working around the clock, dividing his time between helping to plan the control of arguably the most significant public order incident in the city's history across three volatile geographic locations, Cronulla, Maroubra and Lakemba, and relieving as the operations manager of the Southern Region, with its eleven local area commands. After six or seven nights, as the situation in Sydney appeared to be under control, he was ordered back to Southern Region. There, he planned, then led, an operation in and around Wollongong where it was anticipated there would be break-out incidents.

Soon after, Laurence took part in Operation Pendennis, the largest counterterrorism exercise ever to take place in Australia, followed by the biggest series of criminal trials the nation had seen. The operation involved the simultaneous execution of search warrants by New South Wales, Victorian and Federal Police across Sydney and Melbourne, following hundreds of thousands of hours of surveillance, which gathered a huge amount of material giving agencies great insights into terrorist plots, and the information to head them off.

'By the time I put my head on the pillow I had been awake for over thirty hours and worked for twenty hours,' says Laurence. 'But when you spend extended periods in a heightened state of alert, you reach the point where sleeping like a normal person is impossible. It struck me I'd spent a significant portion of my adult life living off adrenalin, dealing with the worst and most dangerous situations that can occur in society. In that world there is no room for fear and you have to condition yourself to override your emotions. It prepared me well for what was to come with Sam.'

At that stage, Laurence was promoted to inspector and asked to return to the Goulburn academy to head up the Operational Safety Training Unit, where he'd worked previously. He agreed and went back, receiving an award after six months from the commander of educational services. But by then, Laurence had met Samantha, and after travelling back and forth between Goulburn and Wollongong, applied to transfer to PORS. Cullen welcomed him with open arms.

It was the start of a whole new phase of frontline policing. On his return to the Bathurst races in 2007 and 2008, this time he was the tactical commander. It was great to be in charge, but always hard work. The first year, it got ugly in the middle of the night. 'Numerous arrests were made, rocks, lit toilet rolls, missiles, fireworks were all thrown, and we were dealing with heavily intoxicated people – limited to a mere twenty-four standard drinks per day!' he says. 'During one intense stand-off, I was in charge of over 100 officers deployed amongst a crowd of several thousand who were threatening to overrun the police compound. I had fully kitted-up riot squad officers and a police helicopter on standby, and it was a highly dangerous situation for most of the night.'

Another massive security exercise was undertaken for the series of meetings between the twenty-one members of the Asia-Pacific Economic Cooperation (APEC) in various venues around Australia in 2007. The event culminated in Sydney where the heads of government of each country congregated for a week from 2 September.

A security perimeter was erected around much of inner-city

Sydney to try and keep people away, and new powers for the police were introduced because of fears of violent protest by various opposition groups. With Cullen the senior tactical commander, Laurence was in charge on the ground and briefed and deployed 650 public order police, 600 from New South Wales and fifty from the Australian Federal Police, then commanded them in the field.

The Saturday saw the biggest of the organised APEC protest rallies, with around 5000 people braving pouring rain to attend. While mostly peaceful, it turned ugly at one stage, with one officer being struck in the face by a dart and another being hit with an iron bar. Seventeen protesters were arrested. Laurence used a forward command vehicle with three people assisting him, each of whom subsequently became tactical commanders, to control the crowd. 'It was the largest deployment of public order police in the history of policing in this country,' he says. 'I was making decisions at such a rapid rate, it took two of us to operate the radios and phones while someone else drove, and Condo [Inspector Paul Condon] became a runner, racing into the field and diving into formations relaying my instructions to team leaders. The whole time all four of us were yelling at each other and bouncing ideas off each other, as we set about managing a protest which within several minutes of setting off had turned nasty. It was an incredible adrenalin surge to operate at these levels and enormously gratifying to see tactical plans come to a productive conclusion.'

And what made it even more worthwhile was coming home to Samantha whenever he was off duty. His life had rhyme and reason all over again.

* * *

Suddenly, the curtains around Samantha's bed were ripped back. Laurence raced over. She was struggling to open her still badly swollen eyes but as she finally managed to open them, he could see her looking around.

As her eyes finally settled on him, he saw the unmistakable flicker of recognition, and realised she was trying to move her body and her arms towards him. Laurence's vision blurred and he felt a heady sense of euphoria completely engulf him.

He kissed Samantha and held her hand, then hugged everyone within arm's reach, over and over again. He could hardly dare believe what he was seeing. It was Samantha back again; they were being given a second chance at life.

Everyone in the ward was beaming at him, thrilled that he'd got his dearest wish. Margaret was there by his side, and they hugged each other as if they'd never stop. 'It was one of those magical moments in time that you wish you could capture and relive over and over again,' he says. 'Margaret and her husband were both smiling and crying. Words couldn't describe my sense of elation and relief. It was as if Sam had been reborn. She had the worst black eyes in the world, her nose was still broken and her head was still in such a huge bandage you could only see the smallest amount of skin, but she knew me! She was back!'

Samantha was still hooked up to all the machines, with tubes down her throat and her arm in a splint. Laurence took his familiar position beside her bed, held her left hand again and gently started explaining where she was, reassuring her that everything was okay. She seemed bewildered, uncomprehending at first, and was still lapsing in and out of consciousness.

Slowly over the next two days, he broke the news to her that she'd been attacked and badly injured, and had been in a coma. As soon as she started to understand, she tried to sit up and started punching with her arms. 'Come on, I'm right,' she whispered. 'Let's get the bastard!'

Laurence smiled as if his heart would burst. 'I was suddenly sure the worst was over,' he says. 'But I later discovered how naive I'd been. In many ways the journey had only just begun.'

PART THREE:

# Fighting Back

# Chapter 11

## A WOMAN POSSESSED

Samantha Barlow still had a long way to go before she was completely out of danger but, as far as anyone could tell, she was now likely to live and hopefully wasn't suffering the kind of brain damage that would leave her impaired. Yet it was early days; she was still confused, and not quite with it.

The doctors reassured Laurence that her state of mind was only to be expected after her brain had undergone such extreme trauma. They thought this might prove to be a passing phase. At least, they hoped it was.

'But it was a scary time,' says Laurence. 'The doctors explained to me that it was like a computer being rebooted, and her cognitive recovery would be uneven as everything came back into line. I was thrilled she'd woken and known me, but it was hard seeing how bewildered she could be, and then stressed because she couldn't remember stuff.

'We knew that the damage to Sam's brain could result in permanent and irretrievable damage to the areas within the brain that controlled movement, speech, memory and a whole range of other cognitive functions. We were all delighted she was alive, but the next phase of her assessment and recovery was not *whether* she would suffer significant mental and physical disability; it was how severe it would be.'

In fact, it quickly became apparent that Samantha could remember absolutely nothing of the attack. That might have been either the permanent effect of her head injuries, or the innate protective mechanism of the brain that blocks out severe psychological trauma, or even a combination of both. 'I remember nothing about it at all,' says Samantha now. 'I can remember setting out for work that morning, parking the car and walking up the hill, then . . . nothing. A big blank.'

Laurence tends to think that was a blessing. 'Sam has a three-month black hole in her memory covering that period but, despite some of the problems that have arisen from this, it's also a good thing,' he says. 'She is unlikely ever to unravel the events that occurred that morning in the park when she was attacked and the living hell she was forced to endure from then on.'

The day after she woke from the coma, she was shown photographs of Lily and Ben. She asked who they were. She'd even forgotten she had children. Gradually, she came to recognise Lily, but Ben was still a mystery to her, and stayed that way for a good week after the coma.

Friends and colleagues who had been dropping by to see her and to sit in the waiting room as a gesture of solidarity were now gradually admitted into the Intensive Care Unit. New South Wales Police Commissioner Andrew Scipione had seen her plenty of times before, and had struck up a good friendship with her parents from his time in the waiting room with them. On the day she came out of her coma, he raced to the hospital to visit her again. He was thrilled to see her awake for the first time and, just as he had when she was asleep, he greeted her. 'I'd spoken to her on a number of occasions while she was in a coma, but of course, she didn't talk back,' he says. 'But this time, she did!

'I'd only said something stupid like, "How are you feeling?", or "How are you going?" And I was so taken aback that she'd answered. It was fantastic! When you think that she had half her head missing, had been attacked so badly by a brick-wielding heroin addict and been left to die and no one had found her for an hour . . . You could see that this woman has a flame in her that never goes out.'

Many of Samantha's other visitors, especially those who hadn't seen her since the attack, were startled both to see the extent of her physical injuries, and to have some extremely nonsensical conversations with her. At first, a few of them thought it might be the result of heavy medication but were told brain surgery generally wasn't uncomfortable, so patients didn't need sedation. It was more about the brain misfiring, and sometimes spectacularly so.

Her boss at Kings Cross, Superintendent Tony Crandell, remembers her wounds looking like a patchwork quilt all across her head. 'But then she woke up and the first thing I saw was a smile, that beautiful smile, and that fabulous personality that sees the positive in everything,' he says. 'She wasn't making much sense to start with, though. She was confused. She wasn't sure why she was in hospital, and she thought she'd just given birth. You could tell she was trying to make sense of it all. She was coherent but she wasn't logical in her thoughts. So we humoured her, and continued to humour her for quite some time, probably a few days if not weeks. But I'll never forget that smile. I thought she wasn't going to make it, so I've never been more pleased to see a person smile than I was that day.'

Deputy Commissioner Dave Owens, her old Maroubra commander, also went in to visit as soon as he was allowed, but he says he didn't even recognise her. Another early visitor was Laurence's boss at the riot squad, Chief Superintendent Steve Cullen, one of the toughest men in the force. 'I didn't want to go into intensive care to see her, but then I finally went in,' he says. 'She opened her eyes, and they were so black and bruised in a face that was just purple. She looked at me and said, "G'day boss," and I just fell apart. Her face was all smashed in, but she was still as cheerful as ever. She should have died that day. It's only the fact that she was such a superb athlete that saved her. She's a champion, an absolute champion.' He left in tears.

Her friends who had been at the hospital for days were thrilled she'd emerged from the coma, and were keen to humour her too. The first time her good friend and Kings Cross workmate Sergeant Perri Hayes saw her, she found it hard to hide her surprise when Samantha blithely asserted she was just back from a day out. 'I saw Sam the night she'd come out of the coma and she said she'd been down to Stanwell Park for the day,' says Hayes. 'I wasn't sure what to make of that. But she was laughing and seemed happy, and I was just so pleased to see her laughing with a brain injury! That made me laugh too. It felt good. She asked after the children in a jovial way, which I thought was good too. She hadn't realised what was going on, but she didn't seem to be in any pain.'

At other times, she was adamant she'd been involved in a car accident. With so much experience in crash investigation, that seemed to make the most sense to her. Then she'd spiral into depression, blaming herself for being so stupid as to have been hit by a car. Over and over again, often up to twelve times a day, Laurence would take her hand and patiently tell her, no, she had been the victim of a robbery and, no, she was in no way responsible for what had happened to her. Now she was safe in hospital, and she just had to concentrate on getting better. Every time Laurence did this, he hoped it might become just a little more ingrained in her memory. But, for everyone, it was an incredibly difficult and emotionally draining experience.

Her other police mate Senior Sergeant Belinda Crowe had seen her twice while she'd been in her coma and had been in floods of tears ever since. 'I'd never seen anything like it, it was awful,' she says. 'I've always been the crier of the group and I even tear up today thinking back to it. But when she came out of the coma, things improved rapidly. But I remember seeing her then and she had no idea what had happened and what was happening around her, which was probably the best thing, really. She was very muddled. I remember her at one stage going through fashion magazines and picking out new handbags and sunglasses to replace the ones that had been stolen. At one stage there in intensive care, her whole life became absorbed with replacing what had been taken. But as soon as she woke up, I knew she'd get better. I knew she'd get through it.'

Her parents, though, were more worried. They'd felt so relieved when their daughter had opened her eyes and recognised them, but they feared she might not improve as much as everyone was hoping. They were also there during that stage of her obsessively wanting to replace her lost things. One day they came in and she was admiring a watch in a magazine, declaring she'd buy it as soon as she came out of hospital.

'So we bought her that watch and it was only afterwards that we thought, should we really have done that?' says Janice Groves. 'But she kept asking why she was in hospital, and would then think she'd just had a baby, Ben, and that's why she was there.

'You'd be talking to her, and other times she'd say she'd been to the races that morning. The first time it happened, I thought, Oh no! But then I looked at the nurse and she'd smile and nod, and we'd just play along with it. I would say, "Have you?" She'd carry on saying she'd had a wonderful time and she won on this race, and won on that. I knew her brain wasn't right. She'd never had a bet in her life! We had Sam back, but not our old Sammy, and we wondered whether we'd ever see her again.'

Slowly, slowly, Samantha's brain started to show signs of recovery. Doctors kept testing her, checking her and asking her questions to look for any changes in her cognitive function. At first, Samantha seemed not to mind, but gradually she grew impatient with being asked the same things all the time, like who she was, where she was, the day and date. 'I know where I am!' she'd snap. 'Don't you?'

Her friend Robin Williams was at her bedside one day when she ran completely out of patience. The doctor had just begun his series of questions when Samantha's eyes started to glaze over. 'Do you know your name?' he asked her.

'Yes,' she said. He waited, but she offered him nothing more.

'Sam,' Williams urged, 'you're meant to say your name.'

Samantha shrugged. 'I can't be bothered today,' she replied. Williams couldn't help laughing. 'That's the real Sam!' she says. 'She doesn't tolerate fools and sometimes she won't give people the time of day. She's got a great sense of humour, and she never lost that.'

Sometimes, she'd be shown flash cards and asked to remember them. If she couldn't, she fell into a pattern of joking with the testers and cajoling them not to write down that she'd got it wrong as she knew she had to pass each test three times in a row to be allowed to advance to the next. Other times, she'd be asked for the names of the prime minister, the New South Wales premier or Sydney's lord mayor, and then the questions would get harder, and harder still. 'Look,' she'd finally say, 'I didn't know that stuff before someone smashed my head in; what hope do I have now? Why don't you ask me something a normal person would know?' Laurence would smile to himself. That was the woman he knew and loved.

But such glimpses started off few and far between. 'Other functions of the brain such as the ability to process information or memory retrieval were not working and appeared to be like a computer with a virus,' he says. 'The lights were on, but there was resistance or faulty wiring that was preventing them from firing up. But watching Sam day after day, you could see it in her eyes – after the swelling had started to go down – that she was determined to break through those internal barriers that were inhibiting her progress. Things were changing before our very eyes.'

Every day and sometimes almost hourly, other areas of the brain would continue to heal and improve, then begin to function normally. For example, one morning review by doctors identified that her sodium levels were not self-regulating. That could be a serious issue as too much sodium in the blood could cause swelling of the brain again and create pressure inside the skull. By the afternoon review the following day, however, it was no longer a problem. That part of her brain had restarted and begun to function normally.

Samantha was given a battery of tasks to complete to try to push the slower parts of her brain into action, or to test whether other areas were firing normally. They'd require enormous levels of effort and concentration and she'd tire easily. Yet she was always determined to do more, to try harder, to see if she could succeed in clearing away more of the fog clouding her brain. She'd request additional memory tests and press Laurence to ask her questions, and she seemed to be constantly processing the information she was being given. But too often, and without warning, the 'real' Samantha would slip away and a stranger would appear in her place.

'Sometimes, it was as though an alien had possessed my wife's body, like Linda Blair's in *The Exorcist*,' says Laurence. 'One minute, Sam would be capable of superhuman things, then, in a split second, her personality could change to a completely different character. I'd be talking to her, then Sam would go off on odd tangents, as if she had multiple personalities. I'd tell her what had happened to her, then she'd accuse me of lying to her and interrogate me relentlessly in a character I came to think of as "Sergeant Sam", then she'd switch to worrying where her belongings were, like jewellery, her phone and the bag she'd had taken. Her emotional state would go from sounding like her old, self-confident, in-control self to accusatory, as she'd question my version of events. Then there'd be confusion as she'd search through her memory for information that was just not there.

'There were moments, too, she'd get angry and fire up, trying to get out of bed, and start trying to swing her arms, saying again that she wanted to "get the bastard" who did this to her. Then she would act and talk like a police sergeant asking questions about the investigation. The final emotion each time would be tears and a sense of uselessness, blaming herself regardless of anything I would say. At first this would happen almost every time she woke up or whenever I entered the Intensive Care Unit, and my world quickly became a completely bizarre and crazy place. I was constantly stunned by how quickly things could change without warning. It was like living with someone who suffers from a severe multiple personality disorder.'

Six days on from the attack, with Samantha now out of physical danger, Laurence allowed himself to finally be persuaded to leave the little room at the hospital where he and Inspector Paul Condon had slept on the floor every night, and check into a hotel just down the road, next door to a favourite pub in Paddington's Oxford Street. The pair had been to the pub, the Three Weeds, a couple of times to grab a quick meal at night while Samantha had been in a coma. One of the few pubs in the area still with an old-fashioned, unadorned interior and a grungy feel, it was a quiet place with good bar meals, a favourite with sports fans whenever a game was on over at the Sydney Football Stadium at Moore Park.

Laurence was under enormous strain and he was all too aware how easy it could be to drink too much in his condition, and how dangerous it would be. Condon laid down the ground rules early on. 'We made it a rule that it was okay to talk to Dr Beer, but that we must not allow his alter ego, Professor Pissed, to surface,' he says. 'So to ensure this, we always had a big feed and after drinking six beers – three double rounds as the first schooner usually disappeared in one or two mouthfuls – Condo would buy us one for the road and put his arm around me and walk me out of the pub.'

That evening, for a change, the pair walked next door to the Arts Hotel. They'd checked in earlier, and Laurence had phoned the hospital then to make sure all was well with Samantha. After their meal and a few drinks, he rang again to reassure himself, and was told she was sleeping peacefully. The nurses asked him not to call during the night, as they'd be busy, and they weren't expecting any problems. They'd call him immediately if there was anything wrong.

By 7 a.m. the next morning, he was on tenterhooks. He hadn't been away from the hospital for so long for a week, and he was anxious and on edge. He called intensive care and said he wanted to know how his wife had got through the night. 'The nurse quite innocently put the phone down,' says Condon. 'She obviously had lots of things going on at the time, and then she picked it back up again and said, "Sorry, just checking, who were you phoning about?"

'At that, Laurence picked the phone up and threw it across the hotel room. I was trying to calm him down, saying, "Mate it's not a biggie, they've got a lot of people to care for. If something had happened, they'd have given you a ring. You've got to take a big breath . . . " But at that he spat the dummy and punched me in the chest. When I'd got my breath back, I said, "Mate, you've got to calm down," but he grabbed the door and threw the door open, nearly ripping it off its hinges, and took off.'

Condon hastily threw on some clothes, pushed his feet into some thongs and chased after him. He saw Laurence cross the road, almost in the path of an oncoming car, and then stride off towards town. Condon decided to follow to keep a wary eye on him as Laurence marched all the way to George Street and down to The Rocks, a distance of nearly 4 kilometres. Hobbling behind him, Condon called one of his bosses, Assistant Commissioner Alan Clarke, commander of the Major Events and Incidents Group who oversaw the riot squad, and he agreed to meet the pair for breakfast. Condon caught Laurence up and told him the plan, and then said they could return to hospital afterwards. But Laurence couldn't be reasoned with. 'I'm not going in there,' he said. 'I'm not going to see her. They don't want me there . . .'

The three had breakfast together, and Laurence finally calmed down. Then Condon's phone rang. It was Samantha's mum. 'Paul, where's Laurence?' she asked. 'Sam's awake and she's asking for him.' Condon turned to Laurence. 'Mate, your wife is in hospital and she's asking for you. How can you say you're not going to go there today? So get your arse into gear, we're going to the hospital.' Laurence snapped out of his fury immediately and raced off, with Condon once again shuffling in hot pursuit.

Another day, Laurence had a call from day care. Lily had been taken sick, and she was being rushed to the paediatric ward of Sutherland Hospital nearby. He ran to his car and drove straight there. Just like Ben the week before at the same hospital, she was diagnosed with an acute respiratory infection.

The paediatrician blanched as he walked in; Laurence could tell he'd recognised him straightaway from all the media that had covered Samantha's attack. The two men shook hands sombrely. 'I don't know what to say . . .' the doctor said. Laurence shrugged. 'You don't need to say anything,' he replied. 'Your eyes have already said it.'

Lily was kept in overnight for observation as she, in turn, was pumped full of medicine. Laurence helped the nurses change her sheets, take her temperature and top up her medications until she was well enough to come back home. 'It felt like someone was treating our family as a voodoo doll,' he says. 'I kept wondering what else fate had in store for me.' He didn't have long to wait. He carried Lily from the hospital to the car and immediately caught sight of a parking ticket on the windscreen. He put Lily down carefully, helped her into the car, then got in himself before putting his head down on the steering wheel and weeping uncontrollably for a full five minutes. He was brought to by the voice of his daughter from the back seat. 'Daddy,' she was saying. 'Daddy, don't cry. It's okay.'

As Laurence inched towards despair, his friends watched on helplessly. 'One of the most difficult things I had to do was watch one of the hardest and toughest men I know, both mentally and physically, slowly fall apart in front of me,' says Condon. 'I was so proud of the way he held himself in public, how strong he was for others, including those other families in the ICU, who he continually spoke to and came to know so well. I was so impressed as I know how hard it had been for him. But, in reality, he was falling apart inside.'

# Chapter 12
# WHAT WILL THE FUTURE LOOK LIKE?

Life at the hospital with Samantha Barlow was rapidly turning into a decidedly uncomfortable version of the movie *50 First Dates*. Just as Drew Barrymore's character, suffering short-term memory loss, would start each day afresh, forgetting that she'd previously been out with her boyfriend, so it was for Laurence, repeating the same story to his wife hour after hour: why she was in hospital, what had happened to her, and what her injuries were.

Like in the film, he surrounded her with familiar things – photographs of the children and her parents, gift cards, letters, presents, his mother's crucifix . . . all items that could be used as conversation pieces and memory prompts for whenever she woke up. But progress was slow. Samantha's short-term memory was proving the last functional area of her brain to begin to work normally again.

There were plenty of light-hearted moments, like when Samantha swore to some visitors she'd been out the previous night conducting random breath tests, had pulled over some cars and locked up some drink-drivers. She was so adamant, they found it hard not to believe her – but for the fact she was still swathed in bandages, and attached to drips and monitors. Another day, she said she'd been off rowing around the Royal National Park. With her mate Robin Williams, she was no less persuasive. 'One day, when she was still delirious, she asked us to smuggle her in some champagne, her favourite sparkling *rosé*,' says Williams. 'She said that would be great, she'd love a glass. I asked her, "But how would we get it in?" I was joking, but she came up with an elaborate plan that she'd obviously thought about carefully, involving putting it in a lemonade bottle and having my daughter smuggle it in under her school blazer.'

Laurence tried to be encouraged by the fact that her fantasies all had a grain of truth in them, since they were an assortment of experiences plucked from her functioning memory of her real past. 'Each of the pieces of her tale was correct, which was a positive, but it was the sequencing of events that was out of order,' he says. 'It appeared that her whole memory was meshed together and she had lost the ability to distinguish different periods in her life or put her life into some kind of chronological order. The danger was that, left uncorrected, these types of stories could become her memory, so very quickly I had to put together a roster of strong people I trusted to sit with Sam during the periods I couldn't be there. When they weren't available, I shut the shop and didn't allow anyone in.

'Sam was an inspiration and improving at a rate no one could ever have dreamt possible, but if this area of her recovery was not managed properly then there was the risk of undoing some of the amazing work done up to that point. I took my cue from the nurses. They would consciously make eye contact, use simple, almost blunt, language and not allow Sam to drift off into her delusion. They'd insist on bringing her back to the reality that she was in the Intensive Care Unit of St Vincent's Hospital and that she was a robbery victim.'

Samantha's neurosurgeon Dr Vanessa Perotti came over two days after she emerged from the coma to take the staples, clips and stitches out of her scalp. She wouldn't normally have done that herself; she would have left it to someone else, but she wanted to see how her patient's scalp was faring. She could see that Samantha was 'off with the fairies' and surmised she was still suffering a degree of hypoxic brain injury – where the brain has been starved of blood and oxygen for a while, as with a stroke.

But she asked Samantha to sit up in bed, and then started taking the staples out with a device rather like an office staple remover. Her scalp looked good but Samantha suddenly went quiet. Dr Perotti stopped for a moment, looked at her and was astonished to see big tears slowly rolling down her face. The doctor was dismayed.

'Sam!' she said. 'I'm so sorry! Have I hurt you?'

Samantha shook her head. She'd realised that her beautiful hair was all gone, and she looked back at her neurosurgeon with a scowl. 'You!' she said. 'You are the worst hairdresser I've ever had!'

It was obvious that Samantha hated being in the hospital and just wanted to go home and be with her kids. After a few days in Paddington, Laurence moved back home so he could at least be with the children at night, to try to return some kind of normality to their lives. The first evening, they were already in bed asleep when he arrived back, so he crept into their rooms, tucked them in and sat and watched them for a while. Finally, he went back downstairs and ate dinner with Samantha's parents and Olivia and Ryan who were staying over. After the meal, he updated them all on how Samantha was doing – and then broke down in tears. 'It was hard, so hard,' he says. 'It was wonderful to be with the kids again but while Ben was a baby and just needed to be comforted, Lily was missing her mum like hell. That first evening Lily woke up screaming for Mummy a couple of times and ran through the house looking for her. It was as tough as anything I had done and would do for the next year or so.'

Yet the hardest thing still about going home was telling Samantha. As soon as he mentioned that he'd have to leave hospital at the end of each day, she would start pointing at imaginary things and telling him to get her clothes, shoes and handbag from her wardrobe so she could come too. He'd then have to talk firmly with her and explain both why he was going home and why she couldn't come with him. Often the conversation would end abruptly with Samantha saying, 'Okay, if you're going, just go!' She would turn her back on him in a gesture that would break his heart. He'd finally dejectedly drag himself out to race to pick up the kids from Bambino's Kindergarten, usually late again because of the exchange.

He didn't want to lie to her, feeling it was important to keep building trust, but instead he started becoming more economical with the truth, saying he had to go to do some work or visit the police station – both tasks he had to do frequently in any case. Somehow, she seemed to find those reasons for leaving much more acceptable, although she'd then want to get up and make him something to eat to take to work, or help him pack his bag, or iron his uniform, forgetting the riot squad dressed in overalls. And it could become problematic too when she asked who'd be looking after the children while he was at work.

Her longing for home, even though she couldn't actually remember where home was, was becoming increasingly difficult to manage. The carers at the kindy had begun taking photos of Lily and Ben for Samantha but when Laurence took them in, they made her even keener to leave hospital. One afternoon, she started whispering to

Laurence that he needed to divert the nurses, or 'prison guards' as she'd started to call them, while she got out of bed. She'd ask him to go and get the car as she was ready to climb out of the window – forgetting they were on the fifth floor of a multi-storey building – and escape.

Another day, things took a more serious turn when she actually decided it was time to go home. Laurence and his riot squad mate Sergeant Brendan Crowe were on either side of her when she started to climb out of bed and, despite both being over 182 centimetres tall, much fitter and stronger than the average person, and with a combined weight of over 220 kilograms, they couldn't hold her down. In the end, she had to be sedated to stop her. There was little respite at night, either. Samantha started phoning him late in the evening and sometimes in the middle of the night, rambling, delusional, crying and sometimes, in moments of apparent lucidity, saying she was scared someone was going to break into the hospital and attack her.

'I found myself lying awake at nights wondering what the hell our future looked like,' says Laurence. 'I was trying to hold everything together but at the same time I was dying from the inside out. The anxiety became all-consuming, preventing me from sleeping or resting. My self-esteem and confidence were shot to pieces and I was scared of myself.'

It was so difficult to behave normally in front of the children, too. Lily in particular was suffering extreme separation anxiety. If Laurence told her that he was off to work, she was clingy, but okay. If he said that he was going to the hospital, she'd scream, cry or withdraw completely. In her two-year-old world, the place she called 'hobsital' was where mummies went – and didn't come back.

Laurence was so stressed, it was getting harder and harder to cope. 'Every day I continued to stumble through the messed-up life that had been forced upon me. It seemed as though it didn't matter what I did, it was wrong. My back was killing me, but I had no time for my own physio or chiropractic sessions, I'd developed tinnitus from so much exposure to loud noise over my career which was driving me insane, I was eating poorly and drinking too much alcohol. I was scared that the rage I was continuing to suppress about the man who'd put us in this position was going to bubble to the surface and I was going to do physical harm to someone. I was losing it.'

Others could see how Laurence was struggling. Kings Cross Superintendent Tony Crandell was becoming increasingly concerned. 'I've never seen a bloke go through so many emotions as him when his wife was on the verge of death,' he says. 'He handled himself well, spoke well, he put his heart on the line and I reckon he put a few years on himself – and on me too! I remember one time he was in the office and he hadn't slept for about five or six days. I said, "Mate, you need some time out. You need to have some sleep." But he said, "No, no, sleep's overrated!" Then he turned. In a split second he became angry. He said he wasn't having rational thoughts, he was angry, he wanted someone to pay. At one point, I actually thought he was going to hit me. I told him I was his friend, not his enemy, and that I was there to help. Eventually he calmed down but it was such an emotional rollercoaster he was on. I had a number of conversations with him about psychologist referrals, however he always refused. In some ways, I almost felt Sam was in a better position, because she was getting medical treatment. I thought, This guy needs help!'

The next morning, Laurence was back at his wife's hospital. At about 11 a.m. she had some physio, so he excused himself and took a quick break to have a cup of coffee with Inspector Paul Condon in the reflective garden out the front. He heard a commotion from the foyer and looked round to see a man on drugs, angry and swearing, being escorted out of the building, through the gardens and onto the pavement beyond, just a few metres away from where he was sitting. The man continued shouting at the security guards and daring them to call the 'dog coppers' so he could 'give it to them too'. Laurence felt the rage build in him, and suddenly realised he was shaking uncontrollably.

He knew he had to do something, so he started walking, Condon again bringing up the rear. He walked quickly along Victoria Street and down William Street towards the city until he came to a small paved section. He stopped there a moment but then saw a group of three men, again obviously out of it on drugs, standing by a sandstone wall. 'I could feel my face flush bright red, my hands clench tightly, my legs tremble, and I was possessed with an overwhelming urge to unleash all my rage upon the three of them,' says Laurence. 'I was ready to explode with potentially catastrophic consequences.'

Condon noticed the tension in his mate as he watched the little group, and moved closer to him. But Laurence shook his head. 'Ready for a real-life demonstration of strength?' he asked. Condon looked confused. Then Laurence walked past the men without saying, or doing, a thing.

Without missing a beat, Condon moved towards him, close enough to put his arm around him as if they were about to pack into a rugby scrum, just in case he needed to stop Laurence doing something he might later regret. 'Real-life demonstration,' said Condon, 'of a mate.' The pair looked at each other, and Laurence laughed. As he did so, it felt like an enormous weight had been lifted from his shoulders as his blood pressure dropped back towards normal and he began to regain his self-control. But he knew it really was time to ask for some help.

Laurence felt annoyed the police force hadn't supplied him with counselling as, in theory, the services of the psychology unit were available to all police families. Finally, however, he made the call and then hoped the person who'd come to see him would be able to offer him a real insight into the mess, and some sound advice on good strategies to help him come to terms with what had happened as well as to manage the challenges that were likely to lie ahead. Condon encouraged him. 'I felt he needed it because I could see he was going insane, literally insane,' he says. 'He was constantly getting angry. I just felt he had to talk to someone other than me. It was at a point where I was starting to lose control of him.'

The psychologist, a young woman in her twenties, arrived when Laurence was sitting alone in the corner of a waiting room at the hospital with a cup of tea between his feet as his hands were trembling so much, he couldn't hold it without spilling the contents. The session didn't start well. Laurence, angry that she hadn't attended before, nor offered help, insisted first on asking her a series of questions, to see if he felt he could trust her. If she didn't reply satisfactorily, he said, he'd ask her to leave. She was taken aback, but agreed to his conditions. 'I was a walking, talking time bomb, and I knew it,' says Laurence. 'But I was filthy at the time with everything. I couldn't walk out of intensive care without someone hugging me, kissing me and offering to pray for me, but professional help had been conspicuously missing in action.'

After the initial few questions, Laurence was unimpressed by her answers, and feeling the session wouldn't work for him, asked her to leave. She refused. He asked her a second time and she refused again. Feeling trapped, he then told her about the incident earlier that morning with the man being escorted out of the hospital and how it had made him feel. She attempted to start a conversation, but Laurence shut her down, and asked her to leave again. This time, she did, but then returned almost immediately, closed the door, sat down and said they needed to talk. He asked her, much more loudly this time, to go. She did.

The psychologist called Condon, who'd been out grabbing a beer and some sushi in a rare break from being at Laurence's side. He rushed back, to find his friend angrily pacing the corridor. Laurence then took out his police ID wallet and tossed it in a bin, and ripped up his business cards, saying he was quitting the force. Condon suggested he go sit in the chapel, and Laurence complied, while Condon went around gathering up his ID and other police items, and putting them in his bag for later.

Laurence sat in the quiet, sipping his tea and slowly calming down. At that point, he suddenly thought, Fuck! What have I done? 'So much for asking someone for help!' he says. 'I felt a night on the drink with some mates at a karaoke bar would have been a similarly useless waste of time, but at least it would have provided me with some respite, something normal that could have restored some sanity and recharged my mental energy. I thought back to something my mum always used to tell me: I never rasied a fool; believe in yourself. And, strangely enough, by the end of the cup of tea I had cleared my head, and felt as though a lead weight had been lifted. I felt cleansed, I felt like I was back in control. Before, I'd been feeling like a victim, someone who'd been smashed from pillar to post and who had buckled under. But now I felt like I was back on my feet and ready to get stuck in again. I'd stood up for myself and called it as I saw it. I'd given her a spray but I'd felt that the unit had deserved it.'

Samantha was always eager for new challenges in her career, and almost from the start set her heart on joining the highway patrol. 'I loved the thought of being out and about instead of stuck in an office,' she says. She was one of the few females in this male-dominated area and was very highly regarded. (Courtesy NSW Police Force)

Samantha always loved the water and was 'quite fearless' from an early age, according to her father.

Samantha, second from right, has been helping people all her life, first through surf lifesaving at the South Maroubra Surf Life Saving Club, then as a police officer. Her lifelong friend Karen Maddock is on the left.

Laurence was sworn in on 14 September 1984. He was twenty years old. 'It was everything I always imagined it would be,' he says.

In 2005 Samantha was the recipient of the NSW Police Medal, issued for ten years of ethical and diligent police service. Commissioner Ken Moroney is on the left.

Senior Sergeant Laurence Barlow in his role as Public Order and Riot Squad Tactical Commander at a protest against the NSW Premier at Wollongong council chambers in 2004.

Samantha and Laurence with baby Ben and toddler Lily, just before her return to work in May 2009. 'I loved my time off with my children; that was very precious to me,' Samantha says.

After the attack, Samantha was left lying in the grass at the back of Arthur Park, drifting in and out of consciousness. She dragged herself to the bus stop. (Courtesy Jimmy Thomson)

Eleven days after the attack, Lily turned two. The staff in intensive care let the Barlows use a conference room for a little party.

Superintendent Tony Crandell remembers Samantha's wounds looking like a patchwork quilt all across her head.

A week into her rehab, Samantha visited NSW Police Commissioner Andrew Scipione in his office: '... she still didn't even have her skull bolted back together properly. But the first thing that struck me was that enormous smile.' (Courtesy Craig Greenhill/Newspix)

Samantha returned to work on 8 March 2011, the hundredth anniversary of International Women's Day. (Courtesy NSW Police Force)

Leaving the force after an outstanding career was one of the hardest things Samantha has ever done. In 2011 she was awarded News Limited's Pride of Australia medal in the Heroism category. (Medal board courtesy Jimmy Thomson)

The newest addition to the Barlow family, Zac, was born in February 2013 when Lily was nearly six and Ben was four and a half. (Courtesy Jimmy Thomson)

But, just as he'd feared, it didn't end there. The psychologist reported him as losing it, and being in need of sedation. He was then forced to spend the next few hours with a doctor and nurse he'd got to know already in intensive care, while they assessed him to decide whether he did, in fact, need sedation. Finally, they agreed he did not.

Yet there was still more to come. The psychologist said she now wanted to talk to Condon, so he'd be better able to help his mate. He was equally unreceptive. 'It was stupid things, like you've got to tell him what to do, and get him out of the hospital,' says Condon. 'I immediately knew that wasn't going to work. You just don't *tell* Laurence to do anything, and it would have taken a depth charge to get him out of hospital.'

It wasn't until six weeks later that Laurence again asked for help and this time found a counsellor much better suited to assist. 'I think the professionals, as well as a true group of your peers, all have their place, but they don't own your journey,' he says. 'The good ones understand that. They are non-judgemental and open to ideas designed to help you "do it your way". The very good ones even make suggestions on how to do this. But the only person with the answers to your life problem, no matter how big it is or how crazy and out of control your life becomes, is you.'

From that point on, Laurence felt a great deal calmer. He drew strength from the way Samantha was battling back, hour by hour, day by day, sometimes making progress, sometimes slipping back, but always with her eye set on the main goal of making it back home to be with her family again. He accepted a helping hand more readily from his friends. And he became even closer to Samantha's parents.

'I remember thinking that I'd only been with Sam for three years, and married to her for five minutes, and I should involve the Groves family more in the decisions I was making,' he says. 'We all loved her dearly and we were all struggling in our different ways. But while they never queried or challenged me about anything, I decided to share the decisions with them more.'

Vernon and Janice Groves were always happy to be a sounding board. They'd watched Laurence almost fall apart under the strain, and then put himself back together again, and were happy he'd regained something of his own self. 'I think it was all affecting him much more than even he was aware of,' says Janice. 'At times, he wasn't really himself.'

The tide of support from strangers continued to help, too. The couple received over 500 cards, letters and emails from people expressing their horror at what had happened, and their heartfelt best wishes. There was the occasional reminder too of the man who'd put Samantha in hospital. One afternoon, an enormous bunch of flowers arrived at intensive care, with an even bigger box of chocolates and a money order. It was from the governor and staff of Long Bay Jail hospital.

Most of all, though, it was Samantha herself who provided the inspiration. Watching her slowly rebuild herself both mentally and physically, never complaining or seeming to feel sorry for herself, Laurence nicknamed her Wonder Woman and the Bionic Woman. Her tolerance for pain amazed hospital staff. A couple of them returned a few times to test her buzzer, convinced it couldn't have been working since she never asked for any extra pain relief. Every time they offered it, she refused. Yes, she agreed, her head was hurting and her stitches hurt, as well as her neck, her back and her hand. But no, she didn't want to take anything, thanks. When they quizzed her why not, she'd just grin. 'I've just had my head smashed in,' she'd say. 'It's supposed to hurt, isn't it?'

No one was in any doubt that Samantha's high level of physical fitness and her psychological training in operational policing, as a member of the Operations Support Group, were major contributors to her recovery. Coupled with that were her trademark motivation and discipline, developed all through her childhood. 'And I could never desert my family,' she says now. 'I'd never abandon my children. Nothing could get in the way of that.'

Every day, she insisted on pushing herself harder, with both the mind tests and the physical rehabilitation. She continued asking for additional tests, or suggesting Laurence hold her up while she completed extra exercises or stretches. 'She's just a freak!' Laurence would laugh with his wife, as the nurses raised their eyebrows. 'You can't kill her. Someone's already tried that and failed.'

# Chapter 13
# THE TIME FOR TEARS IS OVER

On 24 May 2009, eleven days after the attack, Samantha and Laurence Barlow's daughter Lily turned two. Originally, they'd planned a party at a local park and now friends suggested they should perhaps hold some kind of celebration for Lily at the hospital. Laurence was in two minds. It would be easier in some ways to wait until Samantha was out of hospital and just pretend to their daughter that it was her birthday then. But he could understand that it might be a good idea for everyone to get together and celebrate life.

The staff in intensive care were keen and they offered him a conference room to use for a little party. Everyone brought food, decorations and a cake, and there were two guests of honour that day: the birthday girl and Samantha, her shaven head covered in wounds still oozing a combination of blood, fluid and medical creams, and her hand in a splint hooked up to an intravenous line, wheeled down to join in the festivities in her pyjamas.

'I think we were all shocked at how she looked out of bed for the first time,' says Robert Barlow, Laurence's brother. 'She had the big bandage off her head, and all her hair was gone. She had a care nurse nearby and she seemed to be coherent and coping, but her appearance was definitely a shock.'

Samantha has no memory of the day. The photos all show her smiling, but looking uncertain. Everyone else is smiling broadly too, but it's patently obvious they are all feeling the strain, and most had to wipe tears from their eyes as they watched Lily and Ben tentatively approach their mum, uncertain at how different she looked, and sitting in a strange chair. Samantha was obviously eager to see the kids and didn't even wince when Lily clambered onto her lap for a cuddle. Close up, though, Lily took one look at her bruised, swollen face and delivered her verdict. 'Mummy's yucky!' she said. She pushed against her, with the palm of one of her hands coming into contact with Samantha's fractured nose, and lurched forward, scared and confused, to try to scramble away. Samantha carried on smiling, but few doubted that, underneath, her heart must have been breaking.

Someone hastily lit the candles on the birthday cake and tried to start a chorus of 'Happy Birthday'. Most, however, choked on the words, and the song was barely audible. While the cake was being cut, Laurence, joined by his elder children Olivia and Ryan, and Robin and Scot Williams' daughter Casey, tried to sing and complete the actions to Lily's favourite Wiggles song, 'Everybody Clap'. 'It was possibly the hardest thing I have ever done in my life,' he says. 'Despite all of us attempting to appear normal, there was nothing normal about what we were doing. The party had been a tough couple of hours but I'm glad we did it. But it did come at a high price.'

Having now seen the children, Samantha wanted even more to go home and be with them, something that rapidly developed into an obsession consuming all her waking hours. Whenever she thought people weren't looking, she'd try to get out of bed, and she began saying and doing whatever she thought was needed to get her out of the hospital. The doctors advised Laurence that it would be many months before she'd actually be allowed to leave, so he was left trying to work out instead how to bring the two little children into hospital to see her, to a unit full of terminally and critically ill people.

Similarly, for Lily, the experience of being back with her mum confused her and made her miss her presence even more keenly. Before the attack, she would sleep through the night for ten to twelve hours in her own bed, but now she started continually waking up and screaming at night, openly sobbing and calling out, 'Mummy! Mummy!' She constantly needed reassurance that everything was all right, and she always wanted to sleep in the same bed as her dad. Dropping her off at day care five days a week also became a screaming match. Previously, she'd loved going in and would skip, sing and hug everyone as she entered the room. Now, she clung to Laurence and had to be physically prised away, crying and howling. Regular visits to intensive care didn't seem to appease her much, either. In the nights and on the days following each trip, her behaviour simply deteriorated even more. 'Sam and Lily had always been close; it was like the umbilical cord had never been properly severed,' says Laurence. 'And it was heart-breaking now to see how much they were both suffering.'

A couple of days before the party, Laurence was asked to make a statement to the press from the hospital. Journalists had been clamouring for any news of Samantha, and public interest in the case had been intense. The media frenzy showed no sign of abating.

Even within the hospital, people were continually approaching Laurence asking him how his wife was doing.

He wrote out his statement at Kings Cross station, on Samantha's computer in her traffic office, with input from the commissioner's press officer Tony Ritchie and Laurence's brother-in-law Jason Groves, who was continually in touch from his home in London. He spent the evening rehearsing it, then had a practice run the next morning, while Samantha was sleeping, in front of some friends and colleagues outside the Intensive Care Unit.

Just as he was about to go to the second floor to the room where it had been arranged he'd speak to the press, the doors of the unit were flung open. There stood Samantha, supported by a nurse on either side, taking her first few steps since the attack to come to wish her husband luck. He was utterly speechless. 'I realised it really was time to try and start to smile again,' he says. 'We were at last beginning the long journey back to normality. She was incredible.'

Buoyed by what had just happened, he went down and gave the performance of his life. He told his audience that Australia's medical professionals, from its ambulance officers to doctors, nurses to surgeons and support staff, were the equal of the best anywhere else in the world, and that miracles appeared to happen inside the hospital every day. 'I now know where God lives,' he said. 'Level five of St Vincent's Hospital, a place that's staffed by angels.'

For Laurence, it was the perfect opportunity to thank everyone, including their closest friends, the police force and all those people who'd stopped him in the street, telling him they were praying for them. It was also a chance to tell everyone that Samantha was alive and recovering at a rate that defied all the odds. 'It was great to be able to tell everyone at the same time, thanks, but the time for tears was over,' he says. 'I wanted them to know that we should think positively and try to move on. It had been an incredible, unbelievable, dramatic, painfully raw, and shockingly stressful emotional rollercoaster we'd all been on, but I wanted to get everyone refocused on looking forwards rather than backwards. And I wanted to tell the world what an incredible person I was married to.'

As the days went on, Samantha's behaviour seemed to settle down, and the medical team began making preparations to move her out of intensive care and into a high-dependency ward specialising in brain injuries. Everyone in the unit was naturally delighted she was recovering so astonishingly quickly but, by the same token, they were sad to see her go. She was easily the best-known patient there, and other families, even though they were in the middle of their own traumas, all made a point of going over to her to speak to her, touch her leg or kiss her hand and give her cards, flowers or little gifts.

'I think everyone was both overwhelmed by what had happened, and inspired by her incredibly positive attitude and amazing recovery,' says Laurence. 'I saw terminally ill people look at my wife, smile and appear to find a new fighting spirit. I would often then take the time to sit and talk to them, take an interest in their families and reassure them that they would be receiving the best possible care in a place where miracles – just like ours – occurred every day.'

One morning, Laurence came in to the unit and found several nurses sitting on Samantha's bed, poring over the beautiful gifts she was still receiving each day. There'd been so many, Laurence had long lost track of who'd given what so had always felt guilty at being unable to thank all the donors. The little cabal were also flicking through magazines, comparing handbags, the latest iPhone, clothes and jewellery – Samantha and her carers were deciding what should replace the items that had been stolen.

Other times, Samantha would listen intently as hospital staff made plans to visit a local cafe or restaurant, or go away for the weekend. Even while she was confined to bed, she'd excitedly join in, saying she'd meet them there. Everyone was heartened, however, that she was beginning to show interest in life outside the hospital, even if her planning was somewhat unrealistic and premature. Yet it could also be bittersweet: it reinforced how desperately unhappy she was in hospital and how much she was craving a release and return to her old life.

But harnessing that desire to get out was paying huge dividends. It made her even more determined to prove the doctors wrong when they said she couldn't do this, she wouldn't be able to do that, and that she really wasn't ready to push herself at all just yet.

Her old schoolmate Judy Cohen watched her rapid progress without surprise. 'She always wanted to be independent, and she's very strong-willed,' she says. 'As a kid, if she couldn't do something, she'd deliberately work at it until she could. And if someone said she couldn't do something, then she became all the more determined to prove them wrong. It was great to see her recover so quickly. Nothing would hold her back.'

Karen Maddock, her friend from the surf club, agreed. 'Sam's recovery was amazing, but it wasn't unexpected,' she says. 'She never gives up, that girl. She's incredible. At every stop she was told she couldn't do stuff but, true to form, she never accepted it. She never had a negative thought. She decided early on what she was going to do, and that she'd prove them all wrong. Where she gets all that inner strength from, I don't know. Never once did I see her accept that this might affect her life. She never once gave in.

Even at the beginning in hospital, when she had moments of coherence, she'd talk about her future just like a normal person would. That strength comes from somewhere deep inside.'

She truly is her parents' daughter, believes her brother Jason Groves. He is convinced much of that strength comes from them. Their mum and dad were both of a wartime generation who didn't complain, but just buckled down and got on with the job at hand, and they taught their children from an early age to do the same.

'Our father is a very stubborn person too,' Jason says. 'When he was finally selling his business to retire a few years ago, he refused to get help. He was up on a ladder on the side of his building to take down the sign, when he fell off and hit his knee on the way down on a brick ledge and shattered every bone in one of his legs. He still then managed to get himself back into the office to call me but when I suggested he go to hospital, he said, "Don't be ridiculous, it's just a sprain." He wouldn't even go to the doctor!

'Eventually, he did have to go to hospital and the ambulance officers said they didn't know how he even survived the night in the pain he must have been in. Four operations and six weeks in hospital later . . . It's that tradition of being self-effacing diggers who never complained about being in the trenches.'

Her dad Vernon argues, on the other hand, that she could have got her strength of mind instead from her grandfather, his father Harry. In his fifties, he'd been hit by a tram and received severe spinal injuries. He spent two years in a complete body plaster cast. 'They told him he'd never walk again,' says Vernon. 'But he did. He recovered in an amazing way. I think Sam's got some of his determination.' Adds Janice, 'I never really thought she would die. It wasn't an option. She wasn't prepared to accept that. She wanted to stay with her family, not leave them.'

One day in intensive care, Samantha even started talking about buying a motorbike as soon as she got out, an 1100 cc twin-cylinder Ducati Monster. Scot Williams was nonplussed. 'I said, "Really?" But I shouldn't have been surprised. She was always a speed demon, whether about boats or cars, and knowing what she wants has always given her the focus to achieve it. I think that was one of the reasons her recovery was happening so rapidly. She had the determination, drive and vision. Family is everything to her, too, and that drove her too.

'Also, her attitude to setbacks in life was always, "Just suck it up." She'd say that to kids who were whingeing about something, and tell them to accept what had happened, and move on. And that philosophy stood her in very good stead. We used to call her Superwoman. She has no idea how strong she is.'

But another plan for her future that she outlined to anyone who'd listen stopped everyone short. 'One of the very first things she said to me when she woke up was, "When can I come back to work?"' says her old Kings Cross boss, Superintendent Tony Crandell. 'Laurence was in the background, shaking his head and saying, "She's not coming back to work!" I believed him. Of course, I didn't let on to her about that, but I secretly believed that she would never set foot in a police station or put on a suit of blue again.'

No one, it seemed, had any real idea what she was truly capable of.

# Chapter 14
# A RED RAG TO A BULL

It was the small things about Samantha Barlow's gradual recovery that everyone treasured.

Moved out of intensive care after just fourteen days, rather than the three to four weeks the doctors had anticipated, and into a neurological ward for people with brain injuries, she continued to make rapid progress. Her first morning there, on Wednesday 27 May, the children were due to visit and so the nurse came into her room ready to help her to the shower seat. There was no need, Samantha informed her. She'd already showered. And what's more, she added firmly, she'd be doing it herself from now on.

'I remember the nurses were mortified that I'd got myself out of bed and into the shower,' she says. 'But I felt there wasn't that much wrong with me. Besides, I hated feeling so horrible and useless and as if I couldn't do anything for myself. I didn't see anything wrong with showering myself.'

That had been totally unexpected. Samantha could walk by now but was very unsteady on her feet and her head was still heavily bandaged to cover up the skin stretched across the hole in her skull with nothing to protect it were she to fall. It reminded Laurence uncomfortably of the fontanelles on the heads of newborn babies – the gaps between the incompletely formed cranial bones. Her wounds under the stitches had to be cleaned and dressings changed several times a day; she had continual treatments for the fractures on her face, in her spine and in her fingers; her right hand was still in a cast; and, she confided to Laurence, she was feeling dizzy nearly all the time.

Because she was so set on getting home as quickly as possible, and then returning to the police force, she feared that total honesty about her medical problems would only delay her departure from hospital. 'So instead of saying anything, she'd just keep on pushing forward, hopeful that everything would just correct itself or dissipate over time,' says Laurence. 'Denial remained one of her best coping tools. From the moment she woke up from her coma, she remained ever-apologetic for being an inconvenience to everyone, refusing medication, saying she didn't need it, and insisting she was right, she'd be fine.'

Sometimes, Laurence would look at her and know she was lying. 'Look, this is me you're talking to,' he'd chide her. 'I don't care what crap we tell everyone else but if you don't tell me the truth, I can't help you.'

But her tactics worked. After just two days in the ward, she was told she was ready to be transferred across the road to the hospital's Sacred Heart rehabilitation unit.

When Judy Cohen arrived at the hospital to visit her that day, she was turned away from intensive care and told that Samantha was now in rehab. Cohen had argued at first that they must be mistaken. She'd seen her the day she came out of the coma, and she was so sick, that just couldn't be right. The staff, however, were adamant. 'Really?' Cohen had asked. 'Are you *sure*? That can't be possible!'

Finally, she'd allowed herself to be redirected and found Samantha walking in the corridor of her new unit. 'I was blown away,' she says. 'I didn't think a human being could ever recover that quickly. But the physio told me she'd been working very hard. When they told her she could walk for half an hour a day on the treadmill, she did it for two to three hours. Trying to limit her doing anything was like a red rag to a bull.'

While moving to rehab signified real progress, Samantha didn't much like her new home. The unit also served as a palliative facility for terminally ill patients, and she didn't enjoy being around so many elderly and sick people, and others with physical and intellectual disabilities. She became increasingly impatient and was often agitated and easily upset. 'She wasn't prepared to take a passive role in her recovery,' says Laurence. 'It became her mission to know everything, she wanted everything done yesterday, and she wanted to get back in control of a life that was totally out of her control. She wanted her life back.'

She'd never had much patience in the first place; now she became annoyed at the people she saw as trying to slow down her progress. 'I felt I could do anything,' she says. 'I knew I had a big hole in my head, but there were a lot of old people around and I kept asking, "Why am I here? I'm not old!"'

The officer in charge of the investigation into her attack, Detective Sergeant Mat Moss, called her regularly. As someone who'd also nearly lost his life in a senseless attack by a violent thug, he felt he understood a little of what she was going through, and the pair bonded over the phone. 'We drew strength from each other,' says Moss. 'I sensed her resolve within the first ten minutes of speaking to her. I felt, She'll be back! I spoke all the time to Laurence too, telling him what was happening with the case.'

She was also visited by Nicky Glenister, the nursing unit manager from the Intensive Care Unit. 'She was was very determined. She's such a strong woman, and a fighter. Usually rehab can last months and months, but it certainly didn't in her case.'

But it was far from plain sailing. One of Samantha's biggest problems was the lack of sleep. Every time she closed her eyes, she was afraid someone might hurt her. 'So it was much easier not to!' she says. Often restless, she'd then start taking walks around the corridors at night, talking to other people who were awake, or sitting in the TV common room as she didn't like to be alone. One night, she pulled on her tracksuit and running shoes, planning to jog on the treadmill in the gym. The night supervisor, however, refused to allow it, as there was no physio available to supervise her. 'So what am I supposed to do?' asked Samantha, instantly riled. 'Wait till you're not watching, then sneak out and go out for a run around the block? What if I get attacked again?' It didn't help that she'd have vivid nightmares whenever she did manage to get to sleep. She'd wake with a start, terrified that someone was going to climb through the window and hurt her.

At that stage, Robin Williams believes she could easily have felt sorry for herself, and become bitter and angry and lost in a world of complaint and misery. But that wasn't her style. 'I never saw her cry about what had happened to her,' she says. 'She just accepted what had happened and channelled all her energy instead into getting better. She was always trying to sneak out of her room in rehab and do some extra exercises or work in the gym. She was full steam ahead.

'Every minute of every day there was a hurdle to overcome and she wasn't even jumping them; she was knocking them down. It was unbelievable.'

* * *

The man responsible for putting Samantha in this position was still behind bars in Sydney.

Police had wanted to charge Roderick Holohan with attempted murder but they were struggling. Even though he'd said he thought he'd killed her, they knew in court they'd have to prove that he'd set out to murder Samantha, that his actions were deliberate and premeditated. In practice, it's one of the toughest offences on the statute books to get a conviction for: how exactly can you prove intent? The police held talks with the Crown Prosecution Service and took advice from some of the top lawyers in town. Everyone debated the various possibilities long and hard.

Another difficulty was that a couple of the main witnesses for the case against Holohan weren't perhaps the kind of people a jury would necessarily warm to. The prostitute who'd previously taken heroin and had sex with Holohan, then had seen him looking for someone to attack with a brick, might not be considered the most trustworthy of characters. Similarly, the man he'd had a conversation with in their shared holding cell might not stand up particularly well under cross-examination.

On the day Samantha went into rehab, police announced the charge against Holohan was being downgraded from 'attempted murder' to 'aggravated armed robbery causing grievous bodily harm'. It felt terribly unfair, and Samantha was disgusted and outraged. But to those involved, there seemed to be no real alternative.

Shortly after yet another battery of tests by neuropsychologists and rehab specialists, Samantha was declared ready for her first short excursion into the outside world. Her friend Sergeant Perri Hayes had brought her a selection of scarves and a choice of two fashionable hats for her to wear to hide her head injuries, and it was agreed that she, together with Laurence and her three old mates from police college, Hayes, Senior Sergeant Belinda Crowe and Sergeant Sam Harrison, would have a wander down Oxford Street to Paddington, with a stop for coffee at a cafe along the way. As well as giving Samantha a breath of fresh air, the hidden purpose of the outing was to see how well she'd react to street noise, mixing with people, and being in a confined space with all the clamour of a busy cafe. The ultimate goal was for her to take everyone's coffee order, then pay for it, and check she'd received the right change.

Progress turned out to be slow, however. Passers-by kept stopping Samantha and asking her how she was, and if they could give her a hug. She insisted on a few detours of her own too, into a couple of little fashion boutiques and shoe shops. In the shops, other customers came over to say hello, while one asked a shop assistant to take a photo of her with Samantha. She was happy to oblige, if not a little baffled at all the attention.

The little group of five then wended their way to the Ampersand Cafe & Bookstore, a funky second-hand bookshop that also serves coffee and food. There, they found a quiet table to share but, in the excitement of the moment, one of Samantha's friends insisted on taking the coffee order and paying. Laurence would have to wait another day to see how his wife would fare in such a task. 'But it was such a positive day,' says Hayes. 'We had a great laugh and we could all tell it was our old Sam who was coming back. She wasn't making outlandish statements anymore, and she was very coherent.

'I think at that stage she'd really started understanding what had happened, and she started saying she didn't like the man who'd done this to her. She's always been a very independent person and we felt a bit worried that she wasn't maybe accepting as much help as she perhaps needed. We also worried that she was losing her independence. But it was early days. It was the first time she'd been out and it was only for about an hour as she tired easily. It was a wonderful time, though.'

After that, Samantha took a few more trips out of the unit. One afternoon, a nurse suggested they go for a walk into the park just down the street, and asked her if she was up to it. Samantha eagerly agreed. The trip took an unexpected turn, however, when a rough-looking man who'd been begging came over to them. 'There was some hobo there, and he came and spoke to them,' says Samantha's dad Vernon Groves. 'The nurse took fright and got very upset. I think she imagined it would be terrifying for Sam. But Sam didn't seem worried in the least. She just told the nurse not to worry, that she'd look after her! It was quite remarkable.'

A week into her time in rehab, arrangements were made for Samantha to visit New South Wales Police Commissioner Andrew Scipione in his city office and to be interviewed by the media. She called Laurence a few hours before she was due to depart to suggest they go shopping on the way so she could finally buy a new handbag to replace the one that had been stolen. Laurence agreed and arrived at the hospital to find Samantha sitting waiting for him by the lifts. As soon as she saw him, she gave him a hug and said, 'Okay, come on, let's go!'

Laurence hesitated. 'Hang on,' he said. 'I have to sign you out.'

Samantha grabbed his hand and went to step in the lift. 'It's all good,' she replied. 'They said I could go.'

The pair drove over to the massive Westfield shopping centre at Bondi Junction. Laurence circled round and round the underground car park to try to find a space close to an entry to the shops so Samantha wouldn't have far to walk. When he finally found one, he went to slip in, but another driver in an old blue Mazda blocked his way. Just as Laurence was about to remonstrate with him, the other man jumped out of his vehicle and walked over to Laurence's open window. 'It's you, isn't it?' he said. 'The police officer whose wife got attacked?' Laurence nodded. The man went on to say how disgusted he was with what had happened, and asked how Samantha was doing.

At that point, Laurence leant back, pointed to the passenger seat and said, 'You can see for yourself, she's right here!'

Samantha smiled, but immediately the man's face crumpled with emotion. 'I think you're just wonderful,' he told her. He then reached into his back pocket, pulled out his wallet and handed Laurence a $50 note.

'Thanks, mate,' said Laurence, immediately trying to hand it back. 'But we don't need your money.'

The man shook his head. 'No, please have some lunch on me,' he replied. At that, he turned back, jumped into his car and drove away, leaving the couple stunned.

They parked, and then took the escalator up into the centre. Samantha looked around curiously. Always a keen shopper before the attack, she'd known her way around the place intimately. Now, she couldn't remember a thing.

One of the first stands they came to was Pie Face where they ordered two coffees and two toasted sandwiches and sat down at the nearest table while they tried to get their bearings. A lot of people kept looking over at them, recognising them from the media stories. When they'd finished their meal, Laurence went to the cash register and pulled out the $50 note he'd just been given to pay.

The person at the counter, however, smiled, waved his hand and said, 'It's alright. Enjoy!' Laurence was again completely taken aback. 'These were new and humbling experiences,' he says. 'We weren't in uniform and we were in a part of Sydney where we did not live or weren't well known . . . or so we thought! The man who'd given me the money seemed like an ordinary Australian family man, driving a pretty clapped-out car, who doubtless appreciated the true value of $50. But he was so generous and went out of his way to do something kind for us. He, together with the man at the pie shop, helped start to restore some of our lost faith in people. It was a mind-blowing experience.'

They walked around the shopping centre for another two hours, buying that new bag, Samantha trying on clothes and the pair talking, but all the time they were aware of people looking, smiling and nodding at them. A few people even stopped them and said, 'You're amazing!' or 'God bless you both.' When the time finally came for them to leave for the commissioner's office, Laurence's phone rang. It was a mate from the riot squad. He wanted to know what time he was going to be home as the guys at work wanted to deliver a new wide-screen plasma TV set they'd just bought them, having noticed during their babysitting duties that their TV at home had given up the ghost while Samantha was in intensive care. 'It was yet another example of the kindness and generosity that we continued to receive everywhere we went at that time, and still do on occasions years later,' says Laurence. 'Things like that have become a big part of our crazy journey.' He then turned his phone back off so he could enjoy his time with his wife uninterrupted.

The couple then made their way to the police executive offices in the city to provide an update on Samantha's progress. Scipione welcomed Samantha warmly. He was delighted to see her back on her feet so quickly and eager to hear if there was anything she needed. 'I remember that day so clearly,' says Scipione. 'She walked into my office and she had some terrible injuries, she wasn't well and she still didn't even have her skull bolted back together properly. But the first thing that struck me was that enormous smile. It was bigger than Luna Park. I realised then that, despite everything, she was well on her way and getting on with it. And one of the first things she said was, "I'm coming back to work, boss!" I smiled back and said, "You go for it!" I felt it would be an honour to have her back on duty.

'What I love about Sam and her story is that she's been through the horrors of that assault and the nightmare of having to lie alone for an hour before she was found, and then went through all the drama of hospital, yet she determined in her own mind early on that she wouldn't let the things that happened to her shape her destiny. It was what she was going to do in response that was going to pave her way in life. She wasn't going to let that creep rob her of her life and future.'

After talking to Scipione and his senior police about how she was going, the Archbishop of Sydney Cardinal George Pell presented Samantha with a set of rosary beads blessed by Pope Benedict when he'd visited Sydney in 2008 for World Youth Day. She was then interviewed by the media. The investigative team working on her assault were still hopeful the publicity might jog someone's memory and they'd come forward with more evidence to help in their prosecution of her case. True to form, Samantha and Laurence then asked for the photos and film to be taken while she was walking. Her brother Jason Groves had advised them on that. 'We wanted the story to be about Sam's recovery, more about getting better than being a smashed-up police officer,' he says. 'So the images were of her walking and talking. Sam didn't want to be seen as a victim. She's never been a victim, and she never will be.'

As Samantha was ushered in to talk to the press, Laurence turned his phone back on. He noticed that over the last two hours he'd received dozens of calls, texts and emails. As he stared, puzzled, at his phone, one of the commissioner's staff members came over and said Kings Cross police station had been phoning her office too to try to get hold of him.

He excused himself, and made a couple of calls to find out what had been going on. It turned out that Sacred Heart had called the police at Kings Cross to report Samantha as a missing person. Apparently she hadn't signed herself out and, in the absence of any paperwork – and the patient herself – hospital staff had panicked. So it seemed Samantha had finally achieved her dearest wish: her escape from her 'jail'.

Samantha's assailant Roderick Holohan, now beginning to appreciate he could be facing a lengthy spell in jail himself, was beginning to shift from a mood of eager cooperation to sullen anger and self-pity.

The head of the investigation, Detective Sergeant Mat Moss, spoke to him at the Blacktown police station cells. He delivered the official caution that he wasn't obliged to say or do anything, as anything he did would be recorded and later used in evidence. 'Do you understand that?' he asked.

'Yeah,' replied Holohan. 'I know, man. Have you seen today's paper?' It appeared he'd just seen Sydney's *Daily Telegraph*, containing the interview with Samantha and photographs. 'All the time, years I've done inside, I used to give it to cunts like that,' he continued. 'And now I'm one of them. I've had to put myself into protection. My family wants nothing to fuckin' do with me. I can't believe what I've done.' He started to cry.

Moss paused. 'Rod, I don't know what to say to you.' But then he came swiftly to the point of the conversation. 'Would you be prepared to participate in an identification line-up with respect to this matter?'

Although Holohan had said he was appalled at what he'd done, that concern didn't seem to extend to further helping the investigation. 'I've done enough,' he replied. 'No, man, you know I did it. Just leave me in the cell.'

Now Samantha had finally accepted what had happened to her on that dark morning around Kings Cross, she started to ask questions in earnest about the attack. Those questions weren't so much about her assailant or her injuries, however. They were more about whether she could have done anything to avoid the brutal bashing. She'd always considered herself strong, smart and fit, with fast reactions, a sixth sense for when danger might be lurking and well-honed skills in hand-to-hand self-defence, sailing through every level of advanced Operations Support Group tests and training. This event had shattered her self-confidence.

Everyone around her knew, however, that there was nothing she could have done when taken by surprise by a desperate junkie sneaking up on her in the pitch-black from behind, armed with a weapon and not hesitating to use it. Most other people in her position simply wouldn't have survived.

Kings Cross Superintendent Tony Crandell felt enormously sympathetic. 'She was very, very interested in what the physical evidence had to say about whether she'd fought her attacker off,' he says. 'That's her! Any other victim would say, "I was jumped, and that was a cowardly way to attack someone." Anybody can go and pick somebody out of a random crowd and rush them, but she wanted to be sure that she had fought her attacker off and she had attempted to defend herself. There certainly were defensive wounds and she had a badly battered hand to show how hard she defended herself. Believe it or not, I actually think that gave her solace.'

Yet it would still take her a long time to accept that. Perri Hayes says it made her angry for a long time afterwards. 'I think she'll always have a little bit of anger about it because she's so fiercely independent. The fact that he made her feel vulnerable – through no fault of her own – didn't sit right with her. She felt that maybe in some way she may have allowed it to happen. But that's not right. There's no way.'

It did cause her a lot of angst, though, and was to lead to a long period of introspection. As she prepared to leave rehab on Saturday 4 June, after just eight days there rather than the couple of months originally intended, she was still mulling it over.

'To be honest, I never went through that stage of thinking, Why me?' says Samantha. 'I spent much more time thinking, Why couldn't I have fought him off? Why did I have so many injuries? It took me a long time to comprehend that he'd attacked me from behind so I couldn't protect myself. Apparently, he kept going because I wouldn't let go of my bag. So that's good. I wouldn't let him have it. I wouldn't have *ever* let him have it!'

As she turned the situation over and over again in her mind, her brother Jason sympathised with her turmoil. 'She looked at the situation from every angle,' he says. 'She deliberately tried to put the incident to the back of her mind but, deeper down, she looked at it and examined it to check and address every possible chink in her armour. Every possible chink.'

# Chapter 15
# NOT COPING ISN'T AN OPTION

Samantha Barlow's homecoming was a triumph after spending such a short time in hospital, but it was also a time of quiet sadness. As Laurence drove through the streets surrounding their home on Saturday 4 June, Samantha chatted excitedly, thrilled she was at last on her way. But as he rounded the last bend and drove up the driveway to their home, she suddenly fell silent. She didn't recognise a thing.

As she got out of the car and walked to the front door, it was as if she were approaching the house of a stranger. When Laurence opened the door and it still didn't feel at all familiar, she started to get upset. She went in and walked around like a guest in someone else's house, or a prospective purchaser checking out a possible buy. They'd had the house built on the site of an old redbrick cottage she'd owned, and she'd chosen the kitchen and bathrooms, as well as every tile, light fitting, paint colour, carpet and finish. Yet now, six months after they'd moved in, she had no memory of any of it.

'Later, we could see the funny side,' says Laurence. 'Sam was walking around the house, saying how nice the windows or architraves were, and how much she liked the layout and what a great kitchen the house had. But of course she was going to like it – she'd selected everything! Not recognising it did feel like a major setback. But it wasn't until the next few weeks and months that some of the difficulties became apparent. She'd packed away everything for the move there and we're still, four years later, looking for where she might have put some of those things!'

Her friends felt for her. 'She was very confused about where she lived,' says Senior Sergeant Belinda Crowe. 'It was a brand-new house and they'd only just moved in, which probably made it even harder. She said she felt like a stranger in her own house, which must have been so difficult, and upsetting.'

Samantha says even today the house gives her the occasional surprise. She'll be searching for something for the children, and will come upon some good crockery she'd forgotten she had. 'I just didn't have any memory of it all,' she says. 'Maybe I was looking for the old house that used to be here, rather than the new one we'd built. Who knows?'

Yet by far the toughest aspect of Samantha's return home was the continuing level of care she needed. She was still very frail, physically and emotionally, had little energy and found even the smallest of tasks very difficult, although she was determined to do as much for herself as she could. That led to a lot of frustration. She couldn't pick up either of the children because of her vertigo, and the pain from her injuries made it hard to play with them. 'I think I thought I was fine from day one, but I wasn't,' she says now. 'It probably took longer for me to start feeling okay again than I admitted.'

As well, when she was in hospital, she'd been tended by trained doctors, nurses and specialists twenty-four hours a day, seven days a week. While Laurence had watched what they were doing, had asked lots of questions and had tried to learn everything he could from them, he was now the person solely responsible for his wife's recovery. He was qualified in first aid and was an accredited fitness leader with the police force, but nothing could have really prepared him for this. He felt completely underprepared and overwhelmed.

He also had Lily and Ben to care for, two children who had now become much more needy because of the prolonged period of time they'd had without their mum, and a sizeable chunk with their dad absent too. At the same time, Laurence still wasn't well himself. The tonsillitis hadn't gone away and had by now given him swollen glands, neck ache, a high temperature, joint pain, blurred vision and headaches, he had the back pain from the bulging discs, and he felt as though his tinnitus, the ringing in his ears, was steadily driving him mad. Thankfully, however, the lump on his hip had been surgically removed and was found to be a benign cyst.

'It seemed ironic that, at the point in my life where I was being asked to step up and perform like never before, my body was falling apart,' he says. 'But what do you do? You have a choice: either you get upset, whinge and blame everyone else for your problems or you just man up, suck it up and get on with it. Not coping was never an option. Everyone possesses reserves of strength and energy that we're not aware of until tested. What separates survivors from victims is between your ears. And no matter how I felt, or how tough I was doing it, nothing could compare with what my wife had just gone through, and was now living through.'

Laurence's nursing duties began immediately. The back of Samantha's head was still a mess of cuts oozing clear fluid as the skin continued to heal over the hole in her scalp, which pulsed with every heartbeat. She didn't want to know what it looked like, and has still never looked at any photos of her head from those early days. But Laurence had to examine it hourly for the next few months, checking for any signs of infection or new blood. For the first ten days, he also had to change the dressings, bathe and clean out the scars and then smother them in ointment several times a day. It was always painful for Samantha, particularly as the area became terribly itchy with the scars knitting and her hair now beginning to grow back on the flap of skin covering the hole.

It had been a condition of Samantha's early release from rehab that she continue her treatment as an outpatient, and the coordinating rehab expert had drawn up a seemingly endless list of medical professionals she had to see. As well as treatment for her physical injuries, she also had to see people for her loss of memory and sense of taste and smell, constant headaches, back pain and muscular spasms, stress-induced psoriasis over her face and torso, insomnia – since she was typically sleeping only two to three hours a night – nightmares and psychiatric issues.

The first few weeks at home blurred into an almost continual round of appointments with the neurosurgical team, a neuropsychologist, rehab specialists, a forensic psychiatrist, a Feldenkrais practitioner who was an expert in reducing pain and improving mobility through a specialised technique of combining movement, posture and breathing, a vestibular physiotherapist to help with balance and dizziness, a remedial hand therapist, a chiropractor, a remedial masseuse, an ear, nose and throat specialist, a dental surgeon, an ophthalmologist, a plastic surgeon, a dermatologist, a psychologist and a GP. It wasn't unusual to have as many as twenty appointments a week, while the pair also had to make themselves available to police investigators and welfare officers, and participate in any media interviews the police asked them to do.

Reluctantly, Samantha and Laurence agreed to put the children into full-time day care to save them being dragged around to all the appointments and having to either watch their mum being treated, or sit in all the waiting rooms. It proved hugely expensive but the then New South Wales Police Minister Tony Kelly, supported by the shadow minister Mike Gallacher, a former police officer himself who later became the minister, approved some funds for the family and a Federal Government scheme provided a little more.

But financially, it was proving tough. Three weeks after Samantha's release from hospital, the couple had to visit their bank and ask for more money to cover their expenses, by refinancing their house – something they ended up doing no fewer than three times. They'd considered selling their house and buying something smaller and cheaper, to help make ends meet, but knew another move would prove even more stressful for the children, and feel to them like they'd be conceding another major round to Samantha's assailant. And they wanted to avoid that at all costs.

'Our reality was an endless array of doctors' visits, two emotionally confused and emotionally drained children exhibiting signs of stress, and two adults' careers down the toilet and heading for financial ruin,' says Laurence. 'Then there were the psychological issues and the fact we were living in each other's pockets twenty-four hours a day. But now, on top of these, financial stresses became a real problem for us.'

The couple had assumed Samantha would be entitled to significant financial compensation for what had happened to her, and that all treatments would be approved and paid for by the insurance company, leaving them free to focus on her physical and mental recovery. That couldn't have been further from the truth. They visited their solicitor and were told that they could expect a payment from the New South Wales Government's Attorney-General & Justice Department of only between $7500 and $50000 for being a victim of violence, and that they shouldn't bank on getting much from the New South Wales workers compensation scheme – definitely less than a year's salary – as it was broke. What's more, he told them, it would be many years before her matter would be determined and even longer before it was paid. Indeed, at the time of writing, four and a half years on from the attack, they still haven't received a cent.

'Being told that broke Sam's heart,' says Laurence. 'Had she been in a car accident, existing compensation schemes would have provided better cover and entitlements, but the only option left for us became a civil suit against the criminal who attacked her. And how do you get money from a junkie who's spent most of his life in jail? Unfortunately for us, it's not multimillionaires and company CEOs who tend to loiter in dark alleys, take heroin and attack people on their way to work.

'But giving up and *not* going back to work was never an option for Sam. It's all she thought about, twenty-four hours a day. It kept her alive during the dark moments, both in hospital and now she was at home.'

Samantha's neurosurgeon Dr Vanessa Perotti was surprised at what a rapid recovery she was making. 'People with those type of injuries generally don't do as well as she did,' she says. Usually, you only see those kind of injuries in young men who've had car accidents. They'll spend two years in rehab and still be in wheelchairs.

'Probably Sam and Lauren Huxley are the only two people I've seen with these kind of injuries who've ended up going home. But Sam was always strong. Early on, she'd tried to pull out the tube they'd put in. And to have dragged herself towards the road the morning she was attacked . . . I'm stunned at how strong she was.'

In November 2009, Samantha had to return to hospital to have a titanium plate bolted into her skull to replace the section of bone that had been shattered and surgically removed in the first operation. The surgery went without a hitch, with neurosurgeon Dr Malcolm Pell cutting along a large part of the previous scar to reopen her head, lifting a big flap of skin, inserting the plate into position and then returning the flap. Samantha hated the thought of the plate inside her head and shuddered every time she felt it through her skin, but the biggest sacrifice on the day was the loss of the hair that had begun to grow again.

'Once the swelling to Sam's brain subsided, the top of her head became quite sunken in,' says Dr Pell. 'As well, we wanted to protect her brain. If she fell, there was no bone in one area of her skull to stop it getting injured again. So the titanium plate covered the brain to protect it and it's a good material as you can X-ray through it, it's light and it's strong and malleable. There were no problems at all with the cranioplasty. Sam's a young, very fit, very motivated person with a Type A personality. She was always very determined to make a full recovery, which helped her, and always talked about returning to work. I'd say, "Let's see how things go," but for her, it wasn't a question of *if*; it was always *when*.'

On New Year's Eve 2009, she went to another hospital, this time closer to home at St George Hospital in Kogarah, where Lily and Ben had both been born, to have more surgery on her face and nose. Before she went in, the pair booked a holiday to Western Australia and the Northern Territory, as something to look forward to once the rounds of surgery were over. Samantha wanted to get away for another reason too. Just a couple of months after coming home from hospital, her beloved Shar-Pei, Maddie, had died, and she was still reeling from that. For 11 years, woman and dog had been inseparable, she regarded her as the first of her children, and the pair doted on each other. She was devastated when Maddie became so sick in her old age, and she had finally to say goodbye. 'She was my Maddie-moo, a princess, the best dog in the world,' says Samantha, who keeps her ashes in an urn. 'I still can't look at a Sharpei without getting a tear in my eye.'

But, happily, this latest series of treatments, including a rhinoplasty to straighten her nose and dermal fillers for her scars, went well, too.

Her plastic surgeon Dr Damian Marucci had seen her a few months before, when he'd removed the K-wires from her fingers, and was happy with how the rhinoplasty had gone. 'Her nose had deviated to one side so we fixed that and all her other scars had settled and looked good,' he says. 'Often, with trauma injuries, a lot of it is out of your hands. The patient presents to you with a particular deformity or problem, and your job is to try to get things back to as close to normal as possible. Sam's broken nose was a bit of a mess but thankfully she had a very good result. I enjoyed dealing with her. She always had a fantastic attitude, very optimistic, never complained and approached everything in a very proactive way. I feel it's been a real honour to have been involved in her care.'

Early in the new year, Samantha, Laurence and the children finally took off to have a few weeks' break in an attempt to take some time out, regroup and refresh after such a tough time. The trip was partly funded by money donated by police in Chatswood and the New South Wales Police Association, which had both organised fundraising activities for them. 'It was so kind of them,' says Samantha. 'They'll never really know how much it was appreciated!' The little family visited Perth, Margaret River, Broome and finally Darwin and Litchfield National Park, before returning home, ready to face whatever else waited in store.

* * *

Cards and letters continued to flood in for Samantha and journalists were still constantly asking for interviews. She was invited onto the TV show *A Current Affair* to speak about what the couple were going through and, afterwards, the switchboard at the TV station lit up with callers wanting to express their sympathy and pass on their congratulations and admiration. *Woman's Day* magazine also interviewed them, and photographed the whole family, Samantha with her hair just starting to regrow and her right hand strapped up in a splint. It was a good way of letting all the people who'd been kind enough to get in touch know they were doing okay; they were battling through.

Both Samantha and Laurence also appeared at a press conference to thank the two paramedics, Michael Rundle and Seth Leon, who'd first gone to her aid. 'Because of the amazing work they did on May 13 last year, I am able to stand here and thank them personally for the work they did,' she told everyone. Rundle and Leon, as well as St Vincent's Hospital Intensive Care Unit nursing manager Nicky Glenister, were all presented with certificates of appreciation from Dave Owens, in the role of acting commissioner. What's more, Samantha informed the crowd, she was determined one day to go back to work, and was optimistic that, one day, that would happen.

Sometimes, however, that optimism was hard to keep up. Samantha had previously been a great sleeper, someone who relished her time in bed. Now both she and Laurence slept barely two or three hours a night. At times she'd be woken by nightmares, at others by the constant dizziness that prevented her even from lying flat. Instead, she sat up at a 45-degree angle each night, hoping she'd be able to get some rest. Often she and Laurence would put the kids to bed, and then stay up most of the night watching their new TV or DVDs, while doing over and over again the exercises she'd been given by her various physios. 'That TV kept us sane,' says Laurence. 'It was a cheap and safe way of switching off, watching movies, sports or re-runs of favourite TV shows such as the drama about the US military *The Unit*, which I saw so many times, I felt I'd enlisted in the army.' As the sun came up, they'd have a shower, get dressed, wake the kids up and drop them off at day care, then set off on another round of appointments. Keeping so busy had one great advantage. It stopped either of them having time for too much introspection and lapsing into depression.

After a few visits to the dentist, Samantha's teeth were repaired, and the ophthalmologist required only a couple of sessions before declaring her vision was satisfactory too. She was still constantly in a great deal of pain, however, and that took much longer to abate. As well as the skull fractures, there'd also been fractures to the top vertebrae in her neck, which gave her agonising back pain, exacerbated by the time spent lying on her back in hospital, and then lying at the 45-degree angle at home. For this, there were long periods of deep tissue massage, physiotherapy and chiropractic.

Not as much could be done about her senses of smell and of taste, which had both vanished. Dr Pell told her it was often a waiting game. 'The loss of the sense of smell is quite common, even with much more minor brain injuries,' he says. 'The nerves for smell are very sensitive and, with those, you lose the taste sensation too as they're so closely connected. They can return, but often don't.' He told Samantha to be patient, and they might come back of their own accord.

She missed them, though. She'd always enjoyed food but now that was lost to her. Her favourite evening snack had always been a plate of cheese and a glass of red wine. Now when she tried them, she may as well have been eating cardboard and drinking water. She'd also loved cooking, coming from a long line of great cooks, with recipes passed down from her grandmother who'd lived with the family when she was younger. Now it became much more difficult as she was unable to taste her dishes as she went along, and she had no idea if something was burning on the stove until she saw the smoke. After a while, Laurence became too nervous to leave her alone in the kitchen. Even with Ben, it was hard to know when he needed a fresh nappy. Often Lily would be a great help, screwing up her nose and declaring that her little brother was stinky and needed to be changed. 'But I wasn't allowed to pick Ben up, so I wasn't supposed to even change his nappy,' says Samantha. 'So instead, I worked out a way of doing it on the floor.'

She also had to work hard to get over the fear of being attacked again. 'The fear of someone breaking into her hospital room, and later our house after she came home, and hurting her was something she didn't recover from for well over a year,' says Laurence. 'Even after that, it was still the cause of nightmares, and continues to be today. The first year after she returned home we would put the house alarm on downstairs in an attempt to moderate her anxiety.'

Leaving the house was also nerve-racking, which proved difficult with the couple having to spend so much time out of the house seeing specialists. Her brother Jason, often on the phone to her from London, especially in the early hours when she was unable to sleep, wished there was more he could do for her. 'She'd say every time she walked down the street, she worried about any footsteps behind her,' he says. 'If she walked with Laurence, it would be better. But she'd put a brave face on it and say that she'd just have to get used to that again.'

She did resent it, though. 'I used to be a very outgoing, happy and carefree kind of person, but that's been taken from me,' she says. 'Before the assault, I didn't have any fear. I'd do my job without worrying for my own security, and I'd go out without a care in the world. But now I can't go anywhere without Laurence as my personal bodyguard, and I spend my nights checking all the doors and windows to make sure no one can get into the house, and then the rooms and behind doors to make sure no one's already there. I don't feel safe in my own house. I'd love to live in a fort and control who comes in and out.'

Treatment to her shattered hand took a great deal of time. Samantha knew that if she were to stand any chance of getting back to work, she'd have to get her hand back to working normally. At that point, it was horribly deformed. The first, second and fourth fingers on her right hand had each been surgically rebuilt yet were all pointing in different directions, and she was fast reaching the cut-off point where permanent damage would set in. The splint she'd been wearing was designed to keep her hand immobilised and protected, but not to restore movement to the damaged area. Most imagined, looking at her hand, that the only use for it would be as a support to her left. Naturally right-handed, she was already becoming quite adept at signing her name with her left.

On Samantha's first appointment with a hand therapist, her hand was still very swollen and covered in scars where the fingers had been reattached. There was little that could be done except gentle massage, the introduction of new strapping techniques and silicone patches to cover the scar tissue while moulds were taken of the damaged area to create new day and night splints. The therapist hoped to improve the quality of her life with a better-functioning hand; Samantha's aim was much higher.

Soon, she was set on a program of low-intensity, high-repetition exercises six times a day where she had to move each of the fingers through a full range of movement, independently of each other. After a while, she moved on to working with putty similar to children's Play-Doh; it came in different colours based on density and she had to squeeze and manoeuvre it to help the feeling return in her hand. Lily would sit and copy her, doing the same exercises, proudly boasting to Laurence that she was 'helping Mummy'.

That brought painfully back to the couple how much this must all be affecting their children, but there didn't seem to be any way to manage the situation better. Each day Lily would climb onto their bed for a cuddle and innocently ask, 'Do we have to go the doctors today?' She never complained but the disappointment in her voice was obvious. If the kids came along, to try to make it up to them, they'd do as many fun things as they could between appointments, like a trip to the park, the beach or a swimming pool, and maybe have a DVD on in the car on their way. 'It's not as if they had the back garden to play in at home anyway,' says Samantha. 'That was still just dirt, and it would have been dangerous to have let them out in that.' Even today, four years later, they still attempt to make doctors' appointments when the kids are at day care or school. 'The idea is to protect them from worrying about Mummy,' says Laurence. 'It also allows them to be kids and focus on the important things like playing, drawing, and fighting with each other!'

It wasn't long before Samantha and Laurence fell into a routine of taking the exercise charts, splints, buckets and putty with them wherever they went, stopping to do rehab on the side of the road on their way to other appointments, as they had a coffee, even while sitting in waiting rooms to see other doctors, with additional sessions all through the night as they sat and watched TV. Later, hot water became another essential part of the treatment. The therapist showed Laurence how to strap Samantha's hand into a claw-like position as tightly as she could tolerate and she would then plunge her hand into hot water for fifteen minutes at a time, four to six times a day. She'd then go through her stretching exercises before it would be strapped up again into one of the tailored splints.

Her good police mate Senior Sergeant Belinda Crowe called round one day to visit, and watched her, appalled, as she went through some of her hand exercises. 'She'd put on all this strapping, and then drop her hand into near-boiling water!' she says. 'It looked so painful. It was about stretching the tendons out but I could see she was in dreadful pain while she did it.'

Further on, Samantha progressed to immersing her hand in a bucket of uncooked rice to re-sensitise her fingers, particularly the fingertips. After a few surprisingly painful sessions, they had to hide plastic beads, paper clips and hair clips in the rice, and she'd have to search through the rice by feel, to locate and pick them up with her fingertips. 'My philosophy was always: one day at a time, fix it and then move on,' she says. 'I'd give it 200 per cent every time. Never once did I think, No I won't do my exercises tonight. I had no option. If I wanted to get better, I knew I just had to work harder. I felt there was nothing I couldn't do if I worked hard enough.'

As the weeks turned into months, there were review sessions with the hand therapist and the plastic surgeon, different strapping techniques and new splints moulded to fit Samantha's hand: some to hold the fingers together tightly, some to separate them and others to force them into different positions. Laurence was also able to make a contribution. As the chief weapons instructor at Goulburn, he'd found the greatest singular cause of failure to shoot well, particularly in women, was an inability to maintain their wrists locked in the firing position as the trigger is pulled back, thus moving it off target. To help, he'd often recommend that his students do push-ups on their knuckles, where the wrist replicated the firing position, to build and strengthen the small muscles of the fingers, wrists and forearms. For Samantha, these also forced her fingers to bend those last few millimetres into position under her body weight. He also gave her a series of other exercises with weights to help, and bought a spring-loaded wrist-strengthener that allowed her to copy the movement of a trigger, which she carried in her pocket all day long.

'Sam's dogged determination and never-never-never-say-die attitude delivered results that no one could ever have anticipated at the start of the process,' Laurence says. 'After about six months, Sam's right-hand strength had recovered to equal that of the average woman. But that wasn't good enough in Sam's eyes. It was still well below what her left hand was capable of and less than what would be required to rejoin the police's Operations Support Group at some time in the future, ready for fights, wrestles, standing and holding a riot shield, applying handcuffs, and using a gun or a taser. But after about a year of treatment building up to a personal best dead-lift that was one and a half times her body weight, Sam's hand had regained sufficient movement and strength to complete normal everyday functions, and more. It was quite miraculous.'

All the time, there were still myriad other specialists to see. The ongoing dizziness was still plaguing Samantha, and she'd been denied permission to drive, something she'd always loved. She was diagnosed with benign paroxysmal positional vertigo, a dizziness related to something wrong in the inner ear that comes and goes, often without a direct cause, and was referred to a vestibular physiotherapist. He gave her head and balance movements, and instructed Laurence on how he could help her do them at home, too. By the end of the first session, she'd felt an improvement and on the way out, she looked at his appointments book and told him to put her in it every morning at 8 a.m. for the next month. She also practised the movements at home an extra four or five times a day. The exercises increased Samantha's back pain, but she compensated for that by doing more therapy in the pool.

Stress-induced psoriasis had broken out in hive-like welts across Samantha's back, torso, arms, legs, neck and face. They were itchy and embarrassing as they were impossible to hide, particularly when she did therapy at the pool or rehab sessions at the gym. For this, she had to undergo infra-red ray treatment at a skin clinic, with sessions lengthening from a couple of seconds to several minutes a day. Samantha was eventually able to tolerate exposure and intensity among the highest levels offered by the clinic. She also had to use an expensive brand of cream all over her body to soothe the psoriasis, as well as help heal the scarring faster.

'It was incredible,' says her friend Robin Williams. 'She'd be going through all this, but there wasn't any self-pity there. It was all about just getting through it.' In fact, the only time she saw Samantha cry was when the news came through that the court case against her attacker had been delayed. Samantha had been ready for it, hoping it would give her some closure. 'She'd been waiting and waiting and waiting and I think it was the tension that finally got to her,' says Williams. 'That was probably the only time in the whole period she cried.'

Another police friend, Senior Constable Suzie Schwass, visited her and marvelled at her capacity to keep going. 'She was quite amazing,' she says. 'You couldn't imagine the extent of her injuries, but she never complained or felt sorry for herself. She's such an unassuming person but she had an incredible spirit to get through it all. She's my hero.'

* * *

However tough Samantha's fight to get her health back was, it paled beside the battles with the insurance companies to get them to pay for the treatments she needed. With every request, despite being given long letters from her doctors and specialists attesting to how critical they were to her recovery, the companies subjected her to their own series of questionnaires, interviews and examinations. Usually, they'd end in weeks of playing phone-tag and heated arguments. But even then, they'd often knock back applications.

'When the request was made for deep tissue massage, physiotherapy and chiropractic treatments, you would have thought we'd asked them to agree to cut off one of their own limbs – and without anaesthetic,' says Laurence. 'We were told approval might come for one at a time, so we'd have to choose. So we finally chose for them to pay for one, and we paid for the rest. We decided very early in Sam's recovery that if a doctor or a treatment-provider recommended something, we'd do it, whether or not the insurance company approved and paid. If we'd waited for them, Sam would probably still have been in a wheelchair.

'But the daily battles were so ridiculous, they would have been funny if we weren't living through it. A leading psychiatrist in Sydney would give us a massive report that a newly qualified, twenty-year-old OH&S assessor with the insurance company would then reject. Every couple of months the company would reduce their level of support and I would end up in a screaming match with them. We'd then have to ask our doctors for additional reports, and go through all the assessments again, as there was no right of appeal to any third party. It tore my heart out to watch the decline in Sam's spirit every time a request was knocked back or, as she put it, she was "forced to perform like a circus monkey" for another report, feeling like she was being called a liar when she said she needed a particular treatment. Sometimes, we'd just give up and pay for it ourselves.'

It made it even harder that with any sign of improvement in Samantha's condition, financial aid would immediately be cut. She couldn't understand it, assuming it would be in everyone's interests if she regained her health and was able to get back to work and resume paying insurance premiums, rather than claiming. 'The first time on the phone to them, I'd be polite,' she says. 'The second time, I might have a bit of attitude. And the third, I'd have a go. I'd find it traumatic, having to go over and over what had happened, and the extent of my injuries, each time. It seemed to be quite obvious that I wasn't making up a story about being assaulted and getting injured, and it's not like I'd spent time shopping around for doctors when I'd been taken to hospital. I was in a coma – how could I?'

The couple tried to put a fresh spin on the difficulties by using them instead to harden their resolve to get through it. 'In the end, you just have to suck it up and move on,' says Samantha. 'You have to keep on looking forward.' They used their experience to help others, too, with Laurence visiting the parents of another policewoman, Constable Sarah Maxwell, who had been admitted to the same Intensive Care Unit with massive head injuries after being hit by a car while trying to break up a brawl. He was able to reassure them she was in the best hands possible, and talk about the challenges she might face when she came out.

Back home in the garden, 'helped' by Lily and Ben, Laurence dug a hole and planted a Gymea lily. It was the flower he and the wardsman had discussed when Samantha came out of her coma. Every time they felt it was all becoming too much, the sight of the lily would make them feel thankful, all over again, that they'd actually survived.

# Chapter 16
# STARING THE ENEMY DOWN

It was the moment Samantha Barlow had been waiting for ever since she'd first emerged from her coma and understood she'd been attacked. She'd dreamt about this day, planned for it and psyched herself mentally. Now it had finally arrived and she looked at the figure sitting across from her in the courtroom, his shoulders hunched, staring at the floor.

She was disappointed by what she saw. She'd tried not to think too much about Roderick Holohan in the eighteen months since the attack because she didn't want to give him that satisfaction. Besides, she had to preserve all her energy for getting better. But now he was there, she viewed the sinewy Aboriginal man in the dock of the New South Wales Downing Centre District Court with disdain.

'I had no recollection of what he looked like and I deliberately didn't watch any news reports about him,' says Samantha. 'But I'd imagined him to have been a bigger man, considering he'd caused so much damage. He probably looked better in court than he had outside, though, after all those good meals in prison. And I suppose it was all about drug-induced rage and greed rather than size. That can give people incredible strength.'

It was Friday 12 November 2010 and Samantha was finally confronting her attacker. In May, Holohan had pleaded guilty to the new charge of robbery while armed with an offensive weapon, causing grievous bodily harm – a deal struck with the prosecution. Samantha was still seething about the deal, and it had sparked public outrage in the press, on talkback radio and on social media. The hearing had then been set down for June but had been postponed at the last minute, only adding to her anger. 'In his interview with the police, he said he only stopped hitting me because he thought he'd killed me,' says Samantha. 'Then they changed the charge without asking me. I was just told after the fact that they'd done a plea deal. They might have been trying to save me the trouble of testifying and the stress of being cross-examined, but I would much rather have gone to trial and done that for the proper charge. Then they said I looked too well to win a jury's sympathy! But I only got better through my own efforts. It doesn't mean I didn't receive those injuries.'

On the outside, Samantha and Laurence looked like two normal people who'd overcome their obstacles, but in reality they were still locked in grim battles to get Samantha healthy again as well as battles against the insurance company, the compensation authorities and, now, Holohan. They were broke and living on three different credit cards to survive, with the prospect of losing their house at any time. In addition, they'd received legal advice that any attempt to sue the NSW State Parole Authority  for failing to meet its duty of care by not enforcing the parole conditions placed on Samantha's attacker, and not locking him back up the moment he'd broken them, was unlikely to succeeed. Then they'd definitely lose their house paying the costs.

Their only hope for the future appeared to lie in beating the odds to put this all behind them, and both getting back to work.

But for the moment, Samantha was now ready to deliver her victim impact statement to the court and stare down the man who'd cost her the life she'd known and loved, but who – despite his best efforts – couldn't rob her of her future. 'Look at him,' she whispered to Laurence. 'He's nothing. I can do this.' She rose to her feet slowly when the judge beckoned to her and walked over to the witness box. Judge Colin Charteris had previously asked her if she wanted Laurence to read the statement, or wanted him to sit beside her in the box, but she'd declined. She'd spent too much time preparing for this moment.

The evening before, she'd been outraged when Holohan's legal team had demanded she amend her victim impact statement in line with only the facts of the case he admitted. She'd been powerless to refuse. But now, at last, was her time to tell the court what this man had done to her, and cost her. Her knuckles were white from having been squeezing Laurence's hand so tightly. She looked at the judge, the bar table, the media box overflowing with journalists. Then she looked straight at Holohan's face. He was still concentrating on the floor.

She took a deep breath, and began. 'My life completely changed on Wednesday 13 May 2009,' she told the court in a clear, unfaltering voice. 'I went from being a confident, fit, healthy wife and mother of two small children, a daughter aged two and a son seven months old, to a person who almost, and should have, died from the horrific injuries I received from the defendant on that day . . . I was brutally attacked by the defendant and left lying in Arthur Park with multiple injuries. I was left for dead . . .

'The tremendous amount of trauma this caused my husband, children and parents can[not] and never will be understood by anyone. This still, and will always, cause them a significant amount of pain as they didn't know what my prognosis was and what my permanent injuries would be. To have received such horrific injuries at such a young age and through absolutely no provocation from myself towards the defendant is unbelievable . . .'

As she spoke, she glanced at Holohan, daring him to meet her eyes. But his remained fixed resolutely on the ground in front of him. There wasn't any other sound in the court as Judge Charteris listened intently to Samantha outlining the injuries she'd received that day, how no one had stopped to help her as she lay critically injured in the park, her eventual rescue by the police and ambulance officers, and the struggles she'd faced every day since. The last fifteen months, she said, had been a living hell and a nightmare.

'I didn't want to go anywhere by myself because I had a fear of someone else attacking me. I felt weak and vulnerable . . . I couldn't look at the open fresh wounds and I still haven't. It caused, and will always cause me, too much stress to see what the defendant actually did to my head and skull. It causes me continual headaches and flashbacks. My children had to be placed into day care five days a week so I could attend all my doctors' appointments and try to complete as much rehabilitation as possible. No parent wants to place their children, especially when they are so young, in day care five days a week when there was such upheaval to their and our lives. That is when children need their parents most and I was unable to give them that attention because I had such significant injuries and the amount of rehabilitation that I completed daily was tremendous.'

There was a soft murmur in the room as she said how she'd helped people all her life, first through surf lifesaving then as a police officer, frequently putting her own life at risk to save others. The rows of blue in the public gallery nodded in affirmation. Laurence smiled encouragingly at her. 'This incident has taken my old life from me, and I have been forced to rebuild myself into the person I used to be,' she said.

Now came the hardest part. She continued in as strong a voice as she could to outline the agony of going from being a completely self-sufficient person, a wife, the mother of two small children, and a person with a demanding career, to someone unable to do anything for herself. 'Prior to being attacked, I was a very carefree person and had no fears or worries,' she said. 'I was the one who enjoyed helping others both through work, friendships and being an active member of my community. I found it extremely difficult being the person who actually needed the help.

'I still find it traumatising accepting that I was actually the victim and not someone else. I have always been the helper and the person who responded to people's injuries and offered my utmost support and guidance. However, until something like this happens to you, which I wouldn't wish on anyone, you can never begin to even understand it – let alone try and relate to the incident or the injuries inflicted by the defendant.'

Yet it wasn't until she started talking about her dream to have three children that her voice finally began to crack with emotion. She'd hoped to have another baby in 2010, she said, but now she doubted that her body could ever physically or mentally cope with childbirth. 'This is extremely painful and upsetting to have to come to terms with, when this whole incident was caused by the defendant and [he has] therefore basically taken any decisions on my future directly out of my hands.

'These injuries continue to affect mine and my family's futures beyond any possible comprehension. The enormity of the defendant's actions both on my body the day he attacked me and how they continue to affect my day-to-day life and future are catastrophic.

The physical scars, complete loss of smell and taste, mental images and flashbacks are continual reminders. Not even an hour goes past without constant thoughts of my injuries and images of my brutal attack flood my mind. There is nothing peaceful about my life or future with these images constantly plaguing me.'

Tears had now started running down Samantha's face, and she choked back a sob. The judge leant over and asked her if she'd like a break. She nodded silently, and walked outside. Laurence joined her there. 'You're doing great,' he told her, putting his arm around her shoulders. 'Now finish it off. Leave nothing in the tank. This is the only chance we get!' She looked at him and forced a smile. She knew he was right. She took a few more deep breaths, set her shoulders and readied herself to get straight back into the fray.

By the time she walked back into the courtroom, she was fully composed. She continued her speech where she'd left off, saying her battle to get her health back was because she was determined both to get herself better, and to not let the defendant continue to ruin her life. 'I wanted my family back and try to get them to see me how they used to – even though I know deep down that I'm not the same person,' she said. 'My value system has completely changed and I have to enjoy and appreciate every aspect of my family because I know how simply it can all be taken from you in an instant by the intent and actions of any violent, drug-dependent person.'

She still kept looking over at Holohan, hoping that her words might pierce something deep within him. But he didn't stir. He now had his head in his hands and didn't once return her gaze, nor did he even appear as if he was listening. She felt a sense of enormous frustration threaten to overwhelm her as she finished her speech.

'Words cannot describe the tremendous detrimental impact and effect the actions of the defendant has placed on mine, my husband

and children's lives. I have included a small overview to try and capture a glimpse of the actual pain and suffering the defendant has caused me to suffer and endure from the instant he attacked me and now the physical and mental scars and challenges I will face for the rest of my life.'

As she concluded, her eyes blurred with tears. There was absolute silence in court. Sitting there, it took all of her friend Sergeant Perri Hayes' strength not to go over and give her a hug. 'That's the first time, throughout all this, I ever saw her cry,' she says. 'She's very tough, and she's very private and she's been even more like that since this all happened. But I think reading that statement made it all feel very real. And the way the defendant wouldn't look at her drove her insane. You want him to raise his head and at least acknowledge what you're saying. But he didn't, and that was very hard.'

Samantha's old boss, Superintendent Tony Crandell, noticed it too. 'She tried to look at him right in the eye when she was giving her statements, but he wouldn't look at her,' he says. 'He had his head in his hands for most of it and was looking straight down. He didn't even have the decency to look her in the face.'

Crandell went over to Laurence at the end of the hearing, while Samantha was talking to her friends, and asked him how he felt. He'd been surprised, throughout, that Laurence hadn't tried to give Holohan a spray, hadn't said a single word about him. Now, with the sentencing fixed for just over a month away, was his chance. But Laurence shook his head. 'I'm just so proud of my wife,' he said to Crandell. 'Did you see what she did? That was pure courage . . . '

Samantha felt content with the way the day had gone. Holohan had never offered her any kind of apology for the attack, but she wouldn't have believed it was genuine in any case, and felt it couldn't have made any difference. After all, if he'd cared at all about what happened to her, he could have phoned triple 0 as he'd walked away – on his phone or on hers. 'But I was just really conscious in court that I was never going to look away as I read my statement,' she says.

'I wanted to show him I wasn't scared of him, but he wouldn't look me in the eye. I never got that satisfaction, unfortunately. I would've laughed in his face.'

The day after the hearing, Laurence was driving through Hurstville on his way to visit his dad when he suddenly felt as though he couldn't breathe; he was dizzy and faint and was bathed in sweat. His vision blurred and his heart seemed to have slowed down, unable to pump blood around his body. He groaned in agony. It was his second panic attack, and so much worse than the one he'd had in the restaurant Una's, while Samantha was still in intensive care.

'I was losing control, I thought I was about pass out and I became disoriented and couldn't make sense of what was happening,' he says. 'Time became distorted and I remember thinking I was having a heart attack. I stopped at the next red light, knocked the car out of gear and braced myself for the worst, closing my eyes, crossing my arms across my chest and resting my head against the steering wheel, rocking backwards and forwards.

'But somehow I remained conscious, and after a few scary and painful seconds – which felt like several minutes – I could feel the blood return to my face, the pressure release from my chest and things slowly return to normal. As I came to, I could hear car horns blaring and I was able to pull over to the side of the road. When it was over, I felt as though I had an instant hangover and had strained some of the small muscles close to the rib cage in my attempts to force myself to breathe.'

It was only then that Laurence realised how much pressure he was under. Samantha could understand it. 'We were both under a lot of strain and we both felt angry,' she says. 'But it was a different anger. I could use mine to rebuild myself, to choose to get better, but he had to watch me. And he saw it as his job to protect me, and he wasn't there when this happened. But no one takes me to work. I do that myself. So he couldn't have done anything. It was one of those things that was meant to happen, and it did.'

Yet for Laurence, life was beginning to come together in other ways. After nearly eighteen months at home looking after Samantha and the children, taking her to all her appointments and supporting her through all her treatments, he'd finally returned to work. Officially, that is. Emotionally and psychologically, he wasn't there at all.

He'd spent the previous twenty-three years on the frontline in police tactical units, but just wasn't up to returning with his nagging physical injuries like those three still-bulging discs, and the mental pressures he'd been under since the attack. 'In my heart and in my head I knew I could never be a tactical, or even an operational, police officer again as I no longer possessed the clear, critical decision-making skills required when carrying in a gun,' he says. 'If I was in a situation where junkies or a violent Aboriginal offender were involved, how would I react? Would I truly be able to determine the appropriate response?' Instead, Laurence returned to the force as staff officer to his old boss Assistant Commissioner Alan Clarke, the commander of the Major Events and Incidents Group, in charge of the riot squad, among other things. It was meant to be a temporary placement, but Laurence transferred into the position as a permanent role. It didn't take him long to realise his mistake.

The post was a prestigious one, but Laurence found it impossible to adapt to the total change in pace. 'It just wasn't me,' he says.

'The closest I came to danger every day was if I took a sip of my morning coffee too soon. And the irony, of course, for anyone who has a lower back injury is that sitting down behind a desk eight hours a day was actually more painful than climbing in and out of police vehicles or wrestling someone.'

There were occasional challenges, such as being involved in the planning of the Australian police response to the Christchurch earthquake in February 2011, but he quickly came to hate his new position, and himself in it. Deputy Commissioner Dave Owens wasn't surprised. 'He was a square peg in a round hole,' he says. 'It could've worked, but it didn't.'

His old boss at the riot squad, Chief Superintendent Steve Cullen, wasn't sure it would ever have worked. 'He was going to go there on loan but he transferred, so he then couldn't come back again,' he says. 'The position enabled him to work nine to five so he could still assist Sam and look after the children, but it was very, very difficult for him to go from an exceptionally dynamic role to one with a totally different set of priorities. I know he had a bad back but, together with the psychological impact of everything that had happened, that sent him on a downward spiral. It was hard as he'd been earmarked as my successor as commander of the riot squad and he was a very dedicated professional whose circumstances tragically changed. I remember him saying to me once that all he did now was make fucking coffee and tea.

'He took Sam's assault exceptionally poorly and, looking on, Sam took it far better than he did.'

On the day of Roderick Holohan's sentencing hearing, 16 December 2010, both Samantha and Laurence were nervous. A number of police officers had come along in uniform from both Kings Cross and the riot squad to the district court to show their support but the couple had endured so much, they were worried the sentence might be far lighter than they were hoping for and they'd feel further from closure than ever. Among Laurence's mates, there was a genuine fear that he wouldn't be able to stop himself trying to have a go at the prisoner in the dock.

As they filed into the courtroom, however, one of the courtroom officers approached the couple. He was a former police officer who'd once worked with Samantha at Maroubra. He hugged her and shook Laurence's hand warmly. He made a point of looking over his shoulder in the direction of the dock. 'Do you really think I could stop you?' he said with a grin.

Laurence laughed, thankful for the light-hearted distraction. 'Where's the light switch?' he joked back. 'I only need a couple of minutes . . . '

There were quite a few people who thought Laurence might be tempted to launch himself at the man who'd cost the couple so much. Unknown to him, four of his biggest mates had been placed strategically around the room ready to block his path if he tried. 'Everyone expected Laurence to come out and say, "That mongrel who got my wife, I'm going to square him up, I'm going to make sure he pays,"' says Crandell, who'd now moved from Kings Cross to take over Surry Hills. 'But he never did. Never ever. He was almost unemotional towards him. At the sentencing, people were saying to me that I'd better keep an eye on him because he might lose control and he'd attack him in the dock. But there was none of that, not even the suggestion of that. He trained himself to focus on Sam all the time, rather than the offender. He displayed remarkable self-control.'

Holohan's lawyer rose to his feet and talked about his client's difficult background, hoping for clemency. He went over his previous convictions. Someone in the crowd gestured over at Holohan, and muttered, 'He's the most experienced courtroom person here!' He was set to be sentenced that day not only for the assault on Samantha, but also for the assault on the first woman he'd tried to rob the previous evening, who'd fought him off with the help of others rushing to her aid. There was also the break-in at the camera shop that he'd admitted to.

When his lawyer had finished, Judge Charteris addressed the court, recapping Holohan's offences and his 'appalling' criminal past, which included the violent attacks on the young Irishwoman and on a former partner. He pointed out that the brutal attack on Samantha was for just $200, and talked about her injuries and her medical reports. 'One is left with the distinct impression that without the dedicated attention of highly skilled surgeons, Mrs Barlow may well have lost her life,' he said. 'I have taken into account all of those reports. Included is a psychiatric report indicating that the victim continues to have psychological and psychiatric problems . . . Mrs Barlow read a lengthy victim impact statement to the court. I admired the dignified way in which she read it; it was a carefully crafted document. I well understood after hearing her speak the extent of the problems that she has suffered as a result of this cowardly and brutal attack upon her.'

When finally he moved on to the sentences he was going to impose, everyone held their breath. 'As regards the attack upon Mrs Barlow, I accept the Crown's submission that the circumstances of this offence place it in the worst category of offences of this nature,' he said. 'In the commission of the offence itself there are aggravating matters. The use of a rock and the extensive injury suffered by Mrs Barlow demand that the matter be placed in a worst case bracket.' For that, the judge pronounced a sentence of sixteen years and nine months.

Samantha and Laurence had been sitting stiffly near the front of the court, holding each other's hand tightly. At the pronouncement, they squeezed each other's hand, smiled at each other and breathed a sigh of relief. It was longer than they'd dared imagine, almost as long as they'd hoped. It felt like today justice was really about to be done. They barely heard the rest of the proceedings.

The judge went on to say the attack on the other woman was in the middle range of offences and the break and enter on the camera shop was committed while on parole. 'The effect of those three sentences, in which I have convicted the offender of each offence, is a minimum period of fifteen years and nine months, an additional period of five years and three months, being a total sentence of twenty-one years,' said Judge Charteris. He added that the earliest date Holohan would be eligible to be considered for parole was 13 May 2025 – coincidentally, a date that would be the sixteenth anniversary of the attack.

The effect on Holohan was electric. Before, he'd stayed silent, not uttering a word to the court, simply looking down to the ground. But when he heard that he was being sentenced to twenty-one years in jail, he shook his head, gestured and started complaining loudly to his solicitor. 'It was only at that point that he had the courage to look in our direction for just a fleeting glance,' says Laurence. 'It was the only time our eyes made contact.'

All the police officers present were thrilled at such a hefty sentence. Sam's friend Hayes was looking at Holohan's face when the judge read out the jail term. 'I liked the shocked look on his face,' she says. 'He immediately said, "That's bullshit!" I thought, It's good! I hoped Sam and Laurence would be happy with that.'

They were, although they felt even spending the rest of his life behind bars still wouldn't be enough for what he'd put them, and so many other people, through. 'I was satisfied with the sentence,' says Samantha. 'It's as good as it could be, but it won't change anything. It was good I saw him, but that's done and I'll never see him again. I hope he rots in jail. I hope he never gets out alive.'

Outside the court, Samantha, with Laurence at her side, faced the battery of press cameras and microphones. She said the sentencing would allow her to move on with her life, but it would still never be enough for what she had suffered. 'I was walking to work to do the job I love, serving the community of New South Wales,' she said. 'I was brutally bashed and left on the side of the road. Since that day, I have not had the opportunity to do my job, be a mother to my children or the wife to my husband that I wanted to be.

'But despite what this criminal did to me, I would not let him beat me. Today is a significant milestone and now it is behind me I am ready to meet the many challenges that lay ahead, including returning to work. Today we've had some closure, some completion, and we're able to move on and start to enjoy our lives again.' Laurence, holding Samantha's hand, nodded his agreement. 'He was never going to beat us,' he said. 'He was never going to beat the New South Wales Police Force.'

With the proceedings finally over, Laurence drove Samantha home, then raced to the police academy at Goulburn where he'd spent the last two days rehearsing for the ceremony for the formal swearing-in of probationary constables who'd successfully completed their training. He'd applied to the commander of the protocol unit to be involved in some of its future duties, and had been selected for the honour of being the banner ensign – the person responsible for carrying the New South Wales Police banner under armed escort – at the attestation, or passing-out, parade of Class 333, the second-largest in the history of the New South Wales Police Force. Samantha went to her parents' house in Berry to drop off the children then joined him that evening for the official dinner, ready to watch the next day.

Neither anticipated becoming the focus of so much of the ceremony, however. The next morning, Samantha was shown to a seat in the front row and when the then New South Wales Premier Kristina Keneally began addressing her audience of senior police and army officers from both New South Wales and interstate, politicians and other invited dignitaries, she referred explicitly to Samantha as a great example of a modern-day police hero. As the media present heard her words and caught sight of Samantha, they all clustered around her, filming her reaction. Then Keneally repeated Laurence's words from the previous day's press conference: 'He was never going to beat us. He was never going to beat the New South Wales Police Force.'

As she said it, Laurence was standing just before her, holding the banner, with an escort either side, almost bursting with pride. 'Sam was diagonally to my right and, for a couple of minutes, it was as if the parade truly was ours,' he says. 'If there was any doubt left at the impact Sam's incredible recovery had, it was instantly erased as the Premier, along with several thousand relatives and friends – the old and newest members of the police family – took time out to hold her up as an example of a hero and someone others should aspire to be.'

After the parade, Samantha was asked to come up on the dais where Keneally congratulated her on her recovery, asked after Lily and Ben and posed for a photo with her and Police Minister Michael Daley.

For Samantha, it was a great day. But more importantly, it was a timely boost to her continuing campaign to return to work.

# Chapter 17
# REALISING THE DREAM

Samantha Barlow was still obsessed with the thought of getting back to work. At first, it had provided her with a driving force to regain her health but, as she grew in strength and confidence, it became her one, overriding purpose. Even though few others took it seriously, to her, not returning to the police force would feel like a victory for her attacker.

Every time she saw the head neurosurgeon Dr Malcolm Pell, she'd ask him if she was well enough to start training again, to swim, to drive, to get back to a normal life. 'He'd often say, "No, wait a bit longer," but then the next time I saw him, I'd bring the same list back again,' she says. 'He'd say maybe I could do one thing, and then I'd immediately ask for the next. I think in the end I just wore him down.'

The day she received permission to walk in water, she went straight to her local pool and walked a kilometre. When he said it would be fine for her to swim a couple of laps, she started swimming 2 kilometres five times a week – although tumble turns proved problematic until the vertigo subsided. And as soon as Dr Pell gave her permission to go to the gym and begin training gently again, she'd made an appointment with her local Fitness First.

Her first day there had been in January 2010, back when Samantha was still very frail. She was thin and wasn't eating much, having to adjust to the loss of her ability to smell and taste food; her hand was strapped up; and her hair had only just started to grow back, so she wore a cap most of the time. For that initial appointment, Laurence had parked underneath the gym and then held her hand as she clung to the stair railing with the other and hauled herself up the stairs, one by one.

The manager of the club had listened carefully as she told him how she'd been training all her life, but now had to start out again a little more slowly. He'd allocated her a husband-and-wife team of trainers, Glen and Emma Pilcher. 'Her injuries were tremendous, but we looked at her and treated her like any other person coming out of an operation or rehab work,' says Glen Pilcher, who'd previously coached swimmers to a world championship level. 'The idea was that we were going to return to some level of normality, although being careful of her injuries. We didn't want to do anything that was too limiting, that might feel insulting, so we designed a more aggressive approach to her training. I think what she liked was that I treated her like a human being rather than a victim, because she's certainly never been a victim!'

Glen Pilcher was the first new person to enter Samantha's life who wasn't a doctor, nurse or specialist in some way and, at that stage still nervous of strangers, she found it difficult to be open and trusting. Gradually, however, little by little, she became more confident around him. The day she discovered that he and Emma were close friends with the Barlows' own mates, Sergeant Brendan Crowe and Senior Sergeant Belinda Crowe, Lily's godparents, provided another breakthrough. 'In the beginning, it was like the *Titanic* approaching the iceberg!' Glen Pilcher says. 'She wasn't ready to trust me at all, and she never likes to be told what to do. It took us a couple of months to form a good relationship, but after that, it was great. We both love her to bits.'

Samantha made rapid progress. Her training developed from a light session every couple of days to ten sessions a week with weights, group stationary cycling sessions, Pilates, running on the treadmill, rowing, swimming and finally running in the Wanda sandhills. Glen Pilcher had previously coached the Australian Schoolboys rugby union team, some of whom are current members of the Wallabies squad, so he knew all about strength, cardio and endurance training. His major challenge with his new client was trying to hold her back from working too hard.

'Once we started getting good results, and she was seeing she could achieve things, she always tried to go overboard,' says Pilcher. 'I wanted to push her, but make sure she wasn't going to do herself any damage. But her progress was remarkable. She surprised me every day. At the start, she couldn't even do a crunch on the ground because it took her five minutes to get down because of her vertigo. Then she went from not being able to hold a bar to doing Olympic lifting, throwing a ball and boxing, all the kinds of things people had told her she'd never do again. I'd just challenge her and say, "I don't think you'll be able to do this . . ." Then, of course, she'd do it. We wanted to prove them all wrong. I loved it.

'Then they said she'd never be able to go back to work. She said that's what she was determined to do, so we thought, Yes, we'll do it! She's a very special woman.'

Yet it wasn't possible to overcome every problem. In January 2011, Dr Pell informed Samantha that, since her sense of smell and taste hadn't yet returned, it was unlikely to do so in the future. She'd have to face the permanent loss of those senses. Even more devastating was the report that the injury to her brain could possibly also have longer term effects on cognitive function. Samantha received the bad news in silence, and then immediately refocused on more attainable goals. Could she try again to fall pregnant? Could she start driving again? And how about diving? Dr Pell said yes to pregnancy, no to driving just yet, and as for diving, he smiled. 'That can wait until you return to work,' he said, tongue firmly in cheek.

She and Laurence were still getting lost in big shopping centres. One day, most memorably, they couldn't find their car for a good few hours. They'd laugh but it did remind them that they still had a long way to go to get back to some kind of normality. Indeed, at times, they couldn't even remember what 'normal' was. Laurence coined the term 'the new normal'. It seemed to suit their circumstances perfectly.

Wherever they were, they continued to be stopped by well-wishers. Some wanted to buy them lunch, others to pay for their groceries. A builder doing some work on their house asked why the kennel in their garden was empty and, when they told him Samantha's dog, Maddie, had recently died, he insisted on giving them the pick of a litter of golden labradors he'd been breeding, a puppy they immediately named Halle. 'As we walked around the streets of Cronulla, people nodded and said hello to us like they were old family friends,' says Samantha. 'And they still do today. It's a wonderful yet bizarre way to live your life. People sometimes stop me on the beach and say, "I know you!" And sometimes I can't help saying, "No you don't!" I've never liked attention; I just prefer to blend in. But they're always being nice.'

Anonymity certainly seemed a thing of the past. Laurence's cousin Jackie Barnes and her husband Tim visited from the UK for a few weeks, and the four went on a break down the south coast and across to Canberra to pay their respects at the National Police Memorial, a bronze commemorative wall on the shores of Lake Burley Griffin displaying the names of police officers who'd died while in the job. Uppermost in their minds was the thought that Samantha's name could well have been on there too. Stopping off at a fast-food restaurant along the way, they bumped into a former police colleague, now working as a New South Wales Rural Fire Service officer, who asked them how they were. Later, visiting Parliament House, they were shown to seats for question time by another former officer, this time turned security guard, who said the whole place had been following Samantha's recovery closely. On the way home, they pulled in to a service station for petrol, only for a highway patrol car to pull up and the two officers inside, complete strangers, to get out to give Samantha a hug. Tim Barnes was bewildered. 'Tell me,' he said to the pair, 'is there anyone left in Australia who doesn't know who you are?'

Even the most innocent of excursions seemed to end in publicity. In February 2011, Samantha had been picking up a takeaway coffee from a cafe in Cronulla on her way back from the gym when she saw a flyer for the Ritchie Walker Memorial Aquathon – a 1 kilometre open-water swim and a 5 kilometre run to be held two days later at Gunnamatta Bay. As she got into the car, she said to Laurence, 'I want to do this, what do you think?'

'Go for it!' he replied. 'The kids will love it. We'll play in the sand and cheer you on.'

Despite having done no specific training for the event, and not bringing along a wetsuit like most of the other competitors, she got ready in the marshalling area. A friend who saw Laurence with the kids asked him how she was doing. 'Go ask her yourself,' he answered.

'She's over there!' The friend looked stunned. Just as Samantha was about to start, their good mates Robin and Scot Williams, together with their daughter Casey, arrived to join the cheer squad.

Samantha wasn't so happy with her performance, though. Her damaged right hand had locked up in the cold water and she'd received a couple of kicks in the head at the start, which had held her back. It was only later, when she was called up to the front of the presentation area to receive an award, that she realised she'd finished second in her age group, and first in the swim leg. The next week, the local newspaper reported her triumph in full.

'One of the nicest things was the reaction of the kids,' says Laurence. 'They'd been through so much, watching their mum have a near-death experience, so to see her competing in an event and winning a prize was a great buzz for them. The other thing I saw that night for the first time since the coma was a cameo of pre-attack Sam. The spark was back for half an hour or so, and the competitive juices were flowing. It was a return to Sammy Groves, the woman I'd met only a few years earlier who was almost completely killed off, and it removed any of the remaining doubts I had about her not being up to the challenge of returning to work.'

Samantha had spent the end of 2010 and the two months of 2011 going round to each of her doctors and specialists, asking them to support her application to return to work. As she'd done with Dr Pell, she was slowly but surely wearing them all down. Many of her friends were doubtful she was really up to it and tried to dissuade her, but to no avail. 'Everyone was prepared for her not to come back,' says her former Kings Cross colleague, Senior Constable Suzie Schwass. 'But Sam wasn't prepared for that at all.'

Eventually, all of her doctors signed off on a return to work, although they doubtless pictured her in a quiet office job somewhere in the force. She had other ideas, however. Laurence had just gone back to work as the staff officer and hated it, and she could see him gradually falling out of love with the police force as a result. It made her only more determined to go back to a similar role to the one she'd left. While she was off, she'd sat her inspector's exam, so hoped she might soon win a promotion in rank, too.

Her final test was an interview with Assistant Commissioner Mark Murdoch, who'd been her first boss at Kings Cross. Now the commander of the Central Metropolitan Region, he was the one who'd ultimately decide whether she could return to work. 'It was very courageous of her to want to come back to work,' he says. 'I wouldn't have expected anyone in her position to come back, but she clearly had other ideas. She could easily have put the cue in the rack and said she'd had enough. But she'd always set the goal of coming back, and she didn't want to let a lunatic beat her.'

Murdoch wanted to allow her back but with the responsibility for the welfare of 3000-plus officers, he needed to know she was truly up to it. He could see she'd regained her fitness and had already passed most of the tests she'd been set, but he still had misgivings. 'They were primarily about Sam being up to it emotionally and psychologically,' he says. 'She looked fantastic and I had no doubt physically she was up to it, but I worried about her self-confidence. She had to get her headspace right. In highway patrol, they work alone in a car during the day and I wondered if she'd just drive around for four hours, or whether she'd have the confidence and commitment to go out and engage with other people, respond to calls for assistance and pull people over. But she wanted to be back in it at 100 miles per hour.'

Finally, he agreed to put Samantha on restricted duties while she brought herself up to speed on the procedures that had changed while she was away, polished up her operational skills, was re-accredited to carry a firearm and re-did her defensive training. She readily accepted, and was posted to Surry Hills in Sydney's inner city, working three days a week in highway patrol.

Her first day back was 8 March 2011, a couple of months shy of the second anniversary of the attack. The date happened to coincide with the 100th anniversary of International Women's Day. Samantha, just turned thirty-six, imagined she'd be shown her new desk, given a computer, walked around the cars and left to get on with her work. But instead, she was invited to attend an International Women's Day breakfast at Police Headquarters in Parramatta. There, she was greeted by one of the deputy commissioners Catherine Burn, who'd spent many hours at St Vincent's Hospital while she was in a coma and been a huge support during her recovery. Then she was ushered around the room, shaking hands, pausing for photographs and being interviewed by media.

After an hour, she left for the Sydney Police Centre, next door to her new station at Surry Hills. As she arrived, Murdoch and fellow deputy commissioner Dave Owens greeted Samantha with a salute on the steps, before a vast contingent of media. 'It was unbelievable,' says Owens. 'To see her coming back to work after everything she'd been through, and to have achieved all that despite the hurdles . . . Geez! It took her so much fight and determination. It was always her goal to get back but, realistically, I never thought she would. I saluted her, she saluted me back and then I gave her a big hug. It was all so emotional, and I was so pleased to be proved wrong! I was very proud of her.'

Commissioner Andrew Scipione was out of town, but he made a point of speaking to Samantha on the phone. 'We were so proud of her,' he says. 'She worked so hard to get back; it was a superhuman effort. She wouldn't let what had happened define her. It was all about what she was going to do in response. She's such a fighter.'

Samantha was then asked to address the waiting media, and the cameras flashed and the waiting media jostled for position as she took her place before them to say she was sure it would only be a short time before she'd be resuming full operational duties. 'I'd like to think that I've worked damned hard, and I have,' she said. 'My first day back is huge, but I never doubted I'd be back. I'll see everything through to the end. I'm very fortunate in the sense that I was a very strong person before this happened and, if anything, I'm even stronger now. I would not let it beat me.

'It has changed me physically and mentally forever. You can block out most mental images but you can't hide physical scars. My greatest source of strength has come from believing in myself and the support of my husband, Laurence. He has an amazing amount of strength and his continual devotion has seen me through. Without Laurence, this would have been unbearable.'

Joanne Elliott, the media unit supervisor who'd been on duty the morning Samantha had been attacked, watched her interview from the operations room with real pleasure. 'Despite being such a horrible incident, it had such a positive outcome eventually,' she says. 'We all knew Sam and Laurence as such a genuinely lovely couple and it had turned into the kind of feel-good story that you don't get to deal with very often.'

Samatha's trainer Glen Pilcher was even interviewed. 'She's now starting her life again,' he said. 'She was on her way to work when it happened, so now she starts unfortunately two years late to work. But she's back.'

Watching on, Scott Weber, the President of the Police Association of New South Wales, was also delighted to see her return to work. 'Her resolve was extremely strong,' he says. 'She's a fantastic police officer, they both are. Such a tragedy brings it home to us that every time police officers go out onto the street, they might not come back. But Sam had always wanted to do something greater than herself, something for her community, and she'd succeeded in getting back to doing that. She's such a role model for us all, as someone who can dig deep and push through with such incredible perseverance. She's always been a fighter and she's come back more beautiful, more feminine and stronger than ever.'

While Samantha was surprised by all the fuss, her most treasured memory of the day she returned to work was a letter she received from a twelve-year-old schoolgirl from Newcastle, just north of Sydney. She wrote that when she grew up, she wanted to be a policewoman, just like Samantha. 'Today I read about you online and watched you on television,' she wrote. 'When I saw you return to work I felt so inspired by your courage. I am so glad and feel safe that people like you are out there protecting families like mine. Good luck with the rest of your recovery and I personally hope that you get fully better. Your kids are so lucky to have a mum like you. PS: I think you are pretty and beautiful.'

# Chapter 18
# A CONTACT SPORT

Over the next few months, Samantha Barlow worked through the checklist of qualifications and accreditations she needed to return to full duties.

There were mandatory lectures, high-speed vehicle driving re-certification, sitting an annual radar exam and other computerised testing, and she had to requalify as a tester and assessor of other drivers. Three days in, she also took her firearms assessment. This time, thanks to the help Laurence had given her to strengthen her hand and wrist and adjust her stance and drawing technique, as well as identifying that she'd always previously used the wrong eye to focus on the target, she passed with a 100 per cent pass mark – higher than the first time she took it. 'I remember bumping into her and she was back wearing a firearm, pleased as punch,' says Assistant Commissioner Mark Murdoch. 'She was pretty proud of herself!

'It was a good-news story all round. Everyone was glad to see her back. Her colleagues were thrilled, and the community was happy. It was not only a victory for Sam and Laurence, but also for those who knew and supported her and loved her. Lots of people were given a lot by seeing her back at work.'

Before she could return to the Operations Support Group, there was more testing, this time by the same officer who'd been waiting for her that fateful day when she'd never made it. The shuttle runs were set up in the courtyard, looked down upon by almost all of the rest of the building. Aware she was being watched by dozens of officers upstairs, she ran fifteen more than she needed to pass. 'With so many people watching, I wanted to just keep going,' she says later. One of the supervisors immediately tore into the rest of the class for pulling up early, using Samantha as an example of having much more ticker.

She was gradually given greater responsibilities at work. Her boss at Surry Hills, Superintendent Tony Crandell, who'd come over from Kings Cross, was determined to treat her no differently from any other officer – and knew she'd be the first to complain if he did. It meant some tough assignments from a human resources perspective, mentoring more junior officers while they completed performance programs, as well as from an operational viewpoint. She also became a member of the New South Wales Police's Spokeswomen's Network, encouraging other women to advance in the force.

But there were disappointments. While Samantha had been off work, the promotion system had been changed and her results in the inspector's eligibility program weren't good enough. It was the first thing she'd failed in her life, and she was crushed. Had she passed, she and Laurence had already made plans to transfer out of the city to the bush for a while, and the jump in rank would have meant she could spend more time in the office rather than out on the road if the physical side of policing ever became too much. 'That was an enormous setback for her, accepting that she was not as good at being a police manager as she once was,' says Laurence. 'But it shouldn't really have been a surprise considering how much she was still going through.'

Crandell says it was remarkable she even made the assessment in the first place. 'Sam had been off the street for two years, so there's no way she could draw on experience she hadn't had,' he says. 'I think she expected to get through, and it would have suited her addiction for work on the street as well as allowing her to take a managerial role, but it was unrealistic at that stage. It was far too much.'

There were other triumphs, however. In March 2011, at the New South Wales Police Olympics, she won seven silver medals and one bronze medal in the swimming events, and set her sights on the international law enforcement games to be held in the US in early 2012. In May, she was nominated for a News Limited's Pride of Australia medal in the Heroism category. Then, in a lavish ceremony at Government House, it was announced she'd won the medal, and New South Wales Police Commissioner Andrew Scipione handed it to her. News Limited CEO John Hartigan said she was a great example of a truly heroic Australian. 'The thing I take out of this is the indomitable Australian spirit is truly alive,' he said. The Courage medal for 2011 went to blind sportsman Ben Phillips, who turned out to be a participant in the New South Wales Police's Volunteer in Policing program, whereby members of the community work voluntarily to assist police in their duties. He told Samantha what an inspiration he thought she was, and even offered to mind the kids if she ever needed a night out.

That victory came just a week after she was honoured by police nationally, being presented with the revered Hellweg Bravery Award at the Australasian Council of Women in Policing conference in Hobart, opened by Governor General Quentin Bryce. As her name was read out, over 300 fellow policewomen from twenty-six different jurisdictions rose to their feet and gave her an extended standing ovation. Another New South Wales Police deputy commissioner Nick Kaldas said his colleague's strength of character had been an inspiration. 'She has displayed incredible willpower throughout the ordeal and her subsequent recovery,' he said. 'The awards are well deserved, and I congratulate her on all she has achieved.'

Samantha also won the New You award, a national competition held by her gym chain, Fitness First. She was judged the most deserving in the country for her absolute dedication to getting back her life, and her fitness. The ceremony was held in Sydney's Ivy Bar before a phalanx of celebrities, including Olympic swim champion Geoff Huegill and former Spice Girl Mel B.

'My determination to reclaim my life was, and still is, a 24-hour-per-day commitment and my attitude from day one was to return to full fitness and reclaim my life,' she told the judges. 'No one and nothing was going to get in my way, and my personal mantra became, "Never, never, never give up."

'Nobody can fix your life for you; nobody can fix your injuries, lose your excess weight, or improve your health and fitness for you. You have to take ownership of your problem and empower yourself towards finding your solutions. You have to want it more than anything else and be prepared to make sacrifices. Then you need to stop procrastinating and do something about it.'

Yet Samantha had achieved even more than anyone thought possible. In May 2011 she discovered she was pregnant again.

Laurence was still working as the Assistant Commissioner's staff officer, but was hating it more than ever. He'd taken some time off during the court hearings but had returned at the start of 2011 to give it one last crack. Nothing had changed, though, and he found himself dreading every new day.

He still had to attend high-profile operational briefings but now as the minute-taker rather than a decision-maker, and gradually he started to feel that work, instead of being a challenge and a joy, was now 'death by a thousand paper cuts'. His mate Inspector Paul Condon says the dilemma was always that, even if Laurence didn't have a bad back and other injuries, he could never go back to what they used to do. 'I don't think *he* even thought he'd be able to do it anymore,' says Condon. 'I think he'd had post-traumatic stress disorder from all his years in the job, and what happened to Sam tipped him over the edge. But his new job wasn't enough for him. He said he felt like a secretary. He'd been so active and tactical and now felt he was someone just taking notes for the boss. It was the last straw. It destroyed his soul when it came to policing.'

Laurence had also started a Master's degree in public policy at Sydney University and while he was loving that, particularly the ethics class, receiving a series of distinctions and credits as he moved towards qualifying to become a superintendent, the contrast with his role back in the office made him feel even worse.

One of his classmates was Superintendent Pat Paroz, who'd first met Laurence playing rugby league in a mid-week police competition, and then through TRG training. He'd known him as a rough, tough tactical officer and was surprised to find he had other dimensions. 'During what happened to Sam, he'd shown a very family-oriented side, very caring, very protective,' says Paroz. 'I'd always thought he was a big, dumb bloke, and he isn't. Although he doesn't look it, I discovered he's very articulate, very well read and quite a deep thinker. We don't often see that in policing.'

Laurence struggled on but, towards the end of 2011, it was clear he was deeply unhappy. 'I gave it one last try,' he says. 'But it was obvious to everyone I was just kidding myself. It was all over.'

While Samantha loved being back at work, she also had to admit that things were different from what she'd so fondly remembered. For starters, she was different. She'd been to hell and back and was still struggling physically and psychologically, living on a maximum of three hours' sleep a night, seeing a psychiatrist for post-traumatic stress disorder, brain injury and clinical depression, and still having to undergo rehab sessions. So when colleagues complained that they were tired on night shift or didn't like a deployment or had issues with someone else in the office, she didn't have much sympathy. And the job itself was different. When she'd joined, officers did what they were told, and obeyed orders without questioning them. Now, a new generation of police often asked why they had to do something, and why them?

'It seemed a lot of people would far rather complain about the job than just get stuck in and do what they're paid to do,' she says. 'They'd sit back and complain instead of doing something positive about a problem. I thought they should stop thinking like a victim and take control of their lives. But you couldn't really say to people, Get over yourself, be thankful you have your health and are part of the greatest job in the world, and stop whingeing when things don't go your way!'

Laurence felt it keenly too. 'We started to come to the conclusion that we no longer fitted the job, as we found it increasingly difficult to operate or empathise with people who were struggling with what we felt were minor problems,' he says. 'In truth, over time we came to realise that the world never stops spinning, and when life moves on, you can never recapture your old life, the way it once was. You can't go back to the person you used to be.'

As much as Samantha avoided admitting it, she knew she was having problems with the job itself, too. Although she'd been working with a psychiatrist to overcome them, she was still haunted by ghosts from her attack. She no longer enjoyed working alone in a car on highway patrol but, as a supervisor, she could hide that by saying she wanted to work with a different person each shift to get to know them, see how they worked, and assist and mentor them. Her loss of her senses of taste and smell also became an issue almost straightaway. One busy morning there was a gas leak in Darlinghurst and the call came for a highway patrol supervisor to take charge of traffic management. Samantha accepted the job but, as she drove there, she realised she'd have no idea if the gas smell grew stronger, and handed it to someone else instead. She knew she'd be similarly in trouble managing traffic if ever there was a petrol leak.

Tony Crandell felt that was a huge limitation on her abilities as an operational police officer. 'That really hit home to me that she had some serious issues,' he says. 'She would have had a limited time on the street, and that would have hurt her no end. She's not a desk-bound cop like me. She always wanted to be, and always would be, an operational cop.'

Then there was the issue of drink- or drug-affected drivers. Often, in court, the police officer who stopped a driver would be asked if they smelled of liquor or cannabis; she wouldn't have a clue. There could also be problems with the Oleoresin Capsicum spray – pepper spray – that all officers carried. If it were used, she wouldn't be able to smell it, and wouldn't know if she had any on her hands or clothing. With the chemical compound causing the eyes to close, leading to temporary blindness, that was invariably a source of great anxiety. Additionally, if the spray or tear gas were used in a public order incident, she might not realise it. 'I knew that instead of leading these operations, I could now be a potential liability,' she says.

The other thing Samantha was struggling to hide from her colleagues was that her body was not coping well with some of the challenges. Within a few months of her return to work, a driver being pulled over for a random breath test ignored her stop sign and drove straight at her, something that routinely happens to traffic cops, and which had happened many times previously in her career. This time, however, she didn't react quickly enough, and his nearside mirror hit the sign she was holding and she fell to the ground, twisting her back and injuring her knee. Embarrassed to be injured again so soon after returning to work, she didn't tell anyone. It was only when she couldn't get out of bed the next day that she was forced to confess to Laurence what had happened.

When Crandell found out, via an overnight report from another officer, he was outraged. 'I said, "What do you mean she's been hit by a car? That girl should be in cottonwool!" I rang her and she said she'd be fine, she was a bit sore but she'd be back in a day or two. This was a person who'd been bashed to within an inch of her life; she's been hit by a car and she's still coming back in a day or two! It's unheard of, that kind of courage and resilience. She just didn't get it. She said it's part of the job. It's a contact sport. That's the way she thinks. She has a remarkable attitude.'

But it was getting harder to sustain. One night, she was backing up general duties crews who were dealing with a drunken brawl in a hotel on George Street in the city. She tore straight in and helped separate some of the fighters and then, with her partner, wrestled one man, still lashing out, down to the ground, snapped on the handcuffs and arrested him. As they were leading him out to the police vans waiting outside in the rain, he tried to headbutt her, she pulled him to the ground and all three fell into the gutter as the two officers struggled to bring him back under control. Later that night, as she prepared to go home, she realised how much her body was hurting. 'I found my body just wasn't recovering as quickly, or as well, as it used to,' she says. 'Despite all the hard physical training I'd been doing, there still seemed to be a difference between being fit and being "match fit". It was hard to admit to myself, but my body simply couldn't do it anymore.'

Her friends looked on sadly. A number of them had urged her in the past not to go back to work and then, seeing how it was affecting her, to give up sooner rather than later. It was proving painful to watch. Judy Cohen, her old schoolfriend, hadn't been able to understand why, as the mother of two young children, she'd been so insistent on going back and, now pregnant with another, why she wanted to stay. 'I told her I thought she was crazy,' she says. 'She was offered a job two days a week in the office, but she said she hadn't joined the police to sit and file papers.

'I was happy that she felt strong enough to go back, and you could see how much she didn't want to let everything affect her. She wanted to prove that it wouldn't, but it did. What happened was still affecting her physically, socially and emotionally and it felt so sad to see her gradually losing all her ambition and her love for the job. She could see it all slipping away.'

But Karen Maddock felt it was an important part of her recovery. 'She needed to go back as part of the healing process,' she says. 'She might never have forgiven herself if she hadn't done it. But finally she realised she didn't need to do it anymore.'

Her other difficulty was finding enough time for all the training and rehab she was still having to do, as well as looking after herself with her pregnancy. She started arriving at work early to get the day sorted, then would take one hour of annual leave in order to exercise or attend doctors' appointments. She'd also pack any time off with the treatments that she had to complete. After a while, she found she was becoming increasingly tired. With the return to work, the nightmares she often had were also becoming more vivid and frequent in the few hours of sleep she managed to snatch each night. After a period of intense soul-searching, it started to become obvious to both her and Laurence that, despite insisting everything was fine to anyone who asked, returning to her job wasn't going to prove a permanent option. She began approaching each day as if it was her last.

Finally, in October 2011, seven months after her return to work, Samantha and Laurence had a meeting with Crandell in a coffee shop in Walsh Bay and told him she'd decided she couldn't continue; she'd have to apply for a medical discharge. Every single member of her medical team had agreed with her decision. She'd given it everything, but it just wasn't enough. Crandell wasn't surprised. 'I think, deep down, she'd known for a while that she couldn't keep up the pace of operational policing,' he says. 'Having said that, I was always willing to support her. But I was relieved when she came to that view that she couldn't continue on medical advice. In truth, there was only one person who ever said she was suitable for operational duty, and that was Sam Barlow. And she never wanted to do the job at anything less than 100 per cent. But she wanted to prove a point – although she had nothing to prove in my view – and as hard as it was, she decided she had to leave.'

Samantha's police colleague Senior Sergeant Belinda Crowe knew how much the decision was hurting. 'It was always her dream job. We're different: it's a job to me, but for her it was her life.'

It was also a big part of her recovery, believes Sergeant Perri Hayes. 'I wasn't surprised she came back, but I was surprised she came back so soon. I thought it would be much longer. But after achieving that, it was disappointing that she felt she had to go.'

The couple then filled in all the forms, and flew off to Port Douglas for a holiday. Leaving the force was one of the hardest things Samantha had ever done, and she was absolutely devastated it all had to end that way. She was still only thirty-six, and it was tough knowing the career she'd wanted all her life was over.

Laurence's heart went out to her. 'The last thing she wanted to be remembered for was as someone who hung around past their use-by date, like a boxer who has one fight too many,' he says. 'She wanted to leave a positive legacy and not allow any anger, bitterness or disappointment to contaminate the workplace and her memory of it.'

# Chapter 19
# WHAT THE HUMAN SPIRIT CAN ACHIEVE

As the year 2011 drew to a close, Samantha Barlow had kept her decision to leave the police force secret from most people. Now taking time out, she knew her discharge probably wouldn't be approved and become official before the middle of 2012. Happily, as her pregnancy advanced, many just assumed she was off work taking a break.

Apart from the turmoil she still felt about leaving, she was enjoying the rest. She relished the opportunity to spend more time with Lily and Ben, and she'd had a near-perfect pregnancy, with little morning sickness and no complications. The only minor irritant was craving salty foods, like nuts or rice crackers, but not being able to taste them – which made her want them even more. But the children were thrilled about the prospect of a new baby girl about to join them, and came along to a routine scan at St George Private Hospital, six weeks before her due date.

By now Samantha had ballooned and the obstetrician said she was perhaps retaining fluid, and the baby might be as well. As Lily and Ben blew kisses to the monitor, kissing and talking to the baby through Samantha's stomach, the radiographer asked the couple to return the next day for a second scan. They didn't think much about it.

They duly turned up on 17 January 2012 ready for a quick scan, then lunch and a visit to the cinema. It was never to be. The nurse examining Samantha announced she could find no heartbeat from the baby. They all stared at the monitor, Laurence enduring a sickening moment of deja vu after the death of Kyle. Their precious daughter had died overnight, at thirty-four weeks. The couple were taken to a private room, where Samantha sobbed and moaned uncontrollably, while Laurence clung to her tightly, tears streaming down his face too, as they rocked back and forth.

Harper Elizabeth Barlow was stillborn at 6.30 p.m. that evening by emergency caesarean. She looked perfect, with a full head of brown hair and a rosebud mouth. An incredibly active foetus, apparently her umbilical cord had become so tightly twisted, it had cut off the flow of blood and oxygen from mother to daughter. An autopsy later confirmed she'd ultimately caused her own death.

Laurence cut the cord, wrapped Harper in a bunny rug, kissed her, weighed her, dressed her, placed her in a crib and took photos. 'It was so cruel,' he says. 'She looked so normal and was so beautiful, but she was dead.' The couple spent the next few days in the hospital.

Looking back, Samantha feels she took Harper's death much harder than her own near-death. 'It was just so sudden,' she says. 'Everything was so perfect the whole way through. If we'd had any indication that something wasn't right, we would have been prepared, but we didn't. It was really mean in the sense that one day everything was fine, and the next, she was gone. To have gone so long and been so close . . . that's just wrong. Harper was so perfect and she was supposed to be the last part of our family to make it complete.

'For a while, I thought I'd done something wrong. Maybe there'd been something in my food, or I'd taken too much magnesium.

I probably had two sips of wine throughout the whole time, and I thought it might be that. Or maybe I was too active. But I'd worn a heart-rate monitor all the time I was pregnant to make sure I wasn't stressing my body. And my body had been through so much, who's to say that my injuries didn't play a role? In the end, I had to finally accept it was just one of those things you don't have any control over. It's just pretty unfair that we got smashed again.'

Samantha's parents Janice and Vernon visited while they were in hospital, dressing Harper in what would have been her christening gown, but would now be her funeral outfit. Laurence's father George came too, to see his newest grandchild. Mums Like Me, a support group for bereaved parents, delivered a 'memory box'. New South Wales police officer Erin Pavitt, whom Laurence had taught at the police academy and later worked with in Wollongong, had started the organisation after losing her own twin boys in 2009, dedicating herself to helping grieving families ever since.

Their friends arrived as well to express their sympathy. Senior Sergeant Belinda Crowe had spoken to Samantha just the day before, and couldn't believe what had happened. Her husband Sergeant Brendan Crowe was away – part of the continuing hunt for fugitive Malcolm Naden who was eventually caught and jailed for life for two murders – and she turned up, as usual, in tears. 'She's used to me crying, but that was probably the first time Sam cried in front of me, *really* cried. All through her injuries, I never saw her cry. But I felt it was good for her to let it go. It was a big knockback. It was horrible.'

The next afternoon, Laurence brought Lily and Ben in, and they both kissed Harper, hugged her and even began playing imaginary games with her. Lily just remembers how cold she was.

* * *

The morning after they returned home, Laurence's boss from the riot squad, Chief Superintendent Steve Cullen, came over. He told them the police media unit had been inundated with calls and messages of support and the whole force was again rallying behind them. One of the deputy commissioners Nick Kaldas, acting for the commissioner, wanted to offer them an official police funeral for Harper. 'It was very tragic, and so sad, happening so close to the birth date,' says Cullen. 'I said I'd take care of all the funeral arrangements.'

The couple agreed and two days later, on Wednesday 25 January 2012, the funeral began with a single red rose placed on the doorstep of the family's house, followed by a slow march along their street, and then a motorcycle escort by members of Surry Hills Highway Patrol – Samantha's workmates – to the Woronora Cemetery and Crematorium. A police guard of honour was waiting there, made up of Lily and Ben's godfathers, Sergeant Brendan Crowe and Inspector Paul Condon, the men who'd driven Laurence to the hospital the morning Samantha had been attacked, and members of the New South Wales Police's Spokeswomen's Network. They saluted Laurence as, dressed in his police uniform, he walked along the red carpet towards the chapel, carrying Harper's tiny white casket. Samantha, in a black dress, walked in front, holding hands with Lily and Ben. As they mounted the stairs, they were greeted by fellow deputy commissioner Catherine Burn at the entrance.

There was standing room only inside the chapel, with a full contingent of press present, and proceedings were relayed to TV monitors outside. Laurence walked forward and carefully placed the casket on the catafalque as Samantha lit a candle in memory of his mum, Betty, just as she'd done when they married. Janice and Vernon Groves placed flowers on the casket and Lily and Ben came forward to place on it a toy turtle they'd treasured from their holiday in Port Douglas. Both children were still too young to really understand what was happening and both, at different times, asked when Harper could be taken out of her box to play with them again.

The service was conducted by Reverend Neil Percival, the same New South Wales Rural Fire Service chaplain who'd married Samantha and Laurence and baptised Lily and Ben. Laurence made a heartfelt speech, farewelling Harper and talking about how much she'd be missed. 'Life is not fair,' he said. 'Bad things happen to good people too, and sadly babies die every day, and along with them a lifetime of hopes and dreams. But you can't let it beat you or allow yourself to become bitter and twisted or, even worse, simply give up. Sometimes, life chooses us – we don't choose it – and similar to what happened to Sam in May 2009 when she was almost killed whilst walking to work, we are often helpless to do anything to control it.

'What we can do, however, is manage how we choose to respond to the challenges that are thrust upon us by picking ourselves up every time we get knocked down, fight through and rise above the pain we feel, live for today, love and respect one another and not become obsessed with anger while continually looking for someone, or something, to blame. I'm not the best Christian in this room but I have made a point of living my life respecting all religious beliefs and having witnessed a miracle first-hand in May 2009, I know that there is a God, and at times like this I believe that God hurts with us.'

At one point, he looked at the congregation before him and noticed Erin Pavitt from Mums Like Me. It was the first funeral she'd attended since suffering her own loss, and the first time Laurence had seen her for nearly ten years. He smiled warmly at her.

As the couple left the chapel to the strains of the song they'd chosen for Harper, 1927's 'If I Could', they were met with a salute from Cullen, wearing full ceremonial uniform, as a lone piper marched down the driveway and into the distance. Shortly afterwards, there was the crashing of a heavy thunderstorm. It was the last time Laurence was ever to wear a police uniform.

The next few days were again a blur. The ashes were buried in Berry, next to those of Samantha's grandmother, and Laurence had to return a newly-bought pram to the store and cancel the final instalment on a lay-by of baby goods.

They had plenty of visitors too. Among them were Robin and Scot Williams. 'They're such a beautiful couple; how much more can you knock people around?' says Robin Williams. 'They're so tough though; they have true grit. It's Sam's philosophy to just suck it up and get on with things. They're great believers, even after everything they've gone through, that what doesn't kill you makes you stronger. They're very special people.'

And, true to form, Samantha and Laurence still made time for a trip to the obstetrician. Samantha had an important question to ask: When would it be okay to try again for a baby?

Harper's death somehow made Samantha feel her decision not to return to work was definitely the right one. Her brother Jason Groves had watched Harper's funeral online from the UK and noticed a change in her afterwards. 'Her goal was always about going back to work,' he says. 'She didn't want her career to be changed by the assault but losing the baby made it incredibly difficult for her to continue. It made her re-evaluate why it was she wanted to go back to work. It knocked her for six, possibly even more than the attack. Bad people ambush young women all the time, but losing a baby is less comprehensible. It was a horrific blow. She likes to move on from bad things but you can't move on from Harper. She'll always be there.'

Finally, Samantha started breaking the news to everyone that she was leaving the force. Another deputy commissioner Dave Owens, who was also away on sick leave for a back injury he'd sustained in a brawl during a racecourse operation and, he later revealed, a heart condition, had the utmost sympathy for her. He was due to retire on medical grounds at about the same time. 'I was sad to see her leave but I fully respected her decision,' he says. 'She'd had such a hard time, and then to lose the baby . . . It was like she was being tested, and tested, and tested. If it makes you get stronger, I don't think that family could have got any stronger. Enough was enough. It was time for Sam to have a life, and every day is a blessing with her and the kids.'

A date was set for her leaving – Thursday 16 August 2012 – and she was informed an official farewell was being organised. But first, there was one more shadow sitting on the horizon.

Roderick Holohan was appealing the severity of his sentence. His lawyers were arguing, in the case of the attack on Samantha, that Judge Colin Charteris should not have placed it in the worst-case category of offences as there was no gratuitous violence, and he'd used a brick, which was a less dangerous weapon than alternatives. Thus, the sentence the judge had imposed was far too long.

His appeal was heard by three Appeal Court judges on 17 May 2012, four days after the third anniversary of the assault. Their decision was published twelve days later.

Judge Clifton Hoeben said the attack on Samantha was 'brutal and savage', and her injuries 'were horrific and life-threatening.

While the weapon may have only been a rock or house brick, it was used with devastating consequences and was obviously capable of causing serious injury . . . It is clear from his actions that his intention in arming himself with the house brick or rock was not just to threaten . . . but to injure the victim by rendering her helpless after a blow to the head. The attack was explosive in execution and continued while the victim was on the ground to the point the applicant thought he had killed her.'

The sentence on Holohan for the attack on Samantha was upheld, although his attack on the other woman was cut by eighteen months. As a result, his total sentence was reduced from twenty-one years to nineteen and a half years. Samantha was relieved his sentence for the attack on her hadn't been shortened, but still doubts that he'll ever get out of prison alive. 'At least I hope he doesn't,' she says. 'He doesn't deserve to.'

Samantha's farewell turned into another major event. Over 100 people, including New South Wales Police Commissioner Andrew Scipione, New South Wales Police Minister Mike Gallacher, President of the Police Association of New South Wales Scott Weber and a phalanx of VIPs, friends and family, attended the mid-morning ceremony at the Sydney Police Centre in Surry Hills, next door to the station where she'd last worked. Samantha, now thirty-seven, had served eighteen years as a police officer, but was still desperately sad to be leaving.

Everyone there was also desperately sad to see her go.

'I worked very, very hard to get as much of my body back as I could, and I did do a good job,' she told the assembled crowd. 'But if you can't do 100 per cent, then you shouldn't be there. It's a very sad day. I honestly didn't think I would be retiring for decades yet, and I hoped to retire from the police when I was sixty, not to retire at thirty-seven. It's the best job in the world, and I'm very sad I'm not in it now.'

Her speech was greeted with a very long, very loud, standing ovation. Samantha smiled to feel the warmth for her in the room. Laurence beamed with pride.

Scipione responded by saying the vicious attack had robbed Sam of her destiny, and the police force of a potential leader. 'She had a brilliant career and was, potentially, a police commissioner of the future,' he said. Samantha's friends and family smiled at the thought of her one day possibly being a contender for the title of New South Wales' first female police commissioner.

Later, Scipione said privately that her decision to leave was undoubtedly an incredibly difficult one because she did aspire to a much higher rank. 'I think she had all the key ingredients to make it too,' he says. 'She was a fit, young, smart woman who knew her own mind and is very capable. And, of course, she had the remarkable qualities that came out during her struggle.

'But she said if she couldn't give 110 per cent, she couldn't continue. She proved not only to her friends and her workmates, but to me and to herself, that even after such a horrible attack, she still had what it takes. She has bravery, tenacity and an extraordinary commitment that's moved the police force, and the nation.'

She was then presented with the National Police Medal, the National Medal and the Commissioner's Commendation for Service. She also received a presentation from the Commander of Traffic Services for fifteen years of commitment to road safety as well as a plaque from the Commander of the Public Order and Riot Squad, Steve Cullen, for ten years' service to the Operations Support Group.

Among the people coming up to congratulate her was Constable Teneille Keith, the officer who'd been the first to come to her aid that dark, cold morning she was left for dead in Arthur Park. 'Obviously, she didn't know me, she didn't remember anything of that time,' says Keith. 'And she didn't look anything like she did back then! Now she looks fantastic. Laurence introduced us and she thanked me. I'm just so glad we were driving past that day.' Samantha, of course, was very appreciative of all the young officer had done for her that day. 'It was great to meet her,' she says. 'I'm very grateful, and always will be.'

Assistant Commissioner Mark Murdoch watched the proceedings with a heavy heart. Samantha had come a long way since she'd first arrived as a sergeant at Kings Cross, and he regretted seeing her go. 'For a lot of people, it was a very emotional time,' he says. 'I'm always sad when a police officer who I've known and worked with over the years leaves the organisation. You come into the job full of good intentions and high ideals and you want to make a difference. Then it becomes part of your life; it's part of you. It's a big call when it's time to walk away.'

Laurence had signalled his intention to leave too, also on a medical discharge, reluctantly admitting he was no longer physically capable of doing the job. He was being examined and interviewed by doctors about his state of health for a report to be presented to the NSW Commissioner on his future. It looked extremely likely they'd agree he was medically unfit for work and he'd be awarded a pension. Murdoch knew the pair would be sorely missed. 'Sam and Laurence are both good people, not only good police officers,' he says. 'Over the years, they've both given great service to the community of New South Wales. They're good people to whom something horrible happened.

'I think all people, not only police officers, can learn from Sam Barlow. She's a great example of what the human spirit can achieve. She achieved everything she had through sheer determination and guts. It stands as a great example for all people in how they can overcome adversity and achieve what they want to achieve in their lives. Her aim was to come back to work, and she did that. And when she left, she left on her own terms, not those imposed by someone else.'

Her farewell had been arranged by Superintendent Tony Crandell, who had been through so much with the couple over the previous three years. He knew he was going to miss her in many more ways than one. Over the past couple of years, he'd grown used to using the example of Samantha to the rest of his officers whenever the occasion merited it. If someone was having a day off because they had a headache or a sore throat, he'd say, 'Yeah, you know, I reckon Sam Barlow would have had a few headaches in her day! She would have had a few sniffles!'

It was an approach that had yielded miraculous results. 'The sick leave levels at Surry Hills when I came here were some of the highest in the region,' he says. 'They're now some of the lowest! I can't say that's down to the Sam Barlow influence alone, but she's a very good reference point.

'When you talk about courage and you talk about determination, that's Sam Barlow. Sam Barlow could have a sick day as often as she wanted, but she never did because she always wanted to come in and make a difference.'

At the end of the event, Scipione said a fond farewell to his officer. He genuinely meant it. 'Both she and Laurence have given a lot and been through a horrific period and they deserve now to get on with their lives, and we wish them well,' he says.

'While we're sad, and regret her loss, this is the time for her to start thinking of herself and her family and getting stronger and stronger. We wish them the best for the future, and they know they'll always have our support. Who knows what the next chapter holds for them?'

# Chapter 20
# BLEEDING BLUE

It's a sunny Sunday morning and Samantha Barlow is standing on the sand at Cronulla beach, directing a horde of little girls, all dressed in swimsuits, rashies and identical green caps, through their paces. They've been running a series of sprints, learning about the beach flags and having fun with their new friends as part of the under-six Nippers age group of the Cronulla Surf Life Saving Club, one of the oldest in Australia.

There's a broad smile on Samantha's face as she watches the small girls grow in confidence, playing on the sand and then swimming in the pool nearby. 'It's wonderful to see how their swimming has improved over the season,' she says. 'They're getting stronger and more confident all the time. And it's so rewarding to hear the positive comments from both the girls and their parents about how much they look forward to Sunday mornings on the beach.'

It's been four years since Samantha lay fighting for her life in a coma after being brutally beaten and left for dead in a lonely park just off Kings Cross, while her husband Laurence sat distraught by her bedside, hoping against hope at the end of each day that he wouldn't be arranging her funeral. Back then, Samantha had been battered black and blue with terrible injuries that, if she survived, looked set to scar her life horrendously. But today she's fit and active, tanned and pretty. That same old high-beam smile lights up her face, and the lives of those around her.

And she still has that cheery, no-nonsense personality, too. She briskly asks some parents standing on the sidelines to help, and they quickly oblige. It's been like that from the very first day, in late 2012, that she and Laurence took over as managers of the under-six girls. Samantha transferred her membership from the South Maroubra Surf Life Saving Club to Cronulla where her maternal great-grandfather had been a life member back in 1925. For that starter class, she'd been expecting around twelve girls to enrol; she ended up with over sixty.

'The first day down there, Sam was a bit of a celebrity,' says her dad Vernon Groves. 'They knew who she was. The parents were all standing looking at her and she said, "Right, you, you and you . . ." She picked out eight to nine men to help out. One chap said he didn't have a swimsuit. She said, "That doesn't matter, you'll dry!" She earned the parents' respect immediately. They all hopped in and helped her. She's never had a problem getting volunteers since. They know she doesn't put up with rubbish. She gets on and gets everyone organised.'

These days, every Sunday from 7 a.m. to midday, Samantha and Laurence are at the surf club with Ben joinng Lily's group even though he is technically too young. The newest addition to the family, baby Zac, had an early introduction to the club, too. Samantha volunteered with the Nippers right up until the week he was born in February 2013, just a few days before her own thirty-eighth birthday. She missed just one week, then attended with Zac in a pram by her side.

After the under-six session is over, Samantha stays back to teach the bronze medallion course. She chats to a few of the girls and their parents, grabs a takeaway coffee and jumps into her car to drive the five minutes home. There, the family regroups: Laurence, forty-nine, Lily, six, Ben, nearly five, and baby Zac. The two older children are lying at different ends of the sofa, watching cartoons on TV, while Zac gurgles from a baby chair. They take turns to play with him, under Laurence's watchful eye. 'They adore him,' says Samantha. 'They love him to bits. If they could, they'd play with him constantly. He loves it, but I have to yell to them sometimes to get off him. He'll probably end up the toughest of all of us!'

Life for the couple is full. Both remain busy, however, looking after three lively children, ferrying them around to school, preschool and a host of activities like swimming, gymnastics and tennis, while also volunteering at the school to help other children with their reading, its Parents & Citizens committee and the school canteen.

They have had a number of speaking engagements too, and pitch in regularly with fundraising events for causes close to their hearts. In addition, Samantha continues to be a keen member of surf lifesaving and takes a role in instructing and assessing the adult members for their bronze medallion and other qualifications, as well as the Nippers classes – with Lily a keen member, Laurence her assistant and Ben his helper as he's too young to participate just yet. 'She was a member at South Maroubra for nearly twenty years before us,' says the Cronulla club president Robert Short. 'She's a great asset as she has so much experience and long service, and she's obviously committed and dedicated to her important and demanding roles. She's also a really nice person, very positive and friendly with a great smile.'

Samantha also trains constantly at the gym, and competes in various swimming and sports competitions. Then there's her physical rehab with regular visits to the physiotherapist and chiropractor, while both she and Laurence see a psychiatrist regularly to help them overcome the trauma they've been through. While the anniversary each year of Samantha's attack is a sobering occasion, the couple now mark 17 May instead – the day she emerged from the coma – with a celebration for Samantha's 're-birthday'.

The house Samantha once didn't know is still slowly yielding its secrets. The couple recently discovered more glassware they'd forgotten they had; it had been packed and put away while the house was being finished. It was a pleasant surprise. Now, the handsome two-storey house is comfortable and spacious and it at last feels like home. The back garden has long since been landscaped – mostly with the prize money from the Fitness First award – and boasts a pool, play equipment, a kennel for Halle the dog and a grand cubbyhouse for the kids, sitting up high on stilts.

But the couple are planning a move soon. 'It's fair to say we will be living a long way from Sydney and this house at some point,' says Laurence. 'There are too many triggers, too many reminders, here. It might be easier for us all to make a fresh start in a new place.'

Since Samantha's farewell to the police force in August 2012, there's barely been time for her to stop.

Later in the year she attended the New South Wales Police's Spokeswomen's Network conference, where she was acknowledged in many of the speeches. Then she was asked up on stage, with Mums Like Me founder Erin Pavitt, to receive a donation to the organisation, and spoke movingly about how much it had helped her when her daughter Harper had died. She also gave a speech late in 2013 at a network event, and spoke too at the Australasian Council of Women and Policing in Adelaide.

That November, she and Laurence went to the Rotary New South Wales Police Awards evening, for the presentation of a number of awards for excellence in service on the 150th anniversary of the New South Wales Police Force. During the evening, a special award was presented that wasn't listed on the program: Samantha was made a Paul Harris Fellow, a prestigious honour named after Rotary's founder, for humanitarian service to the community. 'It felt like an incredible privilege,' she says. 'It took me completely by surprise, and it was such a great way to say my final goodbye to the police force.'

She also became the inaugural ambassador of the Stride For Stroke charity in the New South Wales South Coast, raising money for the cardiac ward of the local hospital, and went to the New South Wales Central Coast for an event for CareFlight, the organisation dedicated to providing rapid-response critical care to the ill and injured. Back in Sydney, she was asked to speak at a Fitness First evening to raise money for the McGrath Foundation, funding breast cancer nurses. 'Everywhere we went, people treated us like members of their extended families,' says Laurence. 'They invited us to their homes and said how much Sam had inspired them. It was all very humbling.'

Even further afield, people who'd seen them on TV or read about them in newspapers or magazines, and had been touched by their story, would constantly approach them. At an exhibition at Sydney's Darling Harbour to celebrate 150 years of the NSW Police Force, they met a teenager who'd written an HSC paper on inspiration – all about Samantha. On a trip to the Daintree National Park in Far North Queensland, they drove to the isolated Mossman Gorge and then took a walk deeper into the rainforest. There, they were stopped by another pair of walkers who recognised them and asked for a photo. Even on a holiday in Hawaii, the family went on a tour of an active volcano and were standing, lost in awe at the sight, when another man on the tour approached them. 'Are you from Australia?' he asked them. 'From Cronulla? You're those police officers, aren't you? I watched your story all the way through!' The encounter finished in hugs all round.

'I found that loss of anonymity hard at first, but I'm learning to get used to it,' says Samantha. 'It's nice that people say they were inspired by us, though. It's good to think we've given something back.'

However, while all looks well on the surface, life can still be a struggle for the pair. The shadow of what happened is never far from their lives. Every time Samantha brushes or washes her hair, she can feel the scars on her scalp and the edge of the titanium plate inside. 'I hate it!' she grimaces. 'It feels like a constant reminder every time I touch it.'

Samantha still suffers from dizziness and has balance issues, particularly when she stands up too fast, bends down or is somewhere high up, and it might take thirty seconds or so before the feeling subsides. Going on a rollercoaster with the kids and taking part in extreme sports are no longer fun. While the doctors have given her permission to scuba dive again, she's too wary of the consequences of underwater pressure to really enjoy it. Sometimes her sight is blurred and her eyes take time to focus on what she's looking at. 'Whereas Sam once had no fear of anything and enjoyed pushing the boundaries, she is now far more cautious and says that things can hurt,' says Laurence. 'But the impact of her injuries on her daily physical life is minimal compared to what she did go through. People might complain about not getting a good night's sleep, but try to imagine what it's like not to be able to lie flat for eighteen months and then not being able to sleep even three hours a night – sleep that's still regularly disrupted with violent dreams.'

For it's not just the physical scars; the mental ones run even deeper. Samantha's close friend Senior Sergeant Belinda Crowe says she, like many of her friends, can see the evidence of them all the time. 'Sam has changed,' she says. 'She doesn't share as much anymore; you have to prise information out of her. She's a bit mistrustful of people and less tolerant.'

Similarly, Laurence's friends see the changes in him too. 'When I first met Laurence, he was outgoing, friendly, very knowledgeable and a social type of person,' says his good mate Inspector Paul Condon. 'But now he is different. He's cynical, mistrusting, angry, particularly if he has a few drinks. He can't let it go. It's been four years, and he lives it like it happened yesterday. But I can't judge him for that because I'm not in that situation. Still, we're not so close anymore, not like we used to be.'

The man who headed the investigation into the attack on Samantha, Detective Sergeant Mat Moss, who's known Laurence from their days at TRG, feels much the same. 'Laurence has a very strong personality, and he's very dedicated and proud,' he says. 'He joined the police to make a difference. That he's come out the other side is testament to his strength, and their strength together. They needed each other to get through this drama, but they laugh together and are very much in love. Laurence has changed but something like that would change you. He's still the same core of the man. He's angry and he has every right to be. Everyone deals with their grief in a different way.'

But how could something so momentous *not* affect someone for life? Their old friend, former deputy commissioner Dave Owens, feels that strongly. 'I don't know if you ever recover from something like this. You move on and put it to the back of your mind, but it's always there in the background. That's the issue they're both dealing with.'

Both Samantha and Laurence have been diagnosed with Post-Traumatic Stress Disorder (PTSD) and clinical depression, with

Samantha also having to deal with the effects of Traumatic Brain Injury. Laurence sustained PTSD from the years he'd spent on the police frontlines, but it's known that such a disorder often only comes to the fore when something happens to bring the individual to a complete standstill, as with the attack. Experts believe Samantha would have suffered it mostly because of the horrendous ordeal she'd been through but her police work contributed, too. PTSD typically leads to periods of traumatic memories and intense emotions, irritability, depression, insecurity and anxiety. Exercise has proved a powerful anti-depressant for Samantha, although there's no way of predicting what the long-term effects of the brain injury could be.

'That's the big black cloud that hovers over both of us,' says Laurence. 'It's one of the reasons we have such good holidays now. There's no point putting them off until later in life if Sam's health is going to deteriorate. We know only too well now that life can change completely in an instant, so living a long, healthy and happy life is now our biggest challenge.'

But just as Samantha's deep maternal instinct drove her will to survive and then her miraculous recovery, it's also helping her to overcome her problems now. Laurence has his paternal instincts, then there's their place as a member of the police 'family' who came together around them so supportively in their hour of greatest need. The expression 'We bleed blue' has never before felt so real. An even more important factor, however, has been the couple's love for each other and strength as a couple. Love, the professionals believe, can help people find a way through an enormous amount of mental trauma.

Of course, there's still residual anger about the attack that cost them so dearly. Every time something happens, like the murder of eighteen-year-old Thomas Kelly who was king-hit on the streets of Kings Cross in July 2012 not far from where Samantha was assaulted, the horror of their episode returns to haunt them. On any street corner, when Laurence spies a group of drug users, he feels fury rise. 'Sam was always more tolerant than I was,' he says. 'In my thirty years as a cop, I saw a lot of drugs and the misery they caused. They'd steal the eyes out of the back of your head if they could buy drugs. I've always been in favour of zero tolerance. I think all drug users are a waste of life. You look into their eyes, and there's nothing there. I don't see them as victims. Everyone has a choice, and they've chosen to go that way.'

Yet it feels like the couple have the chance of a new beginning, particularly with baby Zac to focus on. While the pregnancy was tinged with anxiety after Harper, and Samantha was on tenterhooks in the weeks before his birth, everything in the end went perfectly smoothly.

The couple are now happy to have more time to dedicate to Zac, Ben and Lily, although nobody knows what effect, if any, this has had on the two eldest. The other day, while staying with her grandparents, Lily woke up in the middle of the night and asked, 'Where's Mummy?' – something she hadn't done for a long time. Yet youngsters often possess a great ability to accept things and move on. 'We probably won't know until much later in life,' says Samantha. 'But hopefully they were too young to know what was really going on at that time. I think I'll wait a long time before I discuss what happened with them.'

But kids are often surprisingly matter-of-fact about life. Samantha's friend Sergeant Perri Hayes says her young daughter went through a phase of distinguishing between Sam and another friend Sam by describing the first as 'Sam who got hit in the head with a brick'. As soon as Samantha started recovering, Hayes gently suggested, 'Why not call Sam Lily and Ben's mum now?' The little girl agreed. 'That was a much better way for a child to distinguish!' smiles Perri. 'And now Sam is able to spend quality time with the children and have a fresh beginning and decide what she'll do next.'

What exactly that will be is currently occupying the minds of both Samantha and Laurence. Being the best parents they can is top of their list of priorities.

'I'm happy to be one of those in-your-face annoying fathers who helps out at school,' Laurence grins. Teaching, after all, was the career he would have chosen had he not joined the police force, and one day he could well move back in that direction, with an interest particularly in teaching ethics. But for now, it will be just volunteering at his local school, and for the kids who need it most. 'I never got to do as much of this as I would have liked when Olivia and Ryan were little as I was often too busy with work and on call, so now I'm really enjoying helping out with lessons, at the gym, coaching sports teams, helping wherever I'm needed. I want our kids, all kids, to have the best start possible.' His brother Robert believes he'll struggle for a while. 'I think he's underestimated how difficult it's going to be to leave the police,' he says. 'I can't picture what else he'll do. He had such variety in his police work. Maybe he could lecture in police studies? But after thirty years in the organisation, it's going to be hard.'

Yet Laurence's kind might not be seen anywhere within the Australian police force much anymore, believes New South Wales Police Commissioner Andrew Scipione. 'He's been thirty-odd years in the job, which is a long time,' he says. 'It's probably something you won't see as we move on to generation X and Y, and they choose to have a number of careers, not just the one. But Laurence has been a very loyal, committed and faithful servant to the job, and it's time for him now to find new challenges, and enjoy his life away from the force.'

As for Samantha, she's also clear about her most ardent wish. 'I want to be a great mum,' she says. 'I wasn't around for a while with Lily and with Ben when he was very small, so I dearly want to make up for that. I want to do my utmost to look after the kids and help them with their sporting hobbies and their studies. That's the most important thing I can do.'

Harper is never too far from their thoughts, either. At Christmas, their tree carries a bell with each of their children's names on it – names also enscribed on the gold medallion Sam wears around her neck every day. 'And when you ask Sam how many children she has,' her close friend Robin Williams reports, 'she always says, "Four."'

Keeping herself well enough to look after the kids as best she can is critical too, and she works out at the gym every day with weights, strength training and cardio exercise. Although the couple are on a tight budget she's recently hired a new personal trainer once a week to help her. Glen Pilcher, who'd proved so vital to her rehab efforts, left Fitness First with his wife, Emma, to set up his own training company, BFS Performance, so taking his place is the gym's training manager Daniel Brims. 'She knows exactly what she wants to achieve, and what she needs to do to get it, and she won't let anyone tell her "No",' says Brims. 'She trains very hard, is very strong and her abilities are much further beyond those of the average woman. She's a fantastic person to work with.'

The increasing number of motivational speaking engagements is giving Samantha the opportunity to pass on some of the lessons she's learnt through her recovery which is very precious too. 'I still find it strange that people want to hear what I have to say, but it's nice,' she says. 'I'm always happy to go along and speak, or chat. If people get something out of it, that's fantastic.

'It's always great to think I might help to make people from all different walks of life feel more empowered about their lives. It gives me a great buzz to give them a hand.'

One day, she might even consider a career in politics. Always keen to help people either through speaking or her community work – just like her parents – she sees that as perhaps offering her a greater chance to play a bigger role. 'I wouldn't mind that at some point,' she says. 'My brother's actively involved in politics in the UK and I've always liked that side of things. I have a great passion to help my community and my country. I'd love to be able to improve things. The thing I've learnt from my experience is that anything can be changed if you want it enough, and are prepared to work for it. If something's wrong, then you work until you fix it, and make it right.'

Whatever Samantha decides to do in the future, no one's in any doubt that she'll achieve any new goals she sets. Everyone's seen how determined, how hard-working and how committed she can be once she sets her mind to something. 'Now the world is her oyster,' says her friend Karen Maddock. 'She'll achieve anything she wants to achieve.'

Laurence's mate Condon agrees. 'Whatever Sam chooses to do, she'll accomplish,' he believes. 'Probably it's good for both of them to be out of the police now as what happened won't be brought up as much. It'll give them the chance to build new memories together.'

Belinda Crowe knows Samantha is enjoying being a stay-at-home mum for the moment, while she continues to build her strength, but believes she won't be content with just that. 'Next, she'll want to be a powerful professional person, and she's going to be looking for challenges for the rest of her life,' she says. 'Or she'll die trying! She'll do lots of amazing things and we'll sit back and say, Wow! She's so inspirational!'

Her old boss, Superintendent Tony Crandell, says any employer would be keen to take her on, sight and skills unseen, 'because you know that she would give you 110 per cent,' he says. 'And if she wasn't good enough, she would be the first person to say so, and her harshest critic. Knowing that, I would take her on in a heartbeat for anything she was interested in. She will rise to the top of anything she wants to do because she's got that enthusiasm, that drive, that determination . . . all those wonderful things you could ever want in a person.'

Samantha's family is simply relieved that the pair seem to have emerged so well from the dark times. 'She's an inspiration,' says her brother Jason. 'I couldn't be prouder. She's absolutely extraordinary. I never cease to be amazed by how incredibly well she's done.' Her mum Janice, too, is thrilled. 'She's done marvellously; they both have,' she says. 'It's sad she had to leave the police as she loved it so much, but she's our Sammy again. We've got her back.'

To friends, she's also an inspiration. Scot Williams says a frequent phrase in his household when they're going through tough times is: What would Sam say or do in these circumstances? And to Moss, Samantha's a champion. 'She's Wonder Woman,' he says. 'She's walked 100 miles over broken glass with no shoes on and come out an absolute goddess. She's very clever and very smart with a great sense of humour and an absolute good sort. I wish her and Laurence a very long, happy and healthy life together, for she's a hero in every sense of the word.'

# HOW TO DEAL WITH A CRISIS

## Laurence Barlow

One of the driving forces for writing this book was to share what this experience has taught us to assist others when they find themselves confronted by a life-changing incident. Surviving the last four years has required reserves of energy, mental strength and resilience we never realised we had.

If our experience can help anyone through their own crisis, then at least something good has come from the horror we were forced to endure and continue to live with every day.

During the many sleepless nights I spent in hospital whilst Sam was in a coma, I grew weary with some of the things people were saying and doing, and, as I reflected on them, I developed an approach that served us well long after we left hospital. It is based on three overlapping principles: respect, empowerment and communication.

### Respect

For almost 30 years I was able to run sieges, command riots, manage investigations, review policy, teach senior Police officers on training courses, relieve as a Commander and make a contribution to major Police operations. But when faced with the most important operation of all involving my wife and family far too many people made the mistake of providing unsolicited advice or thinking they knew what was best for me. When someone's life is crashing down around them, they need your help not your judgement.

### Empowerment

If you don't own the problem, you don't own the solution. Your role is to support the person who is struggling with their challenge no matter how overwhelming it might appear. It takes less effort to help someone stand up than it does to pick them up. It's hard, and not everyone is in possession of the skill to do it, but in many ways it is no different to delegating a task or teaching. A little bit of guidance to get them kick-started will be repaid many times over when they become independent and productive once again.

### Communication

CONNECT – CONNECT – CONNECT.

Connect – find a way to connect with the affected person, be a friend, show some humanity; you are not expected to have all the answers, just love them and show them you care.

Connect – once you have connected and established trust keep communication open.

Connect – once you have found a way to connect help others to do the same.

When applying these three principles, I developed the phrase, 'How can I help you to do it your way?' I consider it a mantra, something that can be recited and used as an opening line in discussion when someone finds themselves facing circumstances they feel inadequately prepared for. It's an attitude, a philosophy, a positive mindset based on empowerment, acknowledging that despite everything that is going on around you, you still retain most of the qualities that made you a productive and valuable member of your organisation, family or community prior to the incident.

## TO HELP OTHERS IN CRISIS

1. You cannot help someone if they have to hold *you* up. It's hard enough for the person involved in a trauma, without having to comfort others who can't contain their emotion. Avoid eye contact until you're strong enough to hold it together.

2. If you want to contact the person at the centre of the tragedy, do it; don't wait to be asked. Don't leave a message with a third person asking them to call you. They won't. Let them know you are around.

3. Don't presume to know what is right for the affected person. If you want to help, *really* listen to them, establish what they need help with, avoid nagging people about sleep, food and other priorities that *you* think are important.

4. Think before you speak. An inappropriate or thoughtless comment can do long-term damage. Work to establish empathy rather than display sympathy.

5. Help people regain control over their life.

6. Don't pre-judge or judge people – everything is right, nothing is wrong, unless it impacts negatively on others.

7. Help create an environment where people are free to be themselves and, if you can, find a way to make them laugh or smile. Humour is infectious and it is almost impossible to laugh without smiling.

8. If you want to bring a gift, respect all requests and attempt to think like the receiver rather than the giver. Not everyone likes or wants flowers.

9. Bring food. Don't tell people to go out and eat.

10. If you're not able to provide direct support or assistance – and not everyone can – say 'Hello', give the person a hug, look for alternate ways of making a contribution and go home and look after your own family.

## TO HELP YOURSELF THROUGH A CRISIS

1. Believe in yourself – life is full of examples of people who have overcome adversity; you will too.

2. Stay focussed, establish your priorities not what other people want or expect. When the euphoria surrounding the incident settles you will be on your own, and at most supported by a close circle of family or friends.

3. NEVER, NEVER, NEVER give up – you will surprise yourself what you can achieve when you want something bad enough.

4. Learn to accept help.

5. Remain open minded to professional assistance.

6. Carry a notepad and pen so you can write down appointments, questions you have, random thoughts, ideas and outstanding tasks. Make sure to ask the experts those questions, seek clarification and don't stress about the unknowns.

7. Lean on friends when you need to, but be careful not to wear them out.

8. Support the supporters – develop some coping strategies for your close friends and family members to deal with future challenges.

9. Find true peer support: people who've been through similar experiences.

10. It's OK to say yes to Dr Beer but avoid Professor Pissed.

11. Develop some coping strategies on dealing with places and memories that have significant meaning to you.

12. Get some normality back into your life as soon as possible, eat well, try to exercise and take a holiday when you can. If you've been through something bad, you need to remind yourself of how beautiful this world is, to appreciate life and to interact with people who don't know you.

13. When you feel strong enough, draw a line in the sand and stop thinking like a victim – take control of your life. Start moving forwards again by taking lots and lots of little steps, rather than re-living the past.

14. Thank people. It takes great courage to step into the unknown and help someone through a crisis. The sad reality is that most people will be conspicuously absent.

15. Do something nice for the people who love you: buy them flowers, a spontaneous gift, or take them out to dinner to show them how much they're appreciated. Because, as we all know, life can change in a heartbeat.

# ACKNOWLEDGEMENTS

There are so many people to thank for helping us get through everything that happened, it's hard to know where to start.

Obviously our families' support was critical for us both, and we'd love to thank Janice, Vernon and Jason Groves, and George and Robert Barlow. Our children too were magnificent – Olivia and Ryan, and then our children together, Lily and Ben and now newcomer Zac, never forgetting Kyle and Harper. You guys give meaning to life, and add so much promise to our future.

A special thanks goes to the NSW Police Force, our extended family. When trouble hit, you supported us more than we could ever have imagined, and we will be forever grateful. We struggle to find the words to reflect our debts to Condo who redefined what it is to be a mate, a man who stood beside me and held me up when my world had collapsed, to Tony Crandell who stood tall during some of the most challenging times imaginable, to commander and trusted friend Steve Cullen and our brothers in the Public Order & Riot Squad, to Mat Moss and members of Strike Force Rendell, and to Brendan and Belinda Crowe. A huge thankyou.

Also, to the men and women of the Kings Cross Local Area

Command: Perri Hayes, Simon Kirby, BJ Kenny (RIP), Angela Moloney, Sophie Hunter, Darren Shott, Matt Mcqueen, Tori Turner and many, many, many others. We shared a journey together that none of us chose, but we could not have been in better company.

So many went far above and beyond the call of duty, like Phil Scott and Teneille Keith who found Sam, Tanya Smith who worked so hard on the investigation, Lisa Groth of the NSW Police Association, NSW Commissioner Andrew Scipione who was there for us at every stage of the journey, his deputy Catherine Burn, Dave Owens, Nick Kaldas ... everyone. You have a special place in our hearts.

We'd also like to thank the ambulance officers Taz and Seth, and at St Vincent's Hospital, the ICU nurses (Airlie, Angela, Corlette, Eliza, Elizabeth, Jackie, Kouta, Leanne, Mark, Sally, Sam ... to name just a few) and the doctors and support carers, and the staff of the rehab unit – everyone who helped Sam on her road to recovery. Your selfless generosity was remarkable at every step.

Other friends were fantastic too. The Williams family, Scot, Robin and Casey, visited twice a day without fail during the month at hospital, and people like Karen Maddock, Mick Austin, Neryl Hales and Auntie Treasure were a great support, while Suzie Schwass helped look after our children as if they were her own. A big hug too for Erin Pavitt from Mums Like Me, while gratitude to the three police ministers Michael Daly, Michael Gallagher and Tony Kelly who also went out of their way to help.

We'd also like to thank the community. We received over 500 cards, letters, emails, presents and bunches of flowers following Sam's attack – so many we couldn't keep a record. Four years later, we are still stopped and hugged by complete strangers. Your support has kept us going through the darkest times, and has been a truly humbling experience.

Thanks too to our agent Selwa Anthony for helping to turn our dream of a book into reality and Penguin for their faith.

And finally, while we are both sad to have left the roles we loved with the NSW Police Force, we salute those who remain, and went before. The spirit and culture of 'the job' is alive and well and, in times of struggle or tragedy, this is never more apparent. We feel privileged to have spent our entire adult lives as members of the largest family in Australia.